To Liz

I hope you enjoy this
and it takes you further
on your journey of discovery

Seth Kurn

Juggling Identities

JUGGLING IDENTITIES

Identity and Authenticity
Among the Crypto-Jews

SETH D. KUNIN

Columbia University Press　New York

Columbia University Press

Publishers Since 1893

New York   Chichester, West Sussex

Copyright © 2009 Columbia University Press

All rights reserved

Library of Congress Cataloging-in-Publication Data

Kunin, Seth Daniel.

Juggling identities : identity and authenticity among the Crypto-Jews / Seth D. Kunin.

p. cm.

Includes bibliographical references and index.

ISBN 978-0-231-14218-2 (cloth : alk. paper)

ISBN 978-0-231-51257-2 (e-book)

1. Crypto Jews—New Mexico—History.   2. Jews—New Mexico—Identity.

3. Jews—New Mexico—History.   I. Title.

F805.J4K86 2009

305.892'40789—dc22

2009000331

Columbia University Press books are printed on permanent and durable acid-free paper.

Printed in the United States of America

c 10 9 8 7 6 5 4 3 2

References to Internet Web sites (URLs) were accurate at the time of writing.
Neither the author nor Columbia University Press is
responsible for URLs that may have expired or changed
since the manuscript was prepared.

CONTENTS

Acknowledgments *vii*

Introduction *1*

1 Diversity and Complexity *23*

2 The Case Against the Authenticity of Crypto-Judaism
in New Mexico *45*

3 The Case for the Authenticity of Crypto-Judaism in New Mexico *82*

4 Ideal Types of Crypto-Jewish Identity *114*

5 Crypto-Jewish Practice: Memory and Bricolage *146*

6 A Postmodern Take on Crypto-Judaism *192*

Conclusion *213*

Theoretical Appendix. (Neo)-Structuralism:
A Basis for Understanding the Transformative Use of
Structure in Crypto-Jewish Culture *223*

Notes *255*

Bibliography *263*

Index *269*

ACKNOWLEDGMENTS

This research for this book would have been impossible without the time and unstinting generosity of the many individuals from the Hispano/crypto-Jewish community who allowed me to spend time with them and interview them, often several times over many years. I would also like to thank my colleagues both in the United States, many of whom are members of the Society for Crypto-Judaic Studies, and in Great Britain for their support and comments, which were an essential part of the development of both the ethnographic and the theoretical aspects of this book. I would particularly like to thank Stanley Hordes, who has been an excellent colleague and a good friend throughout the many years of fieldwork in New Mexico. I should also mention Fay Blake, whose advice and help were instrumental at the beginning of my research, and Heidi Schulman, who helped transcribe some of my many taped interviews at the conclusion of my fieldwork. The preparation for this volume has also been the product of considerable effort on the part of Columbia University Press, and I am particularly grateful to Irene Pavitt, senior manuscript editor, for all her work on and contributions to my manuscript. Finally, I would like to thank my parents and my brother, David, for their support throughout the long period of both researching and writing this book. (I should also mention the patience of my dogs, Quincy, Trotsky, and Pete, and cats, Che and Alex, for their long stays in kennels and catteries during the fieldwork stages of the research.)

In addition, this research would not have been possible without the funding provided by a number of sources: the British Academy, the Estate of Eva Feld, Nottingham University, Aberdeen University, and Durham University.

Juggling Identities

INTRODUCTION

"Crypto-Judaism" is one of many terms generally used to describe the practices of a range of communities whose members outwardly profess one cultural identity as well as having some aspect of a hidden Jewish identity—sometimes religious, cultural, or even historical. Although this word is most commonly used in relation to individuals whose roots are in the Iberian diaspora, crypto-Jews have also been identified in various parts of the Islamic world, particularly Iran, and can perhaps include people from the former Soviet Union or other modern states in which the public practice of Judaism was forbidden. This book specifically examines issues of identity among the crypto-Jews of the American Southwest, primarily New Mexico.

When used in relation to the Iberian diaspora, the word "crypto-Judaism" is neither easily understandable nor uncontested. A number of terms have been suggested, each of which focuses on a particular aspect of the phenomenon and thus reflects the differing interests of both the academics studying it and, most important, the individuals and groups claiming that identity. It should be emphasized that although many of these terms have historical references, I am primarily interested in how and why they are used today.

The word *marrano* was commonly used in scholarship until fairly recently, as in Cecil Roth's *A History of the Marranos* (1932). While the etymology of this term is highly contested, the interpretation of its meaning as "swine" is now commonly accepted by members of the crypto-Jewish community, who therefore regard the word as abusive.[1] Although some individuals choose to use it to describe themselves, it has largely been rejected by both other crypto-Jews and academics.

The term *converso* has been used in reference to both individuals in the past and crypto-Jews of today. It has a specific historical meaning, referring to those who converted from Judaism to Catholicism and their second- and third-generation descendants. While some in the modern community choose to use this word, many have rejected it. They suggest that *converso* emphasizes the wrong thing; it focuses on their ancestors having converted to Catholicism, rather than their having maintained their Jewish identity. For these individuals, the Jewish aspect is the more important and therefore has to be emphasized in the term used to identify them. In this book, the word *converso* refers specifically to individuals in Spain or the Americas who were of Jewish descent, but whose construction of identity—that is, whether they understood themselves to be Jews—is not known. It is important to emphasize that the majority of *conversos* either did not choose to or were not able to maintain their separate Jewish identity and thus were eventually assimilated fully into the Iberian Catholic culture. The distinction between the use of the term "crypto-Jew" and that of the word *converso* in the historical discussions highlights this point.

The terms "crypto-Jew" and "secret Jew" are synonyms. The term "crypto-Jew" was first used in the nineteenth century (Gitlitz 1996:651) and has been widely employed in academic literature to refer to a range of communities with similar cultural forms and historical trajectories. Members of these communities have responded to this term in a number of ways. Some have focused on the word "crypto" and claim that it implies that they are not real Jews; others suggest that any modifier of the word "Jew" is unnecessary and perhaps calls their Judaism into question. One woman from Albuquerque said, "Why use the word 'crypto' or 'secret.' We are Jews; I am a Sephardita."

While this challenge to the terminology is not infrequent, I use "crypto-Jew" in this book. The term is particularly useful, as it emphasizes the aspect of secrecy. If we look at crypto-Jewish identity and culture, secrecy is one of its primary constituents, inseparable from all crypto-Jewish practices. The importance of secrecy is both a significant factor in the historical development of crypto-Judaism, due to the fear of the Inquisition, and a key element in understanding the identity of crypto-Jews today. Even though secrecy is no longer necessary in the United States, many crypto-Jews continue to emphasize it, since it is as much a part of who and what they are as is any other facet of their identity. In this book, though, I narrow the use of this term to refer to individuals who acknowledge some form of Jewish identity or association, rather than merely being descended from Jewish or crypto-Jewish ancestors.

Some crypto-Jews have recently appropriated the term *anusim* (the plural form of the singular *anús* is more frequently used) as the one that best expresses their self-understanding. It means "those who were forced"— that is, the forced converts. Those who use this word emphasize that the conversion of their ancestors was not by choice, but by coercion, and thus not real or sincere. *Anusim* is becoming increasingly popular in the community and may become the preferred term, particularly for those who wish to maintain some aspect of identity separate from that of mainstream Jews.

The statement by the woman from Albuquerque indicates an additional route of nomenclature—that is, the rejection of a separate crypto-Jewish identity. She, as well as others interviewed for this study, has chosen to join mainstream Jewish communities. Although she has a very strong interest in her crypto-Jewish past, she does not regard crypto-Judaism as an ongoing distinct identity. Thus at different times, she aligns herself with either the Jews in general or the Sephardic Jews.[2] While it is important to establish how and why terms are used in this book, nomenclature is also closely related to self-perception. Each of the words just defined has been used by individuals and groups to describe themselves at different times and in different contexts. The term chosen often indicates what is considered most important. Thus *marrano, converso, anusim,* Sephardic Jew, or Jew emphasizes a specific connection, a distinct way of characterizing past and present.

Since the crypto-Jews of New Mexico claim to be descended from *conversos* from fifteenth-century Spain, it maybe helpful to present a brief outline of the historical events that tie the period of significant conversions from Judaism to Catholicism, 1391 to 1492, to the present day. It is important to understand from the outset that some aspects of this history are contested by historians; while I will indicate some points of these arguments, the aim of the discussion is to present the history as understood by the crypto-Jews themselves. In this sense, it is an idealized version of history—although it may be argued that this idealization is true of all historical reconstructions.

Although I later consider some of the details of the arguments about history, particularly in chapters 2 and 3, my main interest in this book is ethnographic, and thus I leave most of the historical questions to be adjudicated by experts in that field.

Historical Context

By the fourteenth century, the Jewish community on the Iberian Peninsula was well established. It had particularly flourished both culturally and economically under Islamic rule and, to a slightly lesser extent, under the new Spanish kingdoms. But there were periods of religious persecution, resulting in conversions both by force and by choice. The period of significant forced conversions began in Seville in 1391, and as many as 100,000 Jews were converted, often at the point of the sword. The process of conversion continued at a very rapid rate until the ultimate expulsion of the remaining Jews from Spain after the reunification of the country in 1492. Some scholars suggest that up to 250,000 Jews were converted during the fifteenth century.

While the number of Jews who were converted either by force or by choice is a question for historians, perhaps the most important consideration for our purposes relates to the self-identification of those who were converted, as it provides the basis for the claim of crypto-Jewish identity by their present-day descendants. Some scholars—for example, Yitzhak Baer (1961, 1966) and Haim Beinart (1981)—believe that a very large proportion of *conversos* continued to adhere secretly to aspects of Judaism; others—for example, Benzion Netanyahu (1966, 1995)—believe that a very small minority continued to affiliate with Judaism after the initial generation. Evidence presented by yet other scholars—particularly David Gitlitz (1996), Renée Melammed (1999), and Stanley Hordes (2005)—supports a third way, suggesting that while many converts did maintain their Jewish identity and perhaps practices, they probably made up a majority of neither *conversos* nor their descendents. It is also likely that the traditions and practices of those who did hold onto aspects of their Jewish identity became progressively restricted to those that did not rely on detailed textual traditions or on communal or public performance.

Perhaps the most important development that shaped crypto-Jewish culture was the establishment of the Inquisition in 1481. It is important to emphasize that the particular role of the Inquisition in fifteenth-century

Spain and in sixteenth- and seventeenth-century New Spain (Mexico) and New Mexico was the prosecution of those Catholics considered to be heretics. Thus the unconverted Jews of Spain, particularly between 1481 and 1492, were not within its jurisdiction. The *conversos* were, however, another matter. A Jew who had converted to Catholicism, whether by choice or by force, and who returned to Judaism or practiced Jewish traditions was considered to be a heretic. Thus *conversos* accused of Judaizing were specific targets of inquisitional interest. Between 1481 and 1488, 750 men and women were executed in Seville, having been convicted of Judaizing; 5,000 more were punished for related acts of "Jewish heresy" (Jacobs 2002:5). Janet Jacobs (2002:5) cites a text from Andrés Bernáldez, who reported of individuals prosecuted by the Inquisition that "All of them were Jews," and stated further that those Jews regarded the events in Spain as equivalent to the persecution of the Israelites in Egypt. Interestingly, this association is also made by crypto-Jews today.

The establishment of the Inquisition probably shaped crypto-Jewish culture in two ways. From the time of the first conversions, crypto-Jews were able to maintain different forms of contact with the Jewish community. Information provided by Gitlitz indicates that this contact could have included the provision of Jewish ritual items and knowledge to the *conversos*. The communication between the two groups is perhaps best exemplified in Gitlitz's (1996) statement: "Despite repeated attempts to keep them separate, by the mid-fifteenth century the Jews and the *conversos* tended to form an extended community" (13). His discussion also indicates that some crypto-Jews attended both Mass and services for such Jewish holidays as Yom Kippur. The documents cited by Gitlitz show that this type of communication was of concern to the Inquisition and thus probably decreased significantly after 1481. Indeed, the influence of the Jewish community on the *conversos* was one of the explicit reasons for the expulsion of the Jews from Spain in 1492. The restriction and eventual end of the contact between Jews and crypto-Jews probably greatly reduced the knowledge base of crypto-Jews and led to a narrowing of the range and complexity of their religious practice.

The second and equally significant effect of the Inquisition on the crypto-Jews was the need for secrecy. Most historians agree, despite a range of views on the effectiveness or ruthlessness of the Inquisition, that its existence led to the performance of Jewish practices and the acknowledgment of Jewish identity by *conversos* to be done in secret. This need probably increased as the Inquisition's understanding of Jewish practices became more sophisticated. The period as a whole was also punctuated by periods of increased persecutions that led to a correspondingly increased need for secrecy. While by the eighteenth century the Inquisition's interest in Judaizing was largely at an end, the cultural effects of the previous years of persecution cannot be overstated. Crypto-Judaism, I suggest, is a culture of secrecy, which is as significant an element as religion. This cultural form owes its development to the Inquisition and its actual and perceived role in crypto-Jewish history.

The year 1492 brought together a number of events that were very important to the future development of crypto-Judaism in the New World. The first two were closely connected. In 1492, Ferdinand and Isabella completed the *reconquista*, ending seven hundred years of Islamic rule on the Iberian Peninsula. This enabled the second event: the expulsion of the Jews from Spain. The focus on a religiously (and perhaps to a degree ethnically) unified Spanish identity was a key part of the religious, cultural, and political identity fundamental to the *reconquista*, particularly as conceived by Ferdinand and Isabella. While this ideology specifically targeted the remaining Muslim population, the Jewish community was also included. The policy culminated in March 1492 with the Edict of Expulsion. About half the Jewish community converted to Catholicism at that time and remained in Spain. Around 100,000 Jews left Spain for Portugal, with the remaining 100,000 going to a wide range of countries, including those in the Ottoman Empire (Gitlitz 1996:26–27). The third event, the discovery of the Americas by Columbus, coincidentally also occurred in the same year. It led to a period of colonial expansion, which provided a place for crypto-Jews and *conversos* to settle that at least initially was beyond the reach of the Inquisition. I am not suggesting that a significant number of the colonists were either *conversos* or crypto-Jews, and most historians would argue that they were a minority; nonetheless, the Inquisition documents cited by Hordes (2005) and others indicate that crypto-Jews were among the settlers in New Spain, and the presence of individuals and communities in the American Southwest claiming crypto-Jewish identity suggests that at least some aspects of the identity and practices of crypto-Judaism were passed down to subsequent generations.

The 100,000 Spanish Jews who went to Portugal in 1492 were initially allowed to maintain their beliefs. In 1496, an edict of expulsion was issued by Manuel I, and it was followed by forced conversion. The evidence suggests that many of the Jews who resisted conversion became crypto-Jews. The Inquisition was established in Portugal in 1540 (Jacobs 2002:8). Crypto-Jews and *conversos* from Portugal were among the settlers of the New World, and crypto-Jewish communities have been identified in the mountains of present-day Portugal.

In spite of attempts to ban the migration of *conversos* to the Americas, a wide range of documentary evidence suggests that *conversos* from Spain were among the colonists in New Spain and parts of South America. Gitlitz (1996:53–60) and other historians (for example, Liebman 1970:47) suggest that these settlers, although a minority of the colonial population, still constituted a significant proportion. This contention is supported by the establishment of the Inquisition in New Spain in 1571. There were several periods of serious persecution of the Judaizers in Mexico, particularly the 1580s and 1590s and the 1640s. While the 1640s marked the last extensive period of persecution, there were sporadic trials during the remainder of the seventeenth century. Gitlitz (1996:58) points out that while the records from the years before 1650 suggest that crypto-Judaism was essentially a communal tradition, the trial documents from the rest of the century indicate its transformation to a more individualistic tradition.

Some scholars, particularly Hordes (2005), associate the move of *conversos* and possibly crypto-Jews to northern Mexico, with the establishment of Nuevo León, and eventually to New Mexico with the initial period of persecution. He argues that the foundation of Nuevo León was led by a man of *converso* descent, Luis de Carvajal, and that a number of the colonists were also *conversos*. His work suggests that this colonial enterprise was in part motivated by a wish to move away from the center of inquisitorial power in Mexico City (Hordes 2005:72–86). In 1589, Carvajal was arrested by the Inquisition. This was followed in 1590 by an illegal foray into what is now New Mexico by his lieutenant governor, Gaspar Castaño de Sosa, who has also been identified as being of *converso* descent. Hordes (2005:85–93) suggests that Castaño de Sosa's move into New Mexico was motivated by a fear of the Inquisition and that many of the colonists who accompanied him were also of *converso* descent. Although Castaño de Sosa's expedition was ultimately terminated, it precipitated an authorized settlement of New Mexico by Juan de Oñate in 1595. Hordes demonstrates that some of the *converso* participants in the settlement of Nuevo León and the foray into New Mexico were included in Oñate's colonization of New Mexico.

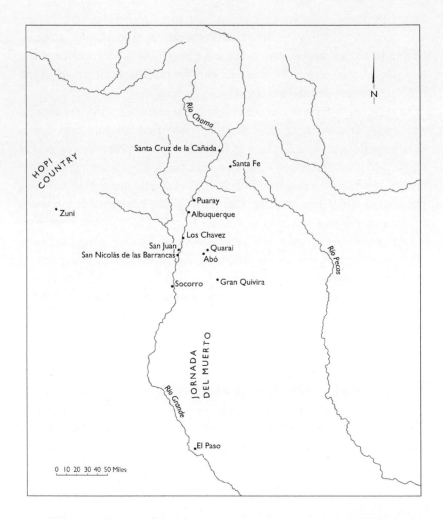

New Mexico in the sixteenth and seventeenth centuries. (Map by Bill Nelson)

Oñate's expedition heralded the settlement of New Mexico by Spain. While *conversos* or their descendents played a part in this initial colonization, no historian suggests that they made up a preponderance of the settlers. It is also important to note that there were waves of settlement, and thus the ancestors of those who claim crypto-Jewish descent may have arrived in New 9 Mexico not only during the years of Spanish colonial dominance, but also after the establishment of Mexico or even after the annexation of northern Mexico by the United States after the Mexican War. Although the colony in New Mexico came under the authority of the Inquisition, the Holy Office did not have a direct presence in New Mexico; individuals accused of heresy were sent to Mexico City for trial.[3] Accusations of Judaizing, and therefore relatively direct evidence for the presence of crypto-Jews in New Mexico, occurred in the first period of settlement, prior to the Pueblo Revolt (1680–1692). For example, Governor Bernardo López de Mendizábal, members of his family, and other prominent members of the community were arrested and tried for Judaizing (Hordes 2005:150–162). After the Pueblo Revolt in New Mexico and more widely in New Spain, accusations of Judaizing by the Inquisition are largely absent from the records. While this may be due to the end of significant Judaizing in the colonies, it may also be due to a change in the focus of the Inquisition to economically and politically more significant targets—with the increased incursions and colonial settlement by Protestant powers in the region. Thus direct evidence for crypto-Judaism in New Mexico largely ceases until the early twentieth century, when there is a brief and tantalizing statement by Mary Austin (1919): "[T]here does not appear to be any of the Spanish Jew among these old settlers, such as may be traced further south in New Mexico" (9–10). The most significant indication of crypto-Judaism did not reemerge until the latter half of the twentieth century, when individuals in the community began to talk publicly about their heritage, leading scholars to become increasingly interested in the possible presence of crypto-Jews in the American Southwest.

Patterns of Colonial Settlement

The geographic location of crypto-Jewish communities and its relation to the shape of crypto-Jewish practices is one of the features of this ethnography. The evidence suggests that crypto-Jews in the remote northern parts of New Mexico maintained a higher degree of communal practice and perhaps a less secret form of crypto-Judaism than did those who lived in closer proximity to the centers of colonial power.

The initial settlement of New Mexico in the period before the Pueblo Revolt largely mapped onto the location of the main Native American pueblos along the Rio Grande, from around Socorro in the south to Taos in the north. The pattern was related both to the role of the colony—that is, as a missionary province—and the accessibility of water and thus the possibility of irrigation and agriculture (Nostrand 1992:32–33). Santa Fe was designated as the capital and became the main location of settlement and colonial power. During this period, Spaniards lived in two forms of settlement: the *villa*, Santa Fe, with some residents holding *encomiendas* (a limited number of tributary awards associated with the pueblos), and *estancias*, land grants for farming and ranching, also associated with the pueblos to maximize the use of Native American labor (Nostrand 1992:35). By the time of the Pueblo Revolt, Nostrand estimates, the Spanish population of New Mexico was 2,500. Santa Fe was the largest settlement, with the rest of the population dispersed along the Rio Grande and with friars and other missionaries based in the pueblos (Nostrand 1992:36).

After the reconquest of the colony from the Pueblo rebels in 1692, the twelve-year hiatus in settlement ended. Two new *villas* were established: Santa Cruz, twenty miles north of Santa Fe, in 1695; and Albuquerque, some sixty miles to the southwest, in 1706 (Nostrand 1992:39–40). During the eighteenth century, Santa Cruz became an important source for colonial expansion. Small settlements were established to the north on both sides of the Rio Grande, and the hometowns of many of the individuals interviewed for this book were founded in the mountainous area to the south of Taos (Nostrand 1992:41). It is important to note that Nostrand's discussion suggests that many of these villages were illegally established by a small number of families, which may support the ethnographic evidence that groups of families with crypto-Jewish identity settled together and that, due to their remoteness from both church and colonial power, they were able to develop a more communal form of practice.

The economy of New Mexico throughout its history has been largely agricultural. Initially, the primary source of income was through agricultural smallholdings. As settlement progressed, there was also an increasing, although always a minority, role for stockmen, particularly sheep farmers

(Nostrand 1992:75–76). The 1790 census indicates that most family heads identified their occupation as farming (Stamatov 2003:10). The Rio Grande core was always more heavily agricultural, while the periphery was more heavily ranching. Although more than 90 percent of the individuals interviewed were no longer involved in any form of farming, most reported that their fathers or grandfathers had been smallholders.

The Hispanos

Throughout this book, I utilize the term "Hispano" in reference to the Hispanic community in New Mexico (as distinct from the word "Anglo," which is used to describe non–Native Americans of non-Hispanic origin). "Hispano" also denotes what some scholars and many Hispanos themselves consider to be a distinctive subculture (Nostrand 1992:7).

Nostrand (1992) suggests that a number of aspects of Hispano culture make it distinctive: language, specific surnames, folklore and art, and the Penitentes. The Spanish traditionally used by Hispanos is of Castilian origin and preserves many archaic grammatical and semantic structures not found in other modern forms of Spanish. Nostrand and other scholars have also identified a particular name-set in the Hispano population; for example, Buechley identified thirty-nine "distinctively New Mexican names" (cited in Nostrand 1992:8). Some given names, as well as surnames, are also specific to the Hispano population. Nostrand (1992) suggests that the folkloric tradition found among the Hispanos is "diffused from Iberia to New Mexico" and preserved in a unique oral tradition (10). The art of the *santero*, in the form of either flat (*retablos*) or three-dimensional (*bultos*) depictions of saints, is also regarded as a distinctive characteristic of the community in New Mexico. The Penitente brotherhood, "a lay Hispano society organized for penance and mutual aid," apparently established in the nineteenth century, also contains many uniquely Hispano features (Nostrand 1992:11–13). The reasons for the distinctiveness of each of these areas, Nostrand (1992:7–19) argues, is twofold:

1. The settlers of New Mexico arrived earlier than those of the other parts of the American Southwest and largely directly from Spain.
2. Once established, the Hispano settlement was isolated.

While these arguments relate to the development of a unique Hispano culture, they also hint at the possible preservation and transmission of a crypto-Jewish subculture within the wider Hispano population.

It is important to emphasize that although the Hispanos consider themselves to be Spanish, this should not be understood as a statement of ethnic origin (in terms of a model of ethnicity based on descent). The term "Spaniard" in New Mexico, unlike in other parts of the Spanish colonial settlement, does not appear to have been reserved for the elite. Nostrand (1992) observes that the class included "the mestizo majority" (14). This point is also emphasized by Ross Frank (1988) in relation to a number of different elements of the community. Thus he argues that *genízaros*, originally baptized Native American slaves, could be referred to as *españoles*. He also notes that there was a more general fluidity to terminology and self-identification based on the negotiation of status (Frank 1998:57). This point is significant, as some scholars have suggested that the claim of Jewish identity by some Hispanos is equivalent to a claim of racial purity. Both in the past and in the present, most individuals do not seem to be excluding the possibility of a more varied origin in their assertions of being *españoles* or crypto-Jews.

The wide use of the term *español* should not be seen as suggesting that New Mexican society was undifferentiated in terms of either status or ethnic origin. It was hierarchical, with those individuals in the highest economic levels claiming the highest status, *español*. This claim, however, was based largely on economic and social standing rather than ethnic or racial origin (Frank 1998:56). While the caste terms used in other parts of the Spanish diaspora were used in New Mexico—for example, mestizo, with *español* at the top—Frank's (1998:57) discussion clearly indicates a strong degree of negotiation of status.[4] This is supported by Suzanne Stamatov (2003:201–203), who suggests that the concept of *limpieza de sangre*—the emphasis on a pure line of Spanish blood—was not a significant feature of the claim of *español* status in New Mexico. She argues that it does not seem to have shaped marriage patterns and that there are correspondingly only very rare cases of marriages between closely related cousins. With the exception of mestizo, none of these caste terms was used in any of the interviews conducted for this book. Many of the individuals who were, in effect, claiming connection with the *español* class also clearly acknowledged a variety of other ethnic elements in their lines of descent.

The Ashkenazic Jews

During the first half of the nineteenth century, New Mexico was linked to the United States by the Santa Fe Trail. It is likely that the first Ashkenazic Jews arrived in New Mexico during that period. The main settlement of Ashkenazic Jews, however, came after the annexation of New Mexico by the United States in 1846, after the Mexican War. The early Jewish settlers were mostly traders and merchants of German origin. Henry Tobias (1990:57) notes that during the initial period, up to 1860, the majority of these men married women from the local Hispano population. Although there is no contemporary evidence that they chose to marry into families identified as crypto-Jewish, several of the individuals from Albuquerque interviewed for this book indicated that their families had intermarried with these men, and they believed that this had been done with the knowledge that the men were Jewish. By 1870, the community was well established, and the majority of Ashkenazic men were marrying women of German Jewish origin (Tobias 1990:57).

The establishment of formal communal structures waited until almost the end of the century. While the first Yom Kippur service was performed in 1860 and the first bar mitzvah was celebrated in 1876, the first synagogue was not founded until 1886. At that time, Temple Montefiore opened in Las Vegas, with Albert Congregation being established ten years later in Albuquerque. Today, Jewish institutions of all varieties are found in many parts of the state, and synagogues representing most denominations of Judaism are found in both Albuquerque and Santa Fe.

Methodological Considerations

Alongside historical and literary methodologies, anthropological or, more specifically, ethnographic methods are particularly useful in coming to an understanding of the way people interact and make meaning of their lives and the world in which they live. These methods form the basis of the research included in this book. The ethnographic methods employed attempt to find a balance between the internal point of view (that is, how people look at themselves and interpret and understand their lives) and the external point of view (that is, the theoretical and comparative assumptions of the observer in his or her attempt to understand the nature of the society that is being observed).

The primary element of the method of anthropological fieldwork employed in this study was participant observation, which has two main aspects: participation in cultural activities and close observation of those activities. The fieldwork for this study was conducted over twelve years, including more than twelve months in the field. During that period, participant observation was used in a variety of contexts. While the most important was participating in and observing activities defined by the informants as crypto-Jewish, the contexts also included family meetings and reunions, informal and formal teaching sessions conducted for and by individuals who claimed crypto-Jewish identity, and annual conferences of the Society for Crypto-Judaic Studies.

This last arena of study might be considered surprising. The conference, as discussed in chapter 1, serves many purposes. On the one hand, it provides a location for academics and others to meet and present papers on the subject from a primarily external perspective. On the other, and even more important, it offers a place where crypto-Jews can meet and learn about and come to an understanding of their heritage. The conference therefore plays a very important role in the process of cultural construction and development for the community itself and is an essential arena of study for the anthropologist if he or she is to understand the nature of present-day crypto-Judaism. The importance of this type of meeting is underscored by the development of similar events, often initiated by crypto-Jews, as a means to communicate with and reach out to individuals who have not had the opportunity to learn about their cultural heritage.

In this discussion, and indeed throughout this book, I use the term "cultural construction." It may be thought by some that it implies that the culture so constructed is therefore inauthentic. But cultural construction and recreation are processes that occur in all cultures and are therefore not related to either authenticity or inauthenticity. Unlike genetic inheritance, which is to a great extent fixed (albeit the new arguments about evo-devo [evolutionary developmental biology] are challenging this), cultural inheritance is passed down through enculturation and education. As such, each individual's cultural inheritance, although to a great extent shared, also includes aspects that are unique, based on the person's experiences and the information available to him or her through those experiences. The appropriation of aspects of culture also includes a degree of negotiation, with individuals at different stages consciously and unconsciously determining which aspects they will accept and which they will reject. In this view, individuals and communities undergo a continuous process of cultural construction, based on their experiences of new information and new social contexts.

This process is as true for the Reform, Conservative, and Orthodox Jew— who upon learning new ideas or approaches adds to or transforms his Jewish experience and or practice—as it is for the crypto-Jew, who through participating in conferences or reading an article or book adds to her understanding of her culture and identity. It should be apparent from this argument that I view culture as undergoing a continuous process of negotiation at all levels and thus being in a continuous state of construction or recreation.

One of the problems with using participant observation in the crypto-Jewish community is that the cultural practices today are largely narrative; that is, many crypto-Jews speak about their experiences rather than perform the practices themselves. This raises issues about memory and the nature of a culture that exists largely in memory. I touch on those issues later, but now suggest that many of the informants regarded talking about and sharing their experiences as a cultural practice, especially when they are sharing with other crypto-Jews in informal or even formal contexts.

The focus on the oral and remembered nature of much of crypto-Judaism leads to the second main method used in this study: unstructured interviews. The primary goal of this research was to determine how individuals who claimed crypto-Jewish heritage constructed meaning for themselves— how they used stories, practices, and interpretations to create a sense of identity and self. Thus the interviews did not seek to focus the discussion or to look for particular themes or issues. The interviews were unstructured and open-ended, following the thoughts and ideas of the interviewees rather than the interests of the interviewer. By this process, I also sought not to shape the informants' expectations or, indeed, the choice of interpretations or which practices to interpret.

It must be stated, however, that two expectations were built into the process. Almost every individual interviewed knew that my interests related to crypto-Judaism; thus that knowledge must have shaped the nature of the informants' responses to some extent. In addition, all the individuals were willing to be interviewed, so people who had nothing to say or did not wish to say anything were not included in the study. On this basis, any study of a subject like crypto-Judaism suffers from a fundamental aspect of observer bias: since the people being observed or interviewed are aware or think they are aware of the subject of study—and therefore may have expectations about what is appropriately included in that subject—they may tailor their responses to address it.

The research for this project was conducted between 1995 and 2007. During those years, more than twelve months were spent in the field— with the longest continuous period of fieldwork being two months. The research was carried out in this way in order to explore longitudinal developments and expressions of identity; on this basis, twenty of the individuals included in the study were interviewed a minimum of two times, with several years between the interviews. The extended period of time also facilitated the exploration of the development of different forms of groupings related to crypto-Jewish identity.

The repeated interviews were intended neither to test the authenticity of the individuals nor to get them to reiterate information from previous occasions, although this often occurred. Rather, they aimed to explore how individuals moving through different contexts and life circumstances expressed their understanding of their identity and how they used different aspects of memory and constructions of the past in relation to their potentially changed self-understanding.

While over 150 individuals were included in the wider purview of the study—that is, observed in different settings, public and private, with greater or lesser degrees of informal conversation—110 individuals (59 women and 51 men) were formally interviewed. Most of the interviews were conducted in individuals' homes; others, in synagogues, conference venues, and restaurants. Although the interviewees included a greater number of women than men, this should not be taken as significant. During the course of the research, I was not concerned with the gender issue and made no conscious attempt to balance the study in order to test particular questions.

The process of including people in the research was somewhat organic, with no attempt to randomize the sample. Initially, I built on existing connections—that is, individuals who attended the conferences of the Society for Crypto-Judaic Studies or who were known to other scholars working in the field. The majority of those included in the study, however, came from working through networks of associations and had been neither connected with public associations nor previously interviewed.

It might be helpful to present an actual example of the procedure. When I arrived in New Mexico in 1995, I had a list of individuals studying crypto-

Judaism, one of whom was a nonacademic who was working in Albuquerque. I arranged a meeting with her to learn about crypto-Judaism. During the meeting, she offered to contact a crypto-Jew who might be willing to talk to me. The next evening, I received a call from my contact. She said that the crypto-Jew had asked that I speak with her rabbi first, to decide if I was an appropriate person to talk to; the rabbi was from the Ultra Orthodox Jewish community (Habad). After I spoke with her rabbi, the crypto-Jew agreed to meet me at the Conservative synagogue, to which she was also connected. Over the summer, I met her several times at the synagogue. On my return to New Mexico the following year, she invited me to her home, where I conducted several interviews. The following year, I again interviewed her at home; during this period, she invited members of her family, who also were exploring their crypto-Jewish identities. During that and the subsequent years, I met with many of these individuals in different settings, and they, in turn, introduced me to other crypto-Jews. This process began (not including the lay-scholar) with a woman who was in many respects a public crypto-Jew. She had been interviewed on other occasions and was a member of a number of Jewish communities. As the network grew, it came to include individuals who never had been interviewed and were in no sense public crypto-Jews; some of them had only a very distant or even no connection with the woman with whom the network had started.

The individuals who participated in this study come from most socioeconomic levels of New Mexican society. The sample included civil servants, lawyers, professors (at both the University of New Mexico and other academic institutions), teachers, students, doctors, owners of small shops and restaurants, artists (working in both vernacular and international styles), retired men and women, nonworking women, small-scale famers, and unemployed individuals. It should be noted from the outset that there was no significant association of either employment or education with a particular expression of crypto-Jewish identity.

Due perhaps to the nature of the networks studied in this project, the majority of the participants were from the area of New Mexico to the north of and including Albuquerque. The families of many of those individuals who were interviewed in Albuquerque had moved to the city in either the current or the previous generation. More than 70 percent of the respondents were members of families that lived in the triangle formed by Taos, Santa Fe, and Las Vegas, New Mexico. Others came from other parts of the state, such as the areas to the south of Albuquerque, especially around Belen, and

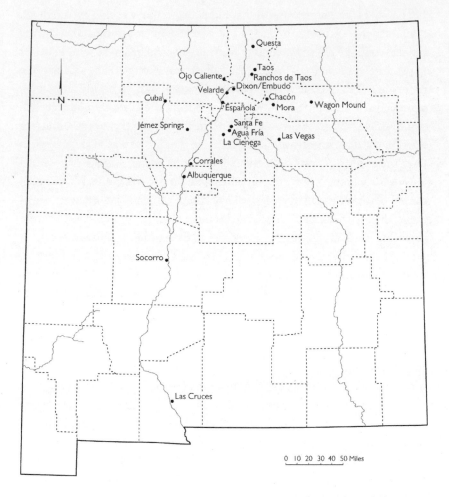

New Mexico in the nineteenth to twenty-first centuries. (Map by Bill Nelson)

to the west of Santa Fe, near Cuba. It should be emphasized that the individuals who participated may not reflect the spread of people with crypto-Jewish identity, as the project was not intended to test geographic dispersion. An analysis of the relationship between identity and geography did, however, have an interesting result. It suggested that in the more remote mountainous areas around Taos, a greater degree of communal crypto-Jewish identity was expressed than in the areas around the former centers of Spanish colonial power—for example, Santa Fe and Albuquerque.

A small majority of the participants, 55 percent, said that their formal religious affiliation was Catholic; all of them and a significant majority of the informants as a whole reported that their grandparents and/or parents were Catholic, most stating clearly that they had never belonged to any other tradition. Of the remaining interviewees, 27 percent were associated with mainstream Protestant denominations, primarily Presbyterian but also Baptist or Episcopal. A small number of respondents, ten, had direct connections with Seventh-Day Adventism, Mormonism, or messianic synagogues or churches. The rest of the participants were nominally or formally associated with one of the mainstream Jewish traditions. I am not indicating their level of crypto-Jewish identification in highlighting their formal religious affiliation. In many cases, as discussed later, formal or even significant participation in a Christian tradition was not regarded as mutually exclusive from a crypto-Jewish identity. Even a majority of those who considered them to be mutually exclusive maintained an external Christian identity, even if it was little more than a mask that they consciously saw as hiding their inward Jewish identity from discovery by their neighbors.

Although other scholars have chosen to use the names of the individuals who participated in their research, I have chosen to maintain the anonymity of my informants. Many of them, who are not part of the public debates, requested that their names not be used. This practice is employed by other anthropologists—for example, Judith Okely in her excellent ethnography *The Traveller-Gypsies* (1983)—and is consistent with the statement of ethnographic ethics developed by the American Anthropological Association,[5] which makes it clear that ethnographers have specific obligations to the people they study and interview in relation to both potential harm and the use of personal identifiers. There is also a good theoretical reason for this anonymization. The individual statements discussed are not meant to indicate purely individual practice; rather, they are used to illustrate views held by a wider group in Hispano society. Thus the anonymous name should be seen as referring to both an individual interview and context and a wider aspect of crypto-Jewish practice and understanding.

Different forms of material culture was another aspect of ethnographic study that played an important role in this research, as discussed in chapter 6. Thus many scholars looking at crypto-Judaism have explored the use of symbols on gravestones, noting, for example, the appearance of six-pointed stars on grave markers throughout New Mexico. A key aspect of our methodology was the view that symbols do not speak for themselves. In the course of this research, I attempted to test the meaning of these symbols, recognizing that there are several horizons of meaning. Thus I was interested in how crypto-Jews unassociated with a gravestone used it as a means of self-authentication. I was also, however, concerned to discover why particular symbols or, on occasion, particular names were originally used. Where possible, therefore, I interviewed families associated with the erection of the stones to find out how they explained the symbols and names.

A good example of the differences between horizons is found in the context of an interview conducted in Albuquerque. The interview was about a particular gravestone on which there were symbols that the respondent associated with crypto-Jewish identity. The marker had been put up in his mother's lifetime. When he was asked how his mother viewed it, he answered that he did not know. I thus potentially had two differing interpretations in each of the horizons. The interviewee related the symbols to his interpretation of a crypto-Jewish past, representing Judaism. His mother may have shared this meaning (as other evidence suggests), but the family may have used the symbols because they liked the shapes or because the symbols had some other, more personal meanings.

Although this discussion has largely been methodological, it is important to touch on some of the theoretical implications of the type of approach taken here. While in its analysis of the data this research seeks to balance external and internal perspectives, it is not directly concerned with the issue of proof of authenticity. In relation to crypto-Judaism, two main approaches claim the right to determine authenticity (or, more usually, inauthenticity). In the first, some scholars utilize an external, allegedly objective academic model. They establish a basis of judgment from a particular disciplinary framework, which usually denies any value to the self-understanding of the communities being studied. They alone (or, occasionally, in concert with other academics) have the right to decide whether a practice or an identity is authentically Jewish or crypto-Jewish. While it is important to learn from such scholars and to take seriously their alternative explanations, it is equally important to take seriously the internal understanding and interpretations of members of a group. The second approach emerges from the mainstream Jewish traditions, in which rabbis, serving as gatekeepers, work within their internally predefined system (that is, Halacha [Jewish law]) to establish authenticity or inauthenticity. While I clearly do not challenge a group's right to establish boundaries, it must be made clear that the group's determination of authenticity is part of its specific internal language game.[6] Thus the mainstream Jewish determination of authenticity can at best be seen as relative to the language game that they are playing and standing alongside the games played by other groups, in this case including the crypto-Jews. The mainstream Jewish game, however, comes into play when crypto-Jews seek admittance to mainstream Jewish communities.

In this study, I regard culture as being closely interrelated with self-understanding. Thus the fact that many of the individuals interviewed consider themselves to be crypto-Jews, and interpret their past (often both their own past experience and the historical past of their families and communities) and present on the basis of this self-understanding, supports their cultural authenticity as crypto-Jews and, indeed, in a technical sense as Jews (although not necessarily thereby acceptable to the mainstream communities). Crypto-Judaism is in our terms an authentic Jewish culture that is worthy of being taken seriously in relation to other Jewish communities. It must, however, be emphasized that this view in no way provides a demonstration of historical authenticity. Historical authenticity (within the context of academic history) relies on documentary evidence and argumentation and can be determined only on that basis. It is outside the scope of this study.

The internal point of view is both the methodological center of our discussion and a key aspect of the theoretical approach. While, as I have suggested, some academic discussions ignore internal interpretations, the method used here considers them to be key data. Thus the meanings attributed by insiders to a particular action or practice or to their definitions of self do not lose their value if they are shown to not have an externally authenticated historical basis. Rather, they are understood as valid interpretations within a living cultural context. While the genesis of an action or a practice (or, indeed, of a people or culture) may be of great interest, in our view the current existential and ethnographic realities are even more significant as they relate to the lives and aspirations of individuals and communities trying to find meaning and value in the world.

ONE
_____

DIVERSITY AND COMPLEXITY

On the surface, the phenomenon of crypto-Judaism may seem simple; that is, crypto-Jews are individuals descended from families that were forcibly converted from Judaism to Catholicism between 1390 and 1492 in Spain (and 1497 in Portugal). In reality, crypto-Judaism was highly complex in the years before 1492; in those after the expulsion of the Jewish community from Spain; and in those of Spanish colonial expansion, which ultimately led to the settlement of New Mexico. This complexity is suggested by the question of the authenticity of the Jews' conversion to Catholicism— the extent to which the conversion was sincere and the aspects of Judaism that were retained and by whom—and by the subsequent choices faced by the _conversos_ in relation to their place of residence and the presence or absence of the Inquisition. The historical complexity is illustrated by the active contemporary debates among rabbis and, indeed, inquisitors about the Jewishness of the people who had converted as well as the current debates among historians about the number of individuals who retained any form of Jewish identity beyond the first generation of _conversos_. The complexity can only have increased in New Mexico up to the present day as a result of both assimilation into the Hispano culture and interaction with non-Hispano groups, ranging from Native Americans to Ashkenazic Jews.

The Society for Crypto-Judaic Studies

The Society for Crypto-Judaic Studies (SCJS) was founded in 1990 by
Stanley Hordes, a historian; Rena Down, a Sephardic Jewish author; and
Joshua Stampfer, a rabbi from Portland, Oregon. Although its initial con-
stituency and interests were essentially academic—and it has maintained
a strong academic base, branching into a wide range of disciplines—the
society has grown to become a highly diverse organization whose members come from a range of backgrounds and express different cultural and
religious identities. Both the historical and the contemporary complexities
of crypto-Judaism are the concern of the SCJS, which has had to wrestle
with the relationship between crypto-Judaism and mainstream Judaism, a
set of issues that have been addressed by rabbis and other scholars of Jewish tradition.

The members of the society can be broadly grouped into three main categories: crypto-Jews, academics, and interested laypeople (who are primarily
Anglo Jews). The SCJS holds annual conferences at which individuals from
all three constituencies speak and participate.

The crypto-Jewish members of the society make up a diverse group. Some
come from families with a long-standing tradition of crypto-Judaism, while
others are searching for spiritual meaning and may have a mystical calling to
Judaism or believe that Judaism offers them a spiritual home. Some have
made formal or informal associations with mainstream Jewish communities, often through conversion or, increasingly, ceremonies of return, while
others identify with non-Jewish traditions—for example, Catholicism, Mormonism, or secular Hispanic culture. Thus these crypto-Jews reflect the diversity of religious and nonreligious traditions found in the Southwest, particularly in New Mexico.

The crypto-Jews who participate in the conferences are also geographically diverse. While many, given the initial focus of the society, come or
came from New Mexico, an increasing number are from other parts of the
Southwest. The conferences have also drawn individuals from Hispanic
and Portuguese communities in other regions of the United States as well
as from such other countries as Spain, Portugal, and Mexico. As the concept of crypto-Judaism has gained wider currency, people from non-
Hispanic populations who believe that there are Spanish elements in their
ancestry have used the conferences as a foundation for exploring these issues in the roots and traditions of their own families.

Even the participants from New Mexico represent a range of geographic areas. As a result of population movements relating to economic forces, most come from large cities—for example, Albuquerque and Santa Fe. This may also be due to the location of the conferences and the limitation of knowledge about either the SCJS or crypto-Judaism to main areas of urban settlement.[1] Many, however, live or have roots in the remote mountainous areas in the north of the state. As discussed later, geography played an important role in shaping the crypto-Jewish experience and developing various forms of crypto-Jewish culture.

The crypto-Jews are diverse not only geographically but also culturally. The boundaries of crypto-Jewish culture are fuzzy: on one side, it overlaps with different forms of Christianity—for example, Catholicism, mainstream Protestant denominations, and Mormonism; on other sides, it increasingly interrelates with different branches of mainstream Judaism—from Reconstructionist to Ultra Orthodox. Various individuals or groups link with Mexican, Hispano, Native American, or Anglo-American cultural forms and, indeed, any and all combinations of these. The difficulty of speaking of crypto-Jewish culture is exacerbated by the intensity of focus on the individual family (or even individual person) rather than on the group, which has characterized much of the crypto-Jewish experience.

Within this diversity, different degrees of knowledge, identification, and assimilation add further complications. This is reflected in the distinction between two groups of crypto-Jews who attend the conferences. One is composed of those who are members of the SCJS and thus are connected to other related associations. They therefore participate in ongoing and, to some degree, public networks of communication and learning. The second group includes those crypto-Jews who come to a conference by chance, having heard about it through the media or, more often, though word of mouth. Many of them are not public crypto-Jews. While they may have a strongly developed crypto-Jewish identity, they often are unconnected with organized networks or associations. Both the public and the non-public crypto-Jews who attend the conferences often use them as a means to both network and explore what their identity means or, indeed, what it could mean to them. These two groups constitute a microcosm of the community; a minority of individuals play an important public role, while the majority maintains the privacy and secrecy that characterize crypto-Judaism.

The academic conferees come from a wide variety of disciplines, including anthropology, history, genetics, Jewish studies, and sociology. Some teach subjects unrelated to crypto-Judaism—for example, management studies—but have an interest in crypto-Judaism or, more generally, Sephardic Judaism. While the majority of the scholars come from the mainstream Jewish community, others are affiliated with various Christian traditions, particularly Catholicism. Some are either rabbis or priests and at times speak from a religious rather than a "purely" academic perspective.

Academics from the Hispanic community with some present or historical connection with crypto-Judaism bridge the divide between the outside, academic role and the inside, crypto-Jewish role. The papers presented by these conferees tend to include both academic argumentation and exploration of self-understanding or -identification, emphasizing one or the other depending on the relative importance of crypto-Judaism in their self-identity. The lay or nonacademic members of the society almost exclusively are of Jewish descent. Some have a general interest in the subject of crypto-Judaism; others regard the crypto-Jews as a community that needs assistance in returning to Judaism. Some individuals "read" the crypto-Jewish story as a narrative through which they can explore their own identities though a range of artistic forms—for example, the novel or dramatic reconstructions of the crypto-Jewish experience.

Although these fictions are more indicative of the individuals who create them than of crypto-Jews, they do raise interesting questions about the use to which mainstream Jews put crypto-Jews as cultural symbols and the way in which crypto-Jews are perceived and received among mainstream Jews as well as non-Jews.

The SCJS Conference

A synthesis of recent meetings of the Society for Crypto-Judaic Studies provides a microcosm for the discussion of the complexities of the crypto-Jewish community and its connections to a variety of groups: academic, religious, and cultural.[2] An annotated outline of a characteristic conference is presented, with the addition of some ethnographic detail, to highlight the nature of the society and to introduce the wider issues in the study of crypto-Judaism.[3]

First Panel: Academic History

The first panel of the conference addresses the subject of history from an academic perspective. Some papers examine the genealogical origins of individuals or families, tracing them back through Mexico to their roots in Spain. Others explore the Inquisition and its definition of Jewish practices as well as the apparent extent of Judaizing in Spain and its colonies in the New World. Some of the historians who participate in this panel may be crypto-Jews themselves and thus have a personal interest in the subject. The main paper in this panel is presented by Stanley Hordes, one of the founders of the SCJS. He is a historian who comes from the Ashkenazi Jewish community. His work has focused on the experience of crypto-Jews in the Spanish colonies, and he has spent considerable time studying crypto-Judaism in New Mexico from an academic historical perspective. His research has been the most public face of the discussion of crypto-Judaism as it is found in the Southwest. It has also been the focus of many challenges, particularly those that question the historical authenticity of crypto-Jewish continuity in New Mexico and the wider Southwest. The issues of authenticity developed in his talk, due in part to addressing those challenges, increasingly have become features of much of the discussion at the SJCS conferences.

The other speaker is of more recent vintage, attending the conference for the first time. He is from the Hispano community and is completing a doctorate in history. While he does have a personal interest in crypto-Judaism in relation to his own family, his paper is historical and analytical. It focuses on the social and economic links among Jews, *conversos*, and Catholics in fifteenth-century Spain.

One of the themes that unites this section and, indeed, many of the other panels is authenticity. Scholars from a number of disciplines—for example, history, folklore, and sociology—have questioned the historical roots of crypto-Judaism in the Southwest. They argue, for example, that it may be a creation of scholars or of the crypto-Jews themselves, who fashioned it on the basis of intentionally or unintentionally misunderstood similarities between Jewish and Judaizing Christian folk practices. Authenticity is an issue of significance not only for many academics but also, not surprisingly, for individuals who identify themselves as crypto-Jews. For academics, the challenge calls into question their data and conclusions. For crypto-Jews, the challenge is understood as an attack on their identity and integrity, as well as the veracity of their memories.

History also plays a number of roles for both academics and crypto-Jews. For academics, the analysis of historical data is, to a large extent, an end in itself. It is part of a process of trying to understand the origins and nature of crypto-Judaism as both a historical and cultural phenomenon. For historians and other academics studying crypto-Judaism, the questions about authenticity raise important issues that have to be addressed in their research and thus are part of a normal academic debate, provided that the challenges are couched in those terms. What is interesting, however, is that the arguments against authenticity often question the integrity of scholars rather than merely the veracity of their research. While it would be fascinating to discover the reasons behind the emotional tone of the challenges, the analysis presented here focuses on the content of the academic debates, not attempting to attribute motives to those who argue either for or against the historical and cultural authenticity of crypto-Judaism.

All identities are authentic as well as constructed by an individual and his or her community. The historical evidence is conclusive in demonstrating a link between the crypto-Jews of New Mexico and the Jews of Spain. It is also probable (although not absolutely demonstrable) that both practices and constructions of self-identification were passed down though the generations. The commonality in the expression of these identities and the similarities in practices found in other parts of the Spanish diaspora—for example, Puerto Rico—strongly support the continuity of practice and identity expressed by modern crypto-Jews in New Mexico.

Second Panel: Personal History

The second historical panel is composed of individuals from the crypto-Jewish community who have in interest in history but do not have professional historical training. Their papers often focus on specific issues that relate to their own families and tend to move the issue of authenticity to the fore. They occasionally make historical connections that would not be made by more academically trained scholars and utilize a wider range of material including memory and family traditions.

Unlike academic historians, these panelists use historical data primarily to authenticate their constructions of identity, particularly in relation to the challenges to that identity in both the academic and the poplar press. History both validates and is validated by present experience and self-understanding.

One paper in the panel explores the associations of a family with a particular Christian religious image found in the Cathedral Basilica of Saint Francis of Assisi in Santa Fe, New Mexico.[4] It is presented by a woman, connected with the society for a long time, whose family comes from New Mexico and who has a personal and family tradition of crypto-Judaism. Using forms of historical argumentation, the paper explores the ways in which the woman's family has interacted with the image through time; it also, perhaps in light of her present understanding of identity, interprets both the image and the interaction with it in crypto-Jewish terms.

The main methodology of the second paper is oral history. The paper is delivered by a lawyer who has been associated with the society for the past few years, particularly since he has been exploring his identity. A member of the Hispano community of New Mexico, he is from a family that did not have an ongoing tradition of crypto-Judaism. He discovered it somewhat by chance and then learned more through discussions with elderly relatives. His paper explores how his discovery of crypto-Jewish or Jewish origins (in genealogical terms) led him to reinterpret his understanding of self in terms of his new understanding of the past. The main historical content of the paper comes from the oral histories provided by the lawyer's elderly relatives who have confirmed and expanded on his chance discovery.

It is important to emphasize that interpretations of the kind found in these papers are authentic. While they may or may not represent historically demonstrable causation or relationships, they do reflect processes that are part of all interactions with culture; they reflect an individual's and the community's appropriation and use of the past to validate and explain present experience.

Memory plays two roles in the papers on history by insiders: as the spur to historical research as the basis for the construction of self-understanding, and in the form of oral history. Many individuals in the crypto-Jewish community report that they have been told at some point in their lives that "Somos judíos" (We are Jews). At times, this statement is associated with a particular branch of the family or even with a specific ancestor. At other times, it merely stands on its own as a family tradition of origins. The tradition becomes the basis for historical or genealogical research, which then is employed to validate the tradition using a societally privileged form—the language and forms of evidence of academic historiography.

But most aspects of a crypto-Jewish past cannot be easily found through the traditional sources of historical analysis. With the help of professional genealogists or historians, many families can trace their genealogies back to Jewish families in Spain. This, however, gives little indication of cultural inheritance. Family trees, baptismal records, or even Inquisition documents do not indicate in unambiguous or uncontroversial ways people's self-understanding or how they understood or followed the practices passed down to them. Although Inquisition records and denunciations do describe practices that were thought to indicate Judaizing, there are serious questions about the status of both the accusations and the lists of practices included. Thus, for example, if the Inquisition had lists of stereotypical practices that were regarded as indications of Judaizing, it is likely that these lists shaped the interpretation of what people were doing and, possibly, limited the inquisitors' view, leading them to ignore practices that were not included on the lists. While Inquisition documents do include confessions, their status is problematic because torture often was used to elicit the confessions. Perhaps a few documents, like those containing the poems of Leonore Carvajal, are strong indications of identity; most, however, can only be taken as suggestive. There is also a significant gap between the end of Inquisition documents related to Judaizing, in the late seventeenth century, and the emergence of modern documentary evidence of crypto-Judaism, in the late twentieth century. Given the lack of documents presenting unambiguous statements of identity and practice, oral history—including memories of individuals' past experiences and families' narratives or traditions—must serve as the primary indicator of cultural heritage as well as the primary mechanism by which that culture is passed from one generation to the next.

The importance of memory in both understanding crypto-Jewish culture and transmitting that culture, however, raises its own set of problems and issues—many of which form a part of the discussions at the SCJS conferences. Memory, although often perceived as a fixed basis of identity, is highly fluid and contextual. Thus, as observed by individuals who have interviewed or spoken to informants, not only crypto-Jews but people from any culture or community may deploy different ranges of memories or indeed different interpretations of the past, depending on the questions asked or the context of the interview or presentation. While some might see this as an insurmountable problem, rendering memory a completely discredited tool for validation or evidence of cultural heritage, it is precisely the fluidity of memory and the importance of contextualization that mark the interaction between identity and culture—neither of which should be understood as a fixed point. Although we tend to think of history, as opposed to memory, as being fixed and therefore authoritative and authentic, history is also prone to fluidity and contextualization, although often on a more conscious or ideological level than memory.

Third Panel: Social Science

The social scientists and individuals from both inside and outside the crypto-Jewish community who focus on culture and practice as found today or in the recent past are included in the third panel, which addresses social scientific issues. The papers discuss a number of interrelated subjects: cultural and religious practices, symbols and symbolism, identity, marriage patterns, and the understanding of genealogy.

The first paper is presented by an anthropologist who has a strong crypto-Jewish tradition in his family, which he has not discussed much in public or academic contexts. He is attending the conference for the first time, and his paper brings together a highly sophisticated anthropological discussion of the nature of memory and the role of memory in his own understanding of his family's crypto-Jewish traditions. The second paper is delivered by an anthropologist who is from the wider Jewish community. Her paper reflects both an interest in the nature of identity and the possible central role of women in passing down cultural and religious practices within crypto-Judaism both currently and historically.

Both historical consciousness and memory, individual and collective, can play important roles in the construction and perception of identity. Crypto-Jews construct their identities in different ways. Most who attend the conference would agree that a conscious understanding of a Jewish past provides the basis of a crypto-Jewish identity. They do not have to consider themselves to be Jewish—indeed, they might have a wide range of religious and cultural associations other than Judaism—but the understanding of origins is regarded as significant. Thus it would be no contradiction to assert that a fully practicing Catholic was also a crypto-Jew. Other participants or interviewees, however, insist that the (or at the very least an) essential element of crypto-Jewish identity is religion: Judaism. Thus for these individuals, one cannot both be a crypto-Jew and practice a religion other than Judaism.

The basis for asserting a crypto-Jewish identity is also complex. It utilizes history, memory, and self-identification. Many crypto-Jews validate their identity through recourse to history. They point to various forms of historical argumentation and/or documentation, and the historical basis often is supported by family tradition. Others validate their identity through different forms of memory, including family memories or traditions and individual memories of events or experiences. The third means of validation comes through self-identification, based on feeling. Thus, for example, an individual may assert that she long had an affinity for Judaism or he had a dream or vision.

Participants at the conference present simple family trees as well as more complex research by historians and genealogists to depict more comprehensive genealogies. Alongside these discussions often are analyses of marriage patterns. These tend to be varied. Some individuals outline a consistent pattern of endogamy—that is, marrying within a limited number of families over a number of generations. Others discuss the alternative pattern of exogamy—that is, marrying outside the group. Some individuals particularly emphasize the varying roots of their families—for example, their Native American, African American, or Hispanic ancestors.

Fourth Panel: Symbols and Practices

The fourth panel consists of individuals from both inside and outside the crypto-Jewish community who are exploring the range of symbols and practices often identified as exemplifying crypto-Judaism. The related areas of symbols and practices are a significant component of the content of papers and discussions at SCJS conferences. The main speaker is a crypto-Jew from New Mexico. He has a strong crypto-Jewish identity and has spent many years trying to understand his family's practices, traditions, and history as well as the wider extent of crypto-Judaism in New Mexico. His paper focuses on the use of symbols on gravestones, particularly trying to identify those that are indicative of crypto-Judaism.

The second paper, presented by an anthropologist from outside the crypto-Jewish community, attempts to develop a theoretically grounded understanding of the nature of symbolism and practice. It also focuses on the way symbols and practices are understood by those who use and follow them, rather than whether they can be proved to be historically Jewish.

One of the features of crypto-Jewish studies, particularly from the non-academic perspective, is the observation that symbols identified as Jewish are used by individuals or communities in different parts of the Spanish diaspora, thus indicating that the people who use them are of Jewish descent. Many conference papers on symbolism attempt to demonstrate that symbols commonly found on gravestones—primarily the six-pointed star, or Star of David, but also pairs of candlesticks or books—can be identified as being solely used by Jews both historically and currently.

The social scientists and the individuals from the crypto-Jewish community tend to analyze symbols and practices in different ways. Occasionally, the confusion between these discourses leads to misunderstanding. The difference between the two approaches is best indicated in relation to symbols. The crypto-Jewish understanding of symbols is that they have fixed meanings, and thus the people who employ any symbol that can be traced back to Jewish traditions in Spain must be Jewish or of Jewish descent. But social scientists and folklorists argue that this approach has several intrinsic flaws.

The academic papers on symbols tend to focus on the theoretical issues relating to symbolism and the need to be very cautious in the interpretation of specific symbols and their meaning in both historical and contemporary contexts. Some papers go further, arguing that particular symbols are generic and thus provide no evidence for the past or present existence of crypto-Judaism. The papers presented by individuals in the crypto-Jewish community often have a different focus. They tend to identify a range of elements, symbolic or otherwise, as being indicators of Judaism and use them as the basis for identifying or affirming Jewish identity. Ultimately, these papers are not about making an objective argument in regard to the nature and meaning of a particular symbol, but are part of the process of self-understanding. The panelists use these symbols as a means to explain, interpret, and connect to their past— to find a material basis for authenticating their culture and identity.

From a perspective that focuses on cultural authenticity, it is a mistake to consider as false the view these papers present. The symbols interpreted as expressions of crypto-Jewish tradition do indeed have the meanings ascribed to them. These meanings, however, belong to the speaker and interpreter rather than to the individual who carved the symbol on a gravestone or made the object in question. These papers bring out the different horizons of meaning that symbols, objects, or indeed practices are able to hold simultaneously.

The distinctions between the methodologies and goals of the academic papers and those of the nonacademic presentations are important to maintain. Although those by academics—at least those by historians, folklorists, and material culture specialists—examine the historical bases and, potentially, the authenticity of the symbols and those by the crypto-Jews use the symbols as a means of understanding and self validation, provided that neither the academics nor the nonacademics confuse these aims, the two forms of discourse can provide insights into crypto-Judaism.

The section of the panel on practice is composed of individuals from the crypto-Jewish community. All three speakers come from the Southwest—Colorado and New Mexico—but have different experiences of practice in their families. The family of the Coloradan retained a set of practices until his generation, many of which continued into his childhood years. His wife's family has a related, although different, set of practices. One of the speakers from New Mexico has a strong connection with her crypto-Jewish identity, even though she is a practicing Protestant. Her family came from northern New Mexico, and she describes living in an almost open community of crypto-Jews who followed both individual and communal practices. The other New Mexican is from a family with a vague tradition of crypto-Judaism. The practices he describes are retrieved from his memories of childhood and from memories of elderly relatives. Very few of the practices persisted beyond his early childhood, and generally he has no idea why they were performed. His paper is a conscious attempt to explore what these memories might mean and specifically asks for assistance in interpreting them.

In addition to some of the questions relating to symbolism, these papers highlight a number of equally significant issues. One is the search for "pure" Jewish forms of practice—particularly those that can be traced back to Spain with little or no change. The practices presented in the papers, however, are rarely so simple. Most were constructed from a wide range of elements that originated in different cultural contexts.

Most practices, for example, have a significant element of secrecy built into them. Thus even where strong aspects of mainstream practice and symbolism remain, the crypto-Jewish ritual differs significantly from the mainstream Jewish one. A good example of this is apparent during Hanukkah. Some families light candles in an eight-branched candelabra that is similar to the *Hanukiah* used by many mainstream Jews. The menorah, however, is in a room without windows to keep it out of sight, as opposed to the traditional Jewish practice of placing the light in a window in order to publicize the miracle of Hanukkah. While this appears on the surface to be a relativity minor change, the addition of secrecy transforms the role of the *Hanukiah* from a public symbol proclaiming acknowledged identity to a private symbol affirming hidden identity.

Other practices include a much wider range of influences. Some borrowed elements from other religions—Catholic, mainstream Protestant, and messianic—while others took elements from the more general cultural environment. In interpreting these practices, it is important to understand their composite nature as well as the implications of different combinations, with different patterns of emphasis and the way they are used and made meaningful by individual crypto-Jews.

Understanding and interpreting practices by the crypto-Jews who perform them is one of the most interesting aspects of this area. Many traditions both followed and passed down in families often have little or no explanation. Thus, for example, many crypto-Jews report that they did not eat pork or use other pig products, but they never knew why. Some claimed that they disliked it; others believed that they and their families were allergic to it. This aspect of the crypto-Jewish experience raises a whole range of questions: If these practices were not interpreted or explained, in what sense are they Jewish? Are they Jewish merely because they are similar to Jewish practices or because they originated as Jewish practices? Is there something essentially Jewish that is passed down, even if the practices are just done and no other aspect of Jewish identity or tradition is present? Ultimately, is the practice itself or the interpretation or explanation of it the more important aspect; that is, are symbols and practices meaningful even if they are unexplained?

The issue of whether the practice is still performed, if it is retained only as part of a family tradition and is no longer performed, or if it is retained only as part of a memory of childhood also raises important questions. Some individuals, perhaps in response to a question or a comment, remember a practice that had been forgotten and that is not part of their current way of living. Such practices often are uninterpreted and uncontextualized. Are these memories of practices that were actually performed and are of Jewish origin, or are they artifacts of the mind's attempt to find (create) order and/or meaning? The relation between cultural forms that are no longer practiced, and reside solely in memory, and the concept of a living culture or identity must be addressed. We should not be surprised that individual crypto-Jews or individuals who are of crypto-Jewish descent take different positions: while many consider these memories to constitute part of a living culture, others regard them as remnants of a past culture that is purely of historical interest.

Beliefs and narratives stand alongside and overlap with symbols and practices. One of the interesting features of many of the papers presented by crypto-Jews is the absence or virtual absence of statements about belief. Perhaps the only clear statement made is negative—that is, what the family did not believe, rather than what it did believe. Thus some papers highlight the rejection of Jesus as god or son of god as the key statement of belief.

If, however, we look beyond strictly theological statements, there are a wide range of beliefs or ways of expressing belief encapsulated in different forms of narrative. Some means of presenting historical events provide statements of belief as well. Some crypto-Jews, for example, describe the expulsion of their ancestors from Spain using the Exodus as a narrative model. Interestingly, in many of these narratives there is an ambiguity about the location of the "promised" land: for some, it is clearly New Mexico; for others or at other points in the narrative, it is Spain; future messianic speculations are more often associated with Spain than with Israel.

Many stories express views about the nature of particular Christian practices or, on a wider level, the relationship between crypto-Jews and their neighbors. Using a humorous tone, one narrative describes how a family was able to avoid baptizing a child or, without anyone realizing, miss taking Communion during a Mass. While these kinds of stories are not explicitly about belief, they do express a strong rejection of central aspects of Christianity. One of the interesting aspects about these narratives is the close relationship between those presented as memories of childhood experiences and those presented as folktales describing the distant past in either New Mexico or Spain.

Fifth Panel: Identity

The interrelated areas of historical consciousness, genealogy and marriage patterns, self-identification, symbolism, practices, and beliefs are the key elements used by crypto-Jews to both construct and express their identity. The term "construct" suggests neither an inauthentic nor a fully conscious process. This process is common to all people, in any cultural context. Culture is not inherited whole cloth in an unchanging form from one generation to the next; rather, it is learned and appropriated by each individual and generation and is changed, both consciously and, more important, unconsciously, by those who take it forward.

The forms of identity constructed by crypto-Jews are highly complex. It is helpful to simplify the data into ideal types. Of course, no individual corresponds exactly to one type or another; rather, the categories create an ordered axis on which individuals or groups can be placed and their identities understood and interpreted. Some of these categories are illustrated by the members of a panel composed of three crypto-Jews who are exploring issues of identity. The first is a woman from northern New Mexico who has a very strong sense of her crypto-Jewish identity. Like the woman, also from northern New Mexico, on the fourth panel, she experienced some communal aspects of crypto-Judaism, but in a much more secretive form and in which families had relationships with several families rather than with a community of families. Her contribution focuses on how her Jewish understanding permeated her experiences and was shaped by a range of practices and traditions. She also introduces the importance of genealogy to her self-understanding. The second panelist expresses a much more transformative understanding and therefore a weaker form of crypto-Jewish identity. He is also from New Mexico, but had a very different childhood experience. He learned of his identity only as a late adolescent and thus was not aware of the Jewish antecedents of his family's practices as he was growing up. The third member, a woman from southern New Mexico, presents a very different identity. She describes a family that was aware of its Jewish heritage and practices, but did not consider them to be constitutive of identity. She considers Judaism to be part of the past and Catholicism to be her religious identity.

The first two categories are the most consistently represented at SCJS conferences, with the second the most commonly represented among both conferees and interviewees for this study. At one end of the axis are individuals who have an ongoing and clearly articulated crypto-Jewish identity. They regard this identity as relatively uncontested; it has been a consistent and conscious part of their lives. Thus, for example, these individuals have a strong understanding of their history and associated genealogy and characteristically embrace a wide range of practices that they interpret as associated with and expressive of that history.

Farther along the axis are individuals whose crypto-Jewish identity is not as deeply rooted as that of the first type. They include those whose families had a tradition of crypto-Judaism that they learned of as adolescents or young adults; some were informed about this identity, while others sought this information from an elderly relative. This group also includes people who discovered their crypto-Jewish heritage through genealogical or historical research. A separate subcategory is composed of individuals who have taken on a crypto-Jewish identity but, unlike the other members of this group, do not have either a family tradition or other forms of evidence on which to base this construction of identity. The reason for including them in this category rather than in a separate one is that they share two key characteristics with those who express a weak form of crypto-Jewish identity: they take on the identity consciously, and they more actively reinterpret their past experiences than do members of the other ideal types.

At the other end of the axis are individuals who in some senses should not be considered crypto-Jews because their distinguishing characteristic is that they do not consider themselves to be crypto-Jews. Like the first ideal type and unlike the second, they recognize the Jewish aspects of their ancestry, even acknowledge the possibility that some of their ancestors were crypto-Jews, and are aware of Jewish or crypto-Jewish practices. Yet they do not consider these to be defining parts of their identity.

This rejection of a crypto-Jewish identity is either religious or cultural. It usually is due to an affiliation with a religion other than Judaism, but adherence to another religious tradition is not in itself sufficient to be included in this category. Other members of this group reject crypto-Jewish identity for cultural reasons. Several interviewees suggested that at some point they had to choose between Hispanic political identity and activism and crypto-Judaism, which they regarded as being mutually exclusive. The individuals who approximate this ideal type are fascinating because they often have the crypto-Jewish identity factors to a strong degree, yet they reject them as constitutive of their identity.

A related category, usually not represented at SCJS conferences, consists of individuals or groups that either are identified by others as crypto-Jews or have practices that are similar to Jewish or crypto-Jewish practices but come from another cultural or religious tradition. The uniting feature of the members of this group is that they do not consider themselves or their practices to be either crypto-Jewish or of Jewish origin. Many associate their practices with a messianic or Seventh-Day Adventist genesis. Commonly, these individuals are misidentified as crypto-Jews because they may worship on Saturday rather than Sunday or are seen to take an interest in

Jewish holidays or other traditions. The individuals in this category who were interviewed for this study were clearly aware of the origins of their practices and did not consider themselves to be crypto-Jews in any way.

As discussed in chapter 2, some scholars, particularly Judith Neulander, consider all crypto-Jews in New Mexico to fall into this final group. The evidence, however, does not support this contention. Most individuals interviewed have no familial connection with Seventh-Day Adventism or other Judaizing traditions. Thus their identity and practices must come from another source. On a broader level, neither Seventh-Day Adventism nor messianic traditions were historically pervasive enough to account for the range and geographic origins of individuals expressing a crypto-Jewish identity. From a different perspective, this argument is also problematic because it, by definition, ignores the identity expressed. It does not consider either the acceptance or the rejection of crypto-Jewish identity to be material to the analysis. The argument developed in this book, however, considers self-definition to be central and thus makes it the defining characteristic of the range of ideal types.

One of the features of these scholars' form of analysis, which is also found in the self-perception of some of the speakers (and in the cultural understanding of those listening to their presentations), is an apparent concretization or essentialization of identity. The discussion seems to slot individuals into a specific identity, with little or no movement or transformation. The ethnography, however, indicates a greater degree of fluidity. At first, they may place themselves in the second or third category, suggesting, for example, that while they have some knowledge of their Jewish past, and it is part of their self-understanding, their Catholic heritage is the more significant aspect of their religious rather than cultural identity. Later, they may place greater emphasis on the Jewish aspects of their heritage, giving Judaism both a cultural and a religious meaning.

One of the interesting features of these changed perceptions of self is an associated change in the use and interpretation of memories. While some individuals may go from citing only a few Jewish aspects of their past, emphasizing the Jewish elements, others seem to move in the opposite direction, deemphasizing their Jewishness. Some might consider these changed uses and interpretations of memory as indicating that one or another statement must be false, but this is a misunderstanding of memory and the cultural and psychological processes related to it. Memory is always bound up with self-perception and interpretation. The memories we evoke and the way we use them are both fluid and highly contextual. These speakers illustrate the inherent fluidity of cultural and religious identity that is characteristic of crypto-Jewish ethnography. It is also, arguably, characteristic of all cultural and religious identities and is particularly consciously deployed in our postmodern world.

Sixth Panel: Genetics

The discussion of genetics and the use of genetics to demonstrate the historical authenticity of crypto-Judaism have become increasingly prominent at SJCS conferences (as well as on Internet sites related to crypto-Judaism). The panel on genetics includes three speakers. The first is the director of a company that traces genetic markers. He has had a long-term interest in genetic patterns related to Judaism and presents a technical paper on the progress of his company's work. The second paper is read by a doctor from New Mexico who has done work on genetic disorders found among Hispanos and, perhaps, crypto-Jews. Her work suggests that some of these disorders are also characteristic of the broader Jewish community, and thus their presence may indicate that Jews and crypto-Jews have a common historical origin. The third paper is presented by a crypto-Jew who has had his DNA tested to authenticate his Jewish origins. He focuses on the importance of using genetic evidence as a basis of authenticity and as a carrier of cultural and religious traditions.

The papers on genetics relate to a number of themes. The issues of authenticity and essentialism are particularly significant. Because of problems relating to the interpretation of historical documents and the question of historical continuity, many crypto-Jews have turned to genetics as a way to demonstrate their authenticity as Jews. They think that the presence of a "Jewish" genetic marker is proof of both a Jewish genetic origin and the continuity of Jewish cultural identity. Underlying many of the discussions is the notion of essentialism. Many speakers regard genes as carrying both biological and cultural information. Thus if someone has "Jewish" genes, he or she is in some deeper sense intrinsically Jewish. While the paper on genetic markers does not include this confusion of genetic and cultural inheritance, it presents statistical evidence of the presence of genetic markers commonly found in individuals of Jewish descent among different communities that emerged from Spain; this is accompanied by a clear underlying assumption that an individual with these markers is an authentic crypto-Jew.

The paper on genetic disorders is of interest to crypto-Jews in relation to both authenticity and health. For some, the presence of "Jewish" genetic disorders is a demonstration of a link with the broader Jewish community and thus of Jewish origins for modern crypto-Jews. Clearly, however, this issue is of particular importance to doctors, aside from any issues relating to identity, as it allows them to properly diagnose and treat disorders that were not expected to affect Hispanos.

Seventh Panel: Religion

The conference also includes participants who are neither academics nor crypto-Jews. Some join the society and attend the conferences for religious (primarily Jewish) reasons, perhaps seeing the crypto-Jews as a lost Jewish community that needs help in returning to Judaism. This group presents an alternative to the largely relativistic stance taken by many of the academic participants. A subcategory of this group is composed of the rabbis who have been members of the society and participants in its conferences from the start. Some of them lead congregations near neighborhoods with individuals of Hispanic descent, and the rabbis are actively engaged in supporting those people who are seeking to become part of mainstream Judaism. Others come from farther afield, often with a slightly more detached attitude. Although these rabbis usually are not actively engaged directly with crypto-Jews, they often present papers exploring how crypto-Jews might be assisted in becoming part of their particular branch of Judaism.

The seventh panel includes two rabbis and a Catholic priest. While both rabbis are Conservative Jews, they come from different parts of North America and have different practical experiences of crypto-Judaism. One works in Canada. Although he has a long-standing interest in crypto-Judaism, crypto-Jews are not part of his rabbinic practice. He addresses, from a rather distanced perspective, the aspects of Jewish law relating to enabling crypto-Jews to return to mainstream Judaism. The second rabbi is from El Paso, Texas, where crypto-Jews form an ongoing and important part of his rabbinic practice. His talk is much more ethnographic, discussing his experiences of helping crypto-Jews become active members of his congregation. The Catholic priest, like the first rabbi, comes to the phenomenon out of interest rather than experience. He explores the issues for modern Catholics in relation to crypto-Jews, focusing on how they can positively relate to the Catholic aspects of their identity and practice.

The issues addressed by the rabbis are a significant and constant theme of SCJS conferences. They focus on the ways in which crypto-Jews and crypto-Judaism can be understood by the dominant traditions of mainstream Judaism. Although Judaism has traditionally, at least for the past two thousand years, had a reasonably clear definition of who is a Jew—that is, a person with a Jewish mother—Jewish communities have begun to diverge in relation to the definition and its application. Thus they respond in different ways to crypto-Jews who seek to join them. The lack of evidence of a consistent inheritance of Judaism through the maternal line has posed a significant obstacle for easy acceptance of crypto-Jews by many Jewish communities. Many of the papers presented by rabbis seek to find mechanisms for overcoming this hurdle and thereby enabling this process without the need for conversion, which is currently demanded by all Jewish traditions other than the American Reform movement.

The Catholic priest is not typical of speakers at the conference. Although Catholicism and, indeed, other forms of Christianity are an important part of crypto-Jewish experience, very few representatives of these churches participate in the society. In part, this is due to the focus of the society on the Jewish aspects of the crypto-Jewish experience. It is also a result of the conflicted relation of many crypto-Jews with their Catholic past. Increasingly, however, the society is attempting not take a particular religious stand, and papers by Christian clergy may be more frequently read at future conferences.

Eighth Panel: Literature and Art

The other papers presented by nonacademics can be divided into two additional categories: historical or sociological topics and various forms of creative writing. The first can be subsumed by the comparable academic papers; they tend to vary in quality to the same extent as their academic counterparts. The second is more interesting, as it projects crypto-Judaism and crypto-Jews into a variety of literary spheres. Although this aspect of the conference has only a peripheral relation to the ethnography covered in this book because most of the individuals involved in these artistic endeavors are not of crypto-Jewish origin, it is of interest inasmuch as it provides insight into how some conferees and members of the mainstream Jewish community might use crypto-Judaism as a means to express their own sense of identity and authenticity or, indeed, as a way to deal with Jewish survival and the Holocaust.

Almost every conference of the SCJS has a panel on this creative aspect of mainstream Jews interacting with crypto-Judaism. The panelists come from a variety of Jewish experiences. Some are Sephardic Jews who often are exploring their own past in literary form and see the crypto-Jews of the past as exemplifying the Jewish experience in Spain. Many of them write historical fiction. Others are Ashkenazic Jews who offer highly romanticized re-creations of either historical or contemporary crypto-Jewish experience. While it is difficult to pigeonhole these texts, they tend to emphasize the exotic or to sexualize the crypto-Jew, perhaps demonstrating in part the orientalist issues raised by Michael Carroll and discussed in chapter 2.

Alongside the literary contributions are other forms of artistic expression, including paintings, sculpture, jewelry, and musical offerings. While the music has tended to be performances of Sephardic music and thus is only indirectly related to crypto-Judaism, it has raised issues of both language and poetic form that may merit future academic exploration. The material artistic works, however, are created by individuals both inside and outside the crypto-Jewish community. Those by the crypto-Jews provide an important insight into the way in which they are appropriating and using symbols and a view into which aspects of their lives they consider important to depict. Some of the artistic work is created by individuals from the Hispano community who do not consider themselves to be crypto-Jews. They consciously utilize crypto-Jewish motifs for different reasons: sometimes the symbols are used to express the presence of crypto-Judaism in New Mexican and Spanish history; other times, to represent a part of their own ancestry (even though it is one that is no longer active); and yet others, to say something about Christianity. The artistic work also both indicates how interaction with mainstream Jews, through the market in folk art, influences how and what artists choose to create and, more important, represents a dialogue within the wider Hispano community on the relation of Judaism and crypto-Judaism to the wider Hispano identity.

Alongside the conferences of the Society for Crypto-Judaic Studies there is a recent development that both adds to the cultural role of the conferences and reveals a latent aspect of the conferences themselves. An additional conference was held on the days before that of the society that was aimed particularly at crypto-Jews as well as others who had an interest in Judaism as a religion rather than as merely a cultural tradition. It aimed to provide these individuals with information to help them join mainstream Jewish communities. The preconference is supported by rabbis who are active in reaching out to the Hispano community and by crypto-Jews who are committed to bringing other crypto-Jews "back" to Judaism. It therefore takes on the role of helping individuals gain both a greater understanding of Judaism and, more significantly for our purposes, an increased knowledge of crypto-Judaism.

Looking at the participation and use of the main SCJS conferences by crypto-Jews over the past years, it is apparent that their role in the enculturation of crypto-Jewish cultural patterns is a significant motivator for crypto-Jews' participation. One significant difference between the conference and the preconference relates to their different attitudes about crypto-Jewish culture. While the preconference takes a particularly positive stance on mainstream Judaism, regarding it as the proper home for crypto-Jews, the conference generally has a more open view, not supporting any specific religious or cultural position. Nonetheless, the conference papers provide cultural data that can be used by crypto-Jews both to help explain features of their own experience and to provide raw material for enhancing their forms of practice.

The society's position is also some what internally contentious. Many members would like it to assume a more active role in supporting or enabling crypto-Jews to move toward Judaism. Up to this point, the more objective stance has been maintained. It is interesting to note, however, that when papers expressing support for taking a positive view of certain Christian traditions are presented—as at a recent conference where three messianic Jews spoke positively about their views of Jesus—there is a good deal of tension and hostility both at the conference and in the subsequent discussions. Similar tension was surfaced when the Catholic priest spoke in positive terms about the relationship of crypto-Judaism to Catholicism.

This outline of the participants in and structure of the Society for Crypto-Judaic Studies conference indicates the huge complexity of crypto-Judaism, which is the subject of the remainder of this book and has led to the challenges to its authenticity.

TWO

THE CASE AGAINST THE AUTHENTICITY OF CRYPTO-JUDAISM IN NEW MEXICO

The authenticity of crypto-Judaism is not only a scholarly question for academics but also a personal matter for crypto-Jews. Although these two groups clearly have different reasons for their interest in authenticity, their approaches to the issue are closely related because they often are responses to challenges made by critics. While these critiques usually appear first in academic publications, they are communicated to the crypto-Jewish and wider communities though the popular press or other forms of mass media. In some ethnographic discussions, these kinds of arguments might be considered background, relating primarily to academic and nonacademic discussion. In this case, and in many other contemporary ethnographic studies, these arguments are as important to those being discussed as to those who discuss them. These debates have framed aspects of crypto-Jews' understanding of themselves and acceptance by others—particularly, Jews who follow mainstream traditions—as authentic Jews.

The challenges to the authenticity of crypto-Judaism—specifically in relation to its manifestations in New Mexico and the wider American Southwest—have come from both scholars, particularly Judith Neulander and Michael Carroll, and some in the Hispano community, which at times overlaps with the crypto-Jewish community. They appear to have a problem with crypto-Judaism that may be connected to particular political agendas in their own community and its relations with the wider "Anglo" communities. We will briefly touch on this at a variety of points during the discussion.

Neulander and Carroll have developed the most significant critiques of both the historical authenticity of crypto-Jews as Jews and the underlying motives and methods of those, both academics and nonacademics, who study crypto-Judaism. Neulander's analysis is the more significant in this respect, as it arises from both fieldwork and scholarship. Carroll's work is second order, considering the published research and thus engages primarily with the motives of the academics in the field rather than the subjects of their study. Neulander's and Carroll's arguments underlie the main challenges to crypto-Jewish authenticity, so they must be understood, tested, and contextualized or disputed—the important academic process that leads to the development of more clearly sustainable approaches. In addition, many of their critiques are based on theoretical assumptions that also have to be examined and, in some cases, challenged. The most important of these assumptions relates to a fundamental misunderstanding of identity and culture based on essentialist models, which focus on some unchanging aspect of identity, be it genetic or otherwise, and seem to underlie arguments presented by both critics of crypto-Judaism and, indeed, crypto-Jews themselves.

Judith Neulander

Judith Neulander's work presents the most substantial critical discussion of both the scholarship on the presence of crypto-Jews in New Mexico and, more important, the authenticity of the Jewish identity of those who claim to be crypto-Jews. (She does not, however, question the phenomenon of crypto-Judaism per se.) To support her critique, she offers alternative explanations for the creation and development of the culture of crypto-Judaism. While Neulander has published some short pieces on the subject, most notably "Crypto-Jews of the Southwest: An Imagined Community" (1994) and "The New Mexican Crypto-Jewish Canon: Choosing to Be 'Chosen' in Millennial Tradition" (1996), her most detailed discussion is in her unpublished dissertation, "Cannibals, Castes, and Crypto-Jews: Premillennial Cosmology in Postcolonial New Mexico" (2001), on which this examination of her work is based. Some of Neulander's ideas have been published in the popular press.

The first chapter of "Cannibals, Castes, and Crypto-Jews" both provides an insight into Neulander's rhetorical strategy and introduces some of the arguments that characterize her work as a whole. Before entering the field, she was concerned that the crypto-Judaism hypothesis seemed to rest on hearsay and thus had no argumentative basis. She cites a number of articles whose authors state that their introduction to crypto-Judaism was based on an anonymous rumor, which she suggests falls into the folkloric category of "friend of a friend tale." According to Neulander (2001:1–3), this common folkloric structure remains consistent in the literature relating to crypto-Judaism, and, from the perspective of folkloric analysis, does not provide adequate evidence for the existence of crypto-Judaism and would be used only by those untrained in ethnology.[1]

If the material collected and analyzed was only indirect and anonymous, as Neulander suggests, it would indeed be problematic and worthy of criticism. She is, however, making a much more significant point—implicitly and, later, explicitly challenging the credentials of the scholars of crypto-Judaism. Suggesting that they are untrained or inappropriately trained in ethnology, she argues that it requires a folklorist to determine the quality of the data collected and thereby the authenticity of the phenomenon of crypto-Judaism (Neulander 2001:1–3). This claim runs throughout her work and ignores the fact that others trained in ethnography—for example, anthropologists and sociologists—are also engaged in studying the crypto-Jewish community.[2]

In her initial chapter, Neulander also introduces the primary theme of her analysis—the misinterpretation of rituals as Jewish because they appear to be Jewish but are, in fact, of non-Jewish origin. She suggests that both the scholars who study Hispano culture and crypto-Judaism in New Mexico and the individuals who claim this background and/or identity in effect created crypto-Judaism in New Mexico as a result of misconstruing practices that, ironically, are vestiges of Christian Pentecostalism.

Neulander initially explores the motives of and theoretical problems found in the work of some of the scholars who have written about crypto-Judaism in New Mexico. She examines some of the issues relating to colonial methods of categorization and extends this paradigm to the work of these postcolonial scholars. The colonial paradigm includes two interrelated levels:

- The use of a taxonomy in which practices that appear similar are assumed to have the same roots
- The search for the lost tribes and the assimilation of newly discovered tribes into that framework (Neulander 2001:8–14)

Neulander makes the rather facile argument that just as the discovery of lost tribes in other ethnographic contexts is "demonstrably unfounded" so is it "demonstrably unfounded" in New Mexico. While there can be no argument with Neulander's general proposition—that colonial interpretations of exotic cultures often attempted to fit them into existing mythic paradigms—her contention that she has demonstrated conclusively that crypto-Judaism in New Mexico is unfounded itself has little ethnographic basis. Neulander's alternative hypotheses are largely unsupported by empirical data and are thus as literary as those that she attributes to her scholarly opponents.

The easy assumption that those who argue for the existence of crypto-Judaism in New Mexico fall into a (post)colonial paradigm of searching for lost tribes (a charge that is not supported by Neulander's citations from their work) is merely a way of not grappling seriously with their line of reasoning. All the academics working on crypto-Judaism, including Neulander herself, come from modern academic disciplines and are trained to be critical within those disciplines. It is therefore important to address their arguments directly, rather than attributing motives to their research. Based on her conclusion that crypto-Judaism is largely the product of postcolonial misinterpretation, Neulander suggests that her study focuses on this process rather than on the nonexistent ethnography of crypto-Judaism itself. Thus she states, quoting her own published work: "It eventually became clear that no ethnography of crypto-Jewish tradition could be done there [New Mexico], for local reconstructions comprised an imagined cultural canon—or a postcolonial traveler's tale—which of necessity, became the focus of my research inquiry (Neulander 1994, 1996 passim)" (Neulander 2001:13). This conclusion, however, forces Neulander to assume that any apparent example of Jewish practice or identity is false and therefore must be explained by a range of largely unsupported hypotheses.

One aspect of Neulander's argument, however, must be taken seriously: it is possible that researchers mistakenly identified common elements of Hispano practice as crypto-Jewish. (The colonial hypothesis cannot be taken seriously, as Neulander provides no evidence in published or unpublished studies to support it.) If it is shown that the practices are consistent in the Hispanic Southwest, then they cannot be regarded as demonstrating or validating crypto-Jewish authenticity.

The issue, however, is not as ethnographically clear-cut as Neulander appears to assume. She implicitly suggests that there can be only one reason why a practice is performed. Thus if, for example, one group lights candles on Friday night for one set of cultural reasons, then all who light candles must be doing so for the same reasons. While this may be true, it may also be that a subset of individuals light candles in adherence to another tradition; their interpretations of this ritual cannot be assumed to be invalid just because others, perhaps even the majority, have a different explanation for the practice. The key point is that the practice in and of itself contains no essentialized meaning. Its meaning comes from the interpretations of those who perform it; if they regard the practice as expressive of their Jewish identity, then that is its meaning. Neulander, however, is correct in a broader sense: practices outside an interpretive context do not authenticate the historicity of crypto-Judaism in New Mexico or, indeed, anywhere else; the meaning given to a practice, such as lighting candles on Friday night, is indicative of its present performance and interpretation, but provides no evidence for its genesis, which may be of Jewish or non-Jewish origin or, indeed, of both.

The point is one of both methodology and, more important, theoretical approach. For Neulander, methodology and theory are focused on the question of etic, or external, authenticity; that is, it is the scholar who determines authenticity. She is not concerned about the self-identities of those being studied. On a number of occasions throughout her work, she suggests that she is interested in ideas, not individuals. As indicated in the earlier quote, Neulander judged there to be no supportable ethnographic evidence of crypto-Judaism in New Mexico, and therefore there must be another explanation for why individuals claim this heritage. If, however, both ideas and practices are examined in relation to an emic, or internal, point of view, then historical authenticity becomes only one issue (although very often a less significant one) within the more important matter of individual and cultural authenticity.

This idea can be illustrated using a practice often identified as crypto-Jewish: how a room is swept. Some individuals, both crypto-Jews and scholars (for example, Halevy 1999), have suggested that crypto-Jews normally sweep a room from the walls to the center, while non-crypto-Jews sweep from the center and out the door. Neulander (2001:17) correctly points to some of the problems with generalizing this practice as an indicator of crypto-Judaism, but seems to conclude that since it may be a common practice, it is therefore not a crypto-Jewish practice. The only way to determine the nature of the practice is by conducting a detailed ethnographic interview and thereby learning how individuals understand and interpret it.

Several people from throughout New Mexico who were interviewed and observed suggested that they sweep into the center of a room because of the injunction to have God's name on the doorposts of their houses, and thus they do not want to sweep dirt out the doors. They mentioned that they do it because it comes from their Jewish heritage. Other interviewees with crypto-Jewish identity, however, did not consider the direction of sweeping a room symbolically significant. For them, this was not a crypto-Jewish practice and should not be interpreted as such. Thus it is personal interpretation that makes an act a crypto-Jewish practice, not the act itself. The interpretation and current cultural meaning are not necessary evidence of the origin of a practice.

Neulander (2001) does not deny per se the existence of crypto-Judaism: "I have never disputed the existence of crypto-Judaism in other parts of the world. Nor have I ever stated anywhere that New Mexican crypto-Judaism cannot exist. I have simply pointed out that, to date, all evidence given to justify claims of a New Mexican crypto-Jewish past, is demonstrably unfounded" (13).[3] She also says that she would be convinced that the phenomenon was real if a diary or other clear examples of material culture were found. These statements, however, merely reiterate the flaws in her work: authenticity is the gift of the scholar, who has the sole right to validate cultural reality, and meaning is carried by material culture rather than by those who use it. In no sense does she accept that an important aspect of any ethnographic study is the views and interpretations of the community and individuals being studied—the folklorist always knows best.

The conflict between the insider and the outsider point of view, and the explicit argument that the outsider is the authoritative judge of authenticity, is both a broader methodological issue in ethnographic studies and an important aspect of Neulander's arguments. Neulander's rhetorical strategy has two parts. The first is to demonstrate the problems in the ethnographic data, from her point of view, such that the data in no way supports the crypto-Jewish hypothesis. The second is to find explanations for why individuals claim this "false" identity. She suggests two main, interrelated motives: using crypto-Judaism both to claim a higher status (that is, a process of racial whitening) and to cover or explain Pentecostal Judaizing traditions. While it may be that both of these are plausible explanations for the presence of crypto-Jewish identity in New Mexico, the mere statement and even discussion of the generalized historical context does not prove that any individual has these specific motives for claiming crypto-Judaic heritage. The only way to test intentions is through extensive empirical study—that is, ethnographic interviews, which requires taking crypto-Jewish ethnography seriously, an approach that Neulander specifically eschews.

While Neulander's dissertation indicates that she spent some time in New Mexico and participated in some interviews, it does not specify the number of interviews, the context of the interviews, the interview methods used, or the amount of time spent in the field. Without this information, it is impossible to test Neulander's theory, which, as we have seen, hypothesizes a set of motives on the part of both the crypto-Jews and the scholars studying crypto-Judaism. Arguably, Neulander is guilty of the crime she attributes to the supporters of the crypto-Jewish hypothesis—the overgeneralization of an empirically untested theory. While her theory is plausible on the surface, and is true of some of the individuals interviewed both by Neulander and for this book, in most respects it suffers from a dearth of supporting ethnographic data, does not fit the self-understanding of crypto-Jews, and is not even historically tenable.

It is important at this point to be explicit about what I am claiming and not claiming. I fully accept the possibility of making false associations based on apparent similarity. This type of misinterpretation can be true both of ethnographers and other scholars and of crypto-Jews (and, indeed, folklorists). In other publications and papers (Kunin 1998, 2001), I have explored this process in relation to symbols on gravestones. These symbols, particularly six-pointed stars, have been used by some crypto-Jews as material evidence of a crypto-Jewish past. But the symbols have no intrinsic meaning. Following the concept of different horizons of interpretation, their meaning is vested in, minimally, two groups: the people who put up the stones and, in a very different sense, those who use the stones today (including the modern crypto-Jewish interpreters). The original meaning can be determined only by conducting ethnographic interviews with the individuals who erected the stones and is clearly distinct from the current interpretation, whether by the family of the deceased who are commemorated by the stones or by the crypto-Jewish interpreters. The present-day interpretations are valid as current understandings of both symbols and identity but not as historical data, which can be provided only by those who chose to use the symbol.

While many of Neulander's warnings about the misinterpretation of practices are important and must be taken seriously, at times it seems that she is so determined not to find any possible evidence of crypto-Jewish presence in New Mexico that she selectively chooses theorists to support her contentions. This is perhaps most clear in her discussion of folk narratives, an area in which she claims specific disciplinary expertise. Utilizing the work of the anthropologists Ruth Benedict (1935) and William Bascom (1969), Neulander implies that folktales are primarily mechanisms for letting off steam. While scholars of myth and folklore would not disagree with this as one possible use of narratives, they would also argue that it is one possibility among many.

The interpretation of any narrative—for example, "The Padre and the Jew" (Neulander 2001:321–324)—may be more multileveled than is suggested by Neulander's rather simplistic analysis, which presents the tale as dealing with only a particular problem related to anticlericalism. The narrative recounts a discussion between a padre and a Jew in which they discuss flowers in the padre's garden:

> —Well, these homely flowers stand for Presbyterian matrimony, and these for the Sultan's matrimony— and so he went on until they came to the most beautiful flowers of all. —These are pretty, Padre. What do they stand for? —They stand for Catholic matrimony. And they kept walking on, and out along the edge was the prickly cactus, and the Jew asked what it stood for. —Oh, I don't want to tell you! You're my friend and I don't want to tell you. And the Jew said to him, since [sic] he wouldn't get mad. —This prickly cactus— the Padre then said —stands for Jewish matrimony. —The prettiest ones— the Jew told him —are useful to wipe where the sun don't shine, but the ones that stand for Jewish matrimony can't be used that way. (Neulander 2001:323)

Neulander's (2001) analysis of the tale suggests that the interpretations offered by crypto-Jews (or academics studying crypto-Judaism), who see it as establishing a boundary between Christian and Jewish categories in which the Jewish category is privileged, are illegitimate because "as Benedict and Bascom have taught us, any tale from a traditional community is less likely to be its mirror image, then to serve its societal needs; among them, to vent collective resentment of oppressive institutions and local authorities" (323–324). She thus assumes that the authoritative interpretation of the narrative is as an expression of resentment against the Catholic Church, with the Jew as cipher. Neulander's discussion misrepresents Benedict by overstating the specific interpretation of "expressing resentment" at the expense of other social functions and ignores all subsequent academic work on the role of folktales. It particularly disregards the possibility of the story having different meanings, depending on the context of the telling and the people both telling and hearing it. Both her explanation and that of the crypto-Jewish interpreters do not reside in the tale itself, but in the individuals telling and using it (with Neulander indeed creating a new level of meaning in the narrative). While "The Padre and the Jew" does not constitute proof of crypto-Jewish presence in New Mexico, it also does not indicate the converse. Thus it is fair to say that a folktale may utilize a symbol, such as the Jew, as a way to criticize the Christian hierarchy as well as to create boundary markers between real and significant categories.

Neulander's discussion also suggests that the use or retelling of this narrative by crypto-Jews is inauthentic. While she admits that "The Padre and the Jew" is well known in New Mexico, she privileges the published version and assumes that any oral version in a slightly different form (without the matrimonial element)[4] must necessarily be based on the published version; thus she suggests that the story was reinvented in 1991, when it was retold to a journalist without the inclusion of the matrimonial element. No evidence is provided to demonstrate that the tale has not been told in different versions and has not been used by crypto-Jews (unless one automatically assumes, as Neulander seems to do, that there are no crypto-Jews in New Mexico). The same narrative can be told by different groups that might claim ownership of it, as does the crypto-Jew whose claim is so clearly denounced by Neulander (2001:324).

Analysis of other folkloric material also suggests that narratives can be subtly transformed in retelling; elements that are no longer relevant to the storyteller, such as matrimony in "The Padre and the Jew," can be dropped. This is possible whether the narrative is traditionally told by crypto-Jews or merely retold by the individual who spoke to the journalist. A good example of such narrative development is found in the Christian retelling of the story of Noah, in which the biblical distinction between pure and impure animals (Genesis 7:2) was removed and often forgotten because it was not relevant in the new context of telling and retelling.

It is essential to ask Neulander a general question about practice, narrative, or material culture: What would she consider to be an object that was self-evidently Jewish and thus in her terms demonstrable evidence of crypto-Judaism? Her discussions suggest that she would expect it to have clear identifying features and be relatively little changed in relation to earlier Jewish practice. This is clearly indicated by a brief tangent in her discussion, in which she attempts to categorize those studying crypto-Judaism as being nonprofessionals or working outside of the areas of their academic competence. She refers to a statement quoted in the popular press as a good example of this, and her discussion is revealing. The person quoted believed that crypto-Jewish practices would have been transformed from earlier Spanish Jewish practices. Neulander contends that this is a misinformed view and that we would expect a strong degree of stability. She argues that "if we were to hazard any expectation of crypto-Jewish survivals at a far distribution from their Iberian homeland, we would expect them not only to closely resemble the form in which they were held when crypto-Jews left home, but we would expect them to resemble those traditions more closely than whatever prevailed in their old home towns" (Neulander 2001:41–42).

Neulander suggests that the individual quoted was influenced by an outdated folkloric principle that the periphery changes faster than the center. This was not necessarily true of the person, and it is not the view taken here. In relation to change, the focus is not on individual cultural items, which may or may not be conservative, but on broader concepts of culture as it moves through time and space. It appears that Neulander and her colleagues are working within a rather outdated model of culture, which assumes it to be relatively monolithic and conservative. Many anthropologists, myself included, consider culture to be much more dynamic and fluid.

The fluidity of culture is perhaps best indicated by Jeanette Rodríguez and Ted Fortier (2007) in a discussion of cultural memory—a context that closely approximates that of the crypto-Jews. According to them, cultural memory is not about "preserving the past per se." It is, rather, a dynamic process of re-creation and reconstruction whose most important feature is the ability to adapt, which is fundamental to the nature of a living and dynamic culture (Rodríguez and Fortier 2007:108).

Arguably, culture as static and monolithic is an academic construct—developed for heuristic purposes rather than as an accurate depiction of human social interactions. Evidence suggests that cultures are pluralistic, with fuzzy and permeable rather than fixed internal and external boundaries. This fluidity suggests constant processes of change, with an appearance of stability rather than its reality.

The issues that relate to the fuzziness of culture are specifically relevant to crypto-Judaism as it is posited by those working in the field. By definition, crypto-Judaism is the mixing of cultural forms: the crypto-Jew has some aspects of Jewish identity and perhaps practice and an external set of Christian identity and practices, as well as a range of other elements—for example, Native American, African American, and Anglo. Given the evidence from most of the individuals interviewed for this study, the outward Christian identity and practices were not simply cover, but constitutive of an individual's identity. In order for Neulander's approach and expectations to be correct, she would have to rely on a theory of compartmentalization in which it would be necessary to keep each cultural aspect separate. While it is possible that such compartmentalization could work for a short period of time, over generations it would break down, and the originally distinct sets of cultural forms would mix, creating a set of hybrid traditions.

The blending of cultural forms is found at every level. While, for example, some interviewees suggested that members of their families consistently married into only other crypto-Jewish families, most described a significant degree of marrying outside the community. Many interviews, as indeed can be seen in Neulander's (2001:80) quotations from and discussion of Anita's interview (which is discussed in detail later) indicate a conflict over practice within a single family. Other respondents reported that, even with marriage between people with similar traditions, each family has its own particular subset of practices. In this ethnographic context, it would be surprising if there was not a pattern of cultural exchange and transformation. Thus the analogy with other folkloric contexts may not be helpful in understanding how crypto-Jewish culture would develop over time, whether in the center or on the periphery.

Neulander's (2001:273–274) expectation of the nature of authentic practices—that is, one that would "closely resemble the form in which they were held when crypto-Jews left home"—is also highlighted in her discussion of naming practices in New Mexico, particularly in relation to the use of the name Adonai. Neulander and other scholars have noted that the name Adonai is occasionally used in the Hispano community. She says that this is conclusive evidence that those with this name are not crypto-Jews because Iberian Jews had a clear aversion to the use of the names of God. She provides proof in a text from the Zohar. This aversion is beyond question, but Neulander's assumption that it was passed down to present-day crypto-Jews is open to challenge. It is impossible to determine what was passed down or not passed down in the five hundred years since Jews left the Iberian Peninsula; thus the fact that individuals do not follow this particular tradition is evidence neither for nor against their being crypto-Jews. Again, Neulander seems to assume that Jewish practices and traditions were transmitted unchanged. If we take the fuzziness of culture seriously, it is possible to suggest an alternative hypothesis: that crypto-Jews adopted the broader Hispanic practice of using the names of God—for example, Jesus—and gave their sons the name that was meaningful to them. Like Neulander's argument, this hypothesis must be tested through interviews, and one informant whose brother was named Adonai stated that the name was indeed an expression of his family's crypto-Jewish identity.

Neulander suggests that the use of the name Adonai has roots in Pentecostal Christianity. Unfortunately, however, she provides no evidence that the families that used this name either were Pentecostal or had other Protestant Judaizing connections, merely implying that that must have been the case. Perhaps more significantly, she offers no documentary evidence that any Pentecostal or other Judaizing church used the word "Adonai" to represent the name of God. In the first half of the twentieth century, when many of these men received this name, Jehovah was the common name used for the Hebrew God in many Christian churches.

Although there are relatively few examples of direct analysis of interviews or other forms of ethnographic practice in Neulander's dissertation as a whole, her way of interacting with this material is significant. She never offers an interpretation that takes an individual's views seriously; her analysis suggests that she has a preconceived view of the data and does not consider alternative hypotheses. Often, as in relation to the retelling of the tale "Matzo in the Hat," Neulander offers insight into the processes of the reconstruction of the past. She, however, ignores the possibility that this reconstruction may be related to an existing identity to which content is being added and reinterpreted (Neulander 2001:116–118). In relation to all the material included in her dissertation, either the interviewees were already in the public eye, as with the material labeled "Carasco," or Neulander was invited to attend interviews by someone already working in the field. She does not provide any evidence that she sought to move outside this narrow range of informants. In other cases—for example, that of Sandoval (Neulander 2001:63–68)—it appears that Neulander worked solely from published material in which an individual was publicly exploring her or his own identity. There is no evidence that Neulander sought to interview these people to test her ideas.

The flaws in Neulander's (2001:80–81) methods are particularly apparent in her discussion of an interview with Anita (whom she interviewed perhaps in conjunction with Stanley Hordes), who talked about her father's practices in relation to the ritual slaughter of animals. Neulander suggests that the informant's material contains a contradiction and that there is a further contradiction in an interview with Anita's son published a year later. According to her, Anita initially said that her father had collected the slaughtered animals' blood for consumption, although there is no direct quotation from the interview on this point. At a later stage in the interview, Anita added a clarification (it is not clear what led to this clarification). Neulander (2001) prefaces her statement with the following: "Anita contradicts herself on her own response to blood consumption, at the same time confirming that her father collected sheep's blood for family consumption, and did not spill it to the ground" (80). The quoted section from Anita's interview indicates a conflict in the family: while her mother liked to eat blood, her father "used to tell us 'don't eat it' . . . cause . . . it's a great sin, you know." In the third version, given by Anita's son, the blood was drained to the ground (Neulander 2001:80–81). This interview has several possible interpretations: Neulander focuses on the changes in the narrative, particularly the statement by the son, and concludes that it is too "contaminated" to be used. If, however, we take Anita's words seriously, the interview suggests that there was a conflict in the family and thus perhaps opposing values and/or traditions. This type of conflict, particularly in families that do not have a tradition of endogamy, was seen at many points in my ethnographic research.

In her discussion of the prohibition on the consumption of blood, Neulander (2001) adds that we can "assume that her [Anita's] father's Pentecostalism included a Hebraized taboo against blood consumption" (80). This assumption needs more support than Neulander provides. At a minimum, we would need evidence that Pentecostal Judaizing in New Mexico or, indeed, elsewhere included the prohibition on the consumption of blood. (Such evidence does not appear to be supported by ethnographic or other sources or documented in Pentecostal literature.) Even if it were available, it would be only one interpretation, an interpretation that would require interviewing individuals to learn their religious or cultural motivations. Neulander seems to have concluded that there was no crypto-Jewish aspect to the father's attitude about the consumption of blood and thus, despite lacking any compelling supporting evidence, attributes Pentecostal religious motivations to him.

It is important, however, to take seriously Neulander's observation of the changes in the narrative between generations. The son was clearly, consciously or unconsciously, presenting a simplified version that emphasizes the crypto-Jewish aspect of his identity. While Neulander is apparently interested in finding uncontaminated cultural forms that are remnants of a historical tradition (although her rhetorical strategy suggests that she is actually interested in demonstrating the opposite) and so questions the information provided by Anita and her son, I am interested in understanding a living and changing community and its cultural context. The type of fluidity demonstrated by the son, of interpretation and reinterpretation, is fundamental to the nature of identity and important at higher levels of community and cultural construction and reconstruction.

The discussion of Anita's material by Neulander (1996:25–26, 2001:76–79) seems to be predicated on her supposition that the Hispano practice of slaughtering is a false parallel with the Jewish practice of *shechita*. She particularly emphasizes that while the Jewish practice requires the draining away of blood, the Hispano practice involves collecting it for consumption. The ethnographic evidence strongly indicates that many crypto-Jews did not eat the blood and, indeed, spilled it on the ground, as prescribed by Jewish tradition. Neulander's argument is also based on a view that *conversos* did not maintain the practice of ritual slaughter, although David Gitlitz (1996:542–548) shows that it was documented well into the seventeenth century.

While all the cases and examples that Neulander provides could be critically examined, in essence they rely on the same theoretical perspective: the misinterpretation of symbols and practices as Jewish because either scholars wish them to be Jewish or, more importantly, crypto-Jews (or, in Neulander's terms, would-be crypto-Jews) wish them to be so. Although Neulander makes important ethnographic points—and, indeed, they have been recognized by others in the field—her analysis, which appears to focus on a single conclusion, is limited and forces the data into a box, ignoring the possibility of a more complex situation. It also has a wider problem: rather than providing one explanation for the misinterpretation of the practices, Neulander deals with each individually. Thus we are forced to assume that a family with a wide range of these practices was simultaneously utilizing a number of bases of misinterpretation. Neulander's arguments would be more convincing either if there were a single method of misinterpretation or if families and individuals followed only a limited subset of the practices.

Neulander does, however, provide two primary meta-explanations for the process of cultural invention that she identifies in New Mexico. It is therefore appropriate to explore the motives that, she argues, explain consistent misinterpretations that she believes characterize the data. I focus here on the processes occurring in the "would-be" crypto-Jewish community, as I have touched on the colonial paradigm, which Neulander suggests provides a key basis for explaining the misreading by scholars outside the crypto-Jewish community.

Neulander's primary explanation of both the practices and the motivations relates to substrata of Pentecostalism in the Hispano community. She suggests that much of the apparently Jewish practices emerged from Judaizing tendencies among various Pentecostal groups. Her argument assumes that a significant number of individuals in New Mexico at one point converted to some form of Pentecostalism, and then either they reverted to Catholicism, or their children consciously or unconsciously misinterpreted their Pentecostal practices as crypto-Jewish practices. A key aspect of Neulander's contention is that many of these Pentecostal groups had a strong identification with biblical Israel and considered themselves to be the new Israel. This identification is the primary reason for the false identification of the members of these churches as Jews.

Neulander's (2001:52) argument is perhaps best illustrated in her discussion of Anita's father. In the interview, Anita stated that her father had become a Pentecostal and that her mother called him "judío." Neulander (2001) assumes, without interviewing the mother or, indeed, apparently even clarifying with Anita what she thought it meant, that "Anita's memory is not in the least confused . . . about her Catholic mother's castigation (with the pejorative 'Jew') of her father's conversion to a Hebraized offshoot of the Wesleyan Church—an organization whose members define themselves as modern day Children of Israel" (52). On the basis of this empirically unsupported assumption, she interprets all his apparently Jewish practices as being of Pentecostal origin.

In this example, Neulander does provide a possible conjunction between crypto-Jewish practices and Pentecostal identity. Nonetheless, there are problems with her analysis. The most significant is her rather simplistic analysis of Pentecostalism. In New Mexico in 1940 (a useful point in time, as most of the individuals interviewed for this study were then children or young adults), there were four Pentecostal groups with significant variations in practice and theology. None of them was very large, with the total number of members not exceeding 750 (Brayer 1940:xii, 172–180), and the penetration of churches was also geographically narrow, with only one church north of Albuquerque. If Neulander was to substantiate her argument, it would be necessary to determine the group to which Anita's father belonged and the nature of the Judaizing practices, if any, in that group.

It is also important not to attribute motives to individuals that are not given (or clearly demonstrated) in an interview. The possible association between membership in a Pentecostal church and the term "judío" remains conjectural without either a clear statement in the interview or a contextual statement in the interview (or from the wider social setting) that the abusive term "Jew" was commonly applied to individuals in the Pentecostal churches by their Catholic neighbors and family members. Neulander also assumes that with the new Israel identity came other Jewish practices, such as those associated with the slaughter of animals. But the Pentecostal literature does not offer evidence for this level of Judaizing practice.

Although there were groups in New Mexico, most notably the Seventh-Day Adventists, that practiced Sabbatarianism—that is, worship on Saturday, the Jewish Sabbath—this was not generally true of the Pentecostals. Neulander sometimes seems to conflate various Christian traditions as a means to account for crypto-Jewish practice.

A significant aspect of Neulander's argument is based on Raphael Patai's (1983) work on Venta Prieta. Patai originally examined an apparently crypto-Jewish community in Mexico and concluded that its "Judaic" practices were·actually the product of a form of Christian fundamentalism similar to Seventh-Day Adventism. (The context was limited and was not extended by Patai to cover all crypto-Jews in Mexico.) Without critiquing Patai's specific analysis, it is important to note a significant difference that renders the analogy between the two ethnographic contexts problematic. Patai focuses on a very narrow geographic area and a relatively limited number of individuals. He demonstrates the clear presence of Seventh-Day Adventism in that community and thus the probability of that tradition being the source of the seemingly Jewish practices. The New Mexico context is very different. Unlike the residents of Venta Prieta, the New Mexicans who claim a crypto-Jewish identity have been found in almost every area of Hispano settlement in the state, from the far south to the far north.

This is further emphasized if we examine the location and size of Sabbatarian religious organizations in New Mexico in 1940, as we did for Pentecostal groups. For example, the Seventh-Day Adventists (established in the state in 1895) had twenty churches, with a total of 700 members, up from 300 in 1907 (Brayer 1940:1). There were two other Sabbatarian groups—two different Churches of God (established in the state in 1927 and 1929, respectively)—with fewer than 350 members in total (Brayer 1940:65–66). While the Seventh-Day Adventists did have some penetration in the north of the state, the majority of the churches and members were south of Albuquerque, as was the case with Pentecostalism. Given the small number of both Pentecostal and Sabbatarian churches and their members, and the limited extent of their penetration in the state, there does not seem to have been a locus of influence, as in Venta Prieta, that would explain the number and spread of individuals who claim crypto-Jewish practice in New Mexico.

Alongside the Pentecostal and Sabbatarian churches were a number of small sects—for example, the Church of the Nazarene, with just over 2,000 members, and the Churches of Christ, with just over 5,000 members. Although there are similarities, neither of these denominations nor similar groups are technically Pentecostal or Sabbaterian. The Churches of Christ are not premillennial in their messianic views and thus do not fit Neulander's general characterization. While it may be that many of these churches viewed themselves as the new Israel, their members did not therefore identify themselves as Jews. A good example of this distinction is found in the Book of Mormon, which distinguishes among the new Israel (that is, the Saints), the gentiles, and the Jews. The term "Jew" is clearly used in a negative sense. This distinction is also found in other contemporary Christian traditions.

Although some individuals may have briefly flirted with one or another Protestant denomination and returned to Catholicism, Neulander would have to provide clear evidence that this was a significant and widespread practice in the mid-twentieth century in order to support her argument. It is just as likely that if individuals were moving between Catholicism and Protestantism, they would have selected the much more popular and widespread traditions of Presbyterianism, Methodism, or Episcopalism—none of which could be characterized as encouraging Judaizing practice. This assumption is supported by the fact that the majority of those who converted to Protestantism from Catholicism chose these mainstream denominations.

In addition to the attitude of Neulander's hypothesis toward the community, assuming that the ethnographer knows more about it than its members and almost totally ignoring the community's self-perception, her approach implies that the individuals being interviewed either had forgotten or chose to lie about events in their very recent past, when they would have had to have been members of Pentecostal churches. The construction of the methods for the research presented in this book took into account the issues relating to possible Pentecostal or other potentially Judaizing influences. The religious context and family background were a feature of all the ethnographic interviews conducted. The majority of the respondents claimed that their families were currently Catholic and, as far as they were aware, had always been so. The next significant group was Presbyterian, the majority from the small communities in the vicinity of Taos. A very small minority was or had family members from a selection of other traditions, including various Pentecostal and Seventh-Day Adventist sects. Those with Adventist backgrounds (only two in the data included in this study) were well aware of the Adventism and attributed many of the practices in their families to it. The two individuals came from the southern part of the state.

An interesting aspect of the movement of individuals from Catholicism to alternative Christian traditions, to which we will return, is the selection of particular forms of Christianity because they allow individuals to express different facets of their identity. While many who claim a crypto-Jewish identity either remain in the church into which they were born or move toward different forms of mainstream Judaism, a number of individuals state that they are attracted to various forms of messianic Judaism or Christianity. These forms are not the source of their Jewish practice (although, as we will see, this is sometimes so) and were not part of their family tradition while they were Catholic. These messianic Judaizing traditions, which are relatively recent in New Mexico, allow them to affirm and practice both halves of their identity: the Jewish and the Christian. Although Neulander might regard this as supporting her theory, I see it as an expression of the complex nature of identities present in New Mexico. It is also possible that this current trend is similar to that discussed by Tomás Atencio (2003), who suggested that conversion to Presbyterianism may have been a way for some crypto-Jews to express a hitherto forbidden form of identity.

The second motive that Neulander attributes to those who claim a crypto-Jewish identity is similarly fraught with problems: an attempt to transform status in a white, European-dominated culture. Thus the claim of being Jewish is a claim of being both white and European, as opposed to being of mixed origin and mestizo (Neulander 2001:139–142). Like Neulander's other arguments, this may be true of some people, who appear to use crypto-Judaism as a way of claiming to be of pure Spanish blood and thus, at least in their own sense of self, of higher social status. The key point, however, is that Neulander presents this hypothesis on the basis of very little ethnographic data, insufficient to make a generalized statement about individuals' motives.

There are, however, serious methodological questions that Neulander has to answer. The most fundamental is the extent to which individuals make statements that illustrate this motive. In my experience, only a small subset of individuals interviewed for my research make claims of pure Spanish descent. Many families are well aware that their genealogies include considerable exchange between groups, often citing descent from non-crypto-Jewish segments of the Hispano and Native American communities. Even when they do not raise the issue of *mestizaje*, they do not seem to use Jewish identity as a marker for whiteness.

This issue is directly addressed by Janet Jacobs (2002), who interviewed fifty individuals claiming crypto-Jewish identity. Close to 50 percent stated that they were descended in part from Native Americans (Jacobs 2002:12–13). In the research conducted for this book, over 60 percent of the respondents acknowledged various forms of nonwhite ancestry, including Mexican, Native American, and African American.

In order to prove her contention, Neulander would have to show that a broad range of Hispanos would consider a claim of Jewish origin to be equivalent to an assertion of whiteness and higher status in the wider Hispano community. She would also need to demonstrate that a claim of being of Spanish descent stigmatized by Jewish origins would be preferable to claiming pure Spanish descent without the taint of any foreign blood.[5] The material from the interviews conducted for this study do not support this understanding by crypto-Jews, the majority of whom do not regard the claim of being Jewish as altering their social status in any way. Indeed, some individuals have suggested that the claim of Jewish identity has led to anti-Semitism and thus reduced their quality of life rather than raised it.

The research conducted by Neulander and that undertaken for this book differ in the nature of the individuals interviewed. Neulander's work gives no evidence of having interviewed people other than those who were already publicly expressing their Jewish identity; indeed, their crypto-Jewish heritage allowed them to access outlets that would have been closed to them in other circumstances. Most of the individuals interviewed for this study had not been interviewed and were not in any sense publicly expressing their crypto-Jewish identity; it seems very implausible that they would enjoy any change in status through their private understanding of identity.

Neulander's work must be seen as a problematic but important contribution to crypto-Jewish studies. The issues she raises, particularly in relation to misidentification, are significant and must be explored in any discussion of crypto-Jewish authenticity. Neulander's two hypotheses, however, due to their attitude toward internal understandings and their lack of empirical support, do not seem to be generalizable. Her key assumption, which guides her work, is that none of the practices or other aspects of crypto-Jewish culture in New Mexico are convincing evidence of its presence in the state. Although at times she denies this view of her work, it seems implicit in the rhetorical structure of her research as a whole. The fact, however, that there is no evidence that she chooses to find convincing is not in itself proof that crypto-Judaism is a false canon. (Neulander uses the term "canon" to indicate that it is the authoritative generally accepted analysis.) In looking at the evidence for or against, it is essential both not to assume that it is necessarily authentic and not to regard it as a "social pathology," which is Neulander's (2001:141) explicit position.

Further, given the absence of an empirical basis for either of her theses and the fact that many of the individuals who claim this descent can also demonstrate connections with Jewish ancestors (Hordes 2005), it is more plausible to accept their internal view of a crypto-Jewish identity. It should be noted that while I find the persistence of identity the most plausible hypothesis, this does not necessarily include the historical persistence of any particular ritual practice or form. Some practices may have historical roots, while others may arise from the processes discussed later in relation to bricolage or may be explained through the specific processes outlined in Neulander's groundbreaking work.

In more recent years, Neulander has moved into an area that is of increasing significance in crypto-Jewish studies and constructions of identity: genetics. She is one of the named authors of an article (Sutton et al. 2006) that claims to disprove "substantial" crypto-Jewish heritage in New Mexico on the basis of evidence from the Y chromosome.

While it is not my purpose here to examine the details of the genetics or to challenge the empirical data, it is important to ask whether the article actually does what it claims to do. It demonstrates that the markers on the Y chromosome of the male population of New Mexico are statistically similar to those of the male population of the Iberian Peninsula—with the unsurprising exception of some contribution from Native Americans. This evidence suggests that the contribution of Jews to the male gene pool in New Mexico is at the same level as that in Spain and Portugal. If we take into account the historical evidence that perhaps as many as 250,000 Jews were converted to Catholicism between 1391 and 1492, and that these individuals were a factor in the gene pools of Spain and Portugal, then the genetic evidence provided by Sutton and his colleagues indicates that the same degree of Jewish ancestry is found in New Mexico. Thus far from indicating the absence of crypto-Jews (or, more precisely, potential crypto-Jews), the evidence indicates the possibility of their presence.

The article concludes with the statement that "the crypto-Jewish scenario proposed by [Stanley] Hordes (1993, 1996) is refuted by these results. The criticisms of Neulander (1994, 1996) are well founded" (Sutton et al. 2006:108). This is overstating the results of the genetic research significantly. If Hordes's arguments rested solely on a "substantial" crypto-Jewish presence in New Mexico, the genetic results would indicate that it is no more substantial than in Iberia. His work, however, does not depend on this premise, but demonstrates the presence of crypto-Jews among the settlers and the descent of modern crypto-Jews from those settlers. This does not demand a substantial Jewish contribution to the New Mexican gene pool, but merely that there be some individuals of crypto-Jewish descent; no one contends that a significant percentage of New Mexicans either are of Jewish descent or are crypto-Jews. To take the article seriously would be to deny the existence of crypto-Jews (or individuals of Jewish descent) in Iberia and, most likely, in other parts of the Hispanic world. This view is certainly counter to the evidence found in many parts of that extended community.

Sutton and his colleagues may be focusing on Hordes's discussion of the motives of the crypto-Jews who chose to settle in New Mexico, suggesting that a significant number chose to settle there because of its geographic distance from centers of power. While this is an interesting aspect of Hordes's argument, it cannot be proved with the available documentary evidence. He does not imply that all or even a substantial number of the settlers were crypto-Jews, but suggests a reason for those who were. The argument about motives is additionally separable from the wider argument of whether crypto-Jews might be a proportion of the population of New

Mexico—at a similar level to that found in other parts of the Hispanic diaspora. Even if it is false or cannot be demonstrated, it in no way undermines the genetic evidence that individuals of Jewish descent were present in New Mexico.

Sutton and his colleagues also make a significant error in claiming to solve a cultural question using biological data. The biological data can only set the parameters for the number of potential crypto-Jews; it says nothing about the cultural issues of identity and practice. Hordes argues that due to the relative weakness of colonial authorities in New Mexico, crypto-Jews would have been better able to maintain their identity there than in some other parts of the Hispanic world. This would suggest that the number of crypto-Jews is actually not the significant issue for New Mexico. Ironically, the article indicates that individuals of Jewish descent were in New Mexico (as they were in Spain), and thus rather than falsifying "the crypto-Jewish scenario proposed by Hordes" (Sutton et al. 2006:108), it actually significantly challenges the proposals made by Judith Neulander.[6]

Michael Carroll

Michael Carroll (2002) explicitly seeks to examine two interrelated issues: (1) the "truth" or authenticity of crypto-Judaism as a historical phenomenon and (2) the "puzzling patterns associated with the CJNM [crypto-Jews in New Mexico] hypothesis that seem unrelated to the matter of 'truth' per se" (2).[7] The second concerns the underlying motives of the scholars studying crypto-Judaism, which Carroll places in the categories of "ethnographic analogy" and "orientalism." Although these issues are intertwined in Carroll's analysis and, indeed, his arguments against authenticity are ultimately based on his discussion of motives, for the sake of clarity they will be disentangled and examined separately.

Carroll, a sociologist, opens his examination with reference to an article published in a general-interest magazine (Ferry and Nathan 2000). This article was based largely on the work of Judith Neulander and challenges the authenticity of crypto-Jews as historically Jewish. He suggests that Barbara Ferry and Debbie Nathan were concerned with "historical truth," which should also concern all those who study crypto-Judaism. Carroll's interest in "historical truth," with its association with the "modern" rather than the "postmodern," is rather ironic in the context of his article as a whole. Both of his main theoretical tools—"ethnographic analogy" and "orientalism"—arguably are part of the postmodern critique of objective academic study, with Edward Said's (2003) concept of orientalism explicitly challenging some of the most significant assumptions underlying the study of "objective" history.

Thus in the context of his own analysis, one might legitimately ask Carroll: Whose history? If, as he argues, ethnography and history are implicated in the societal contexts in which the anthropologist and historian work, how can any historical, anthropological, or, indeed, critical sociological study ever claim the unique and authoritative version of the historical, anthropological, or sociological truth? Indeed, one might ask whether there can be one history and whether any history can claim authenticity in relation to other histories or, in relation to Carroll's work, one sociology. Thus in the context of the crypto-Jewish material, why should the view of history offered by Ferry and Nathan, Neulander, or Carroll be more legitimate than that of the crypto-Jews or perhaps even the scholars whose work Carroll challenges? While authors of a popular article may be forgiven for using a problematic model of truth or "history," a sociologist who employs postmodern theoretical models must recognize the possibility of multiple truths and multiple histories.

While in Carroll's own terms the goal of determining historical authenticity or truth is illegitimate, the cultural context of the academic discussions both pro and con (including his own) is an important and possibly fruitful area for second-order debate. It is perhaps not insignificant that despite his opening remarks, Carroll never really engages the empirical questions, but presents an extended discussion of the nature of the scholarship. He assumes that challenging the motives and cultural context of the scholars who argue for the existence of crypto-Judaism undermines both the validity of their arguments and the existence of the individuals and communities that they analyze. It should be clear from the outset that this type of reasoning would, by definition, undermine all scholarship, as it is impossible to find any scholar who has no motives in his or her engagement in research. It is necessary to demonstrate that these motives have had a material influence on the findings of the research, not just that they may be present.

Despite the logical inconsistency that Carroll's view of "historical truth" raises, it is important to understand the presupposition about truth that underlies his work. His arguments as a whole are premised on the plausibility (or perhaps the probability) of the hypotheses put forward by Neulander and their popularization by Ferry and Nathan. His discussion assumes that any scholar who does not find Neulander's work convincing must have nonacademic motives for ignoring its evident truth or plausibility. While there is no reason to criticize Carroll for his choice of academic arguments, it is worth asking why his position (and, by implication, that of Neulander and of Ferry and Nathan) is motivated solely by objective analysis, while that of the academics on the other side of the debate is motivated by ethnographic analogy (in relation to the Holocaust) and orientalism. His contentions are not prefaced by an in-depth analysis of the two sides of the argument about crypto-Judaism and a demonstration of why one is more compelling than the other. Thus one might ask the same question of Carroll that he asks of the scholars who accept the crypto-Jewish hypothesis: Why do you cling to the rejection of this hypothesis so strongly? Carroll's (2002) main arguments, however, are not directly about truth, but about "the puzzling patterns associated with the CJNM hypothesis" (2). These patterns are puzzling only if one automatically assumes that the hypothesis is false.

To prove its falsity, Carroll deploys the ideas of ethnographic analogy and orientalism. The concept of ethnographic analogy is largely derived from the work of James Clifford (1994:205–228) and that of orientalism from the work of Edward Said, although, interestingly, Carroll does not cite Said's original groundbreaking book, *Orientalism* (1978, 2003).

Carroll suggests that ethnographic analogy is embedded in ethnographic description. On the surface, ethnography is presented as a descriptive analysis of a particular culture or aspect of a culture. Underlying this apparently objective description, however, is a second "story" that reflects the cultural situatedness of the ethnographer. Thus in the same way that the postmodern reader creates the text that she is reading—by interpreting it through her own cultural concerns—the ethnographer provides a reading of culture that is shaped by his own cultural context. On the basis of this theoretical perspective, Carroll (2002:10–12) suggests that the "CJNM hypothesis" is shaped by the imposition of modern experiences, particularly the Holocaust, on the past.

In some respects, Carroll's argument is convincing, particularly when he discusses the changes in scholarship about the Inquisition. The view of the Inquisition before the 1970s was shaped largely by the experience of the Holocaust and, one might add, the development of Jewish identity in relation to Israel. Therefore, pre-1970s scholarship overemphasized both the power and ruthlessness of the Inquisition by analogy with the Nazi persecution of the European Jews and the precarious situation of the Diaspora Jews as a minority (that is, outside Israel). In research conducted since the 1970s, there has been a progressive reconsideration of this view and increasing skepticism about the power of both the Inquisition and inquisitors.[8] It is perhaps significant that one of the scholars whom Carroll cites as being part of this change is Stanley Hordes, one of the principal historians of crypto-Judaism in New Mexico and the Americas.

Carroll then moves the concept of ethnographic analogy to the current scholarship on crypto-Judaism in New Mexico. In spite of the change in historical scholarship about the Inquisition that he notes, he assumes that the analogy found in the earlier scholarship is retained—that is, the Inquisition is equated with the Gestapo and the treatment of the Jews in Spain as "analogous" to that of the Jews in Europe during the Holocaust. The analogy in relation to "so-called" living crypto-Jews is, however, transformed as a result of perhaps ambiguous feelings about the Holocaust. The "crypto-Jews" represent a Holocaust as it might have been rather than as it was; that is, they survived rather than being wiped out. Carroll suggests that many scholars tightly "embrace" the CJNM hypothesis because of this analogy.

While it is certainly not difficult to find some aspects of this analogy, particularly in Jewish organizations that are in effect searching for the "lost tribes," even in these cases the analogy must be taken as implicit and is never explicitly developed. But even underlying evidence for the argument does not appear in the work of the academic historians or other scholars who study crypto-Judaism. Indeed, in presenting this explanation for the embrace of CJNM by scholars, Carroll never cites any specific evidence from academic scholarship (or any specific evidence at all). On the basis of his analysis, we might be forgiven for thinking that the analogy he is discussing is purely in his own mind. This raises some interesting questions about his work that are outside the purview of this discussion. It is also somewhat ironic that one of the scholars whom he cites as challenging the notion of the Inquisition as all powerful, Stanley Hordes, is also one of the scholars whom he suggests is holding fast to this very idea.

If we move away from the specifics of Carroll's analysis to the issue of ethnographic analogy and the role of the anthropologist, the historian, or any other academic in shaping or creating the material that they analyze, we support Clifford's theoretical arguments: readers do provide the basis of interpretation of the texts they read. Thus the "ethnographies" that anthropologists and historians produce do offer significant insight into their own cultural positioning. Nonetheless, this perspective does not deny that there is a text or a set of people and cultural behaviors being analyzed. While the ethnographers of crypto-Judaism may have their own cultural analogies, this does not in any sense provide a basis for challenging the authenticity of the people being studied. If Carroll wants to use this argument, he would have to jettison academic (and nonacademic) discussion of any topic in the sciences, social sciences, and humanities as being subject to the argument. The use of this concept also provides no basis for understanding why individuals in the Hispano community claim the identity or history of crypto-Judaism unless we consider them to be mendacious or deluded.

Before we examine the details of Carroll's application of the orientalist paradigm to crypto-Judaism, it is worthwhile to address the broader question of whether this concept should be or can be applied to the analysis of crypto-Judaism. Carroll cites a number of scholars who point to a process of orientalizing the Southwest by Anglo writers. While the arguments behind the application of this model to both the Pueblo and Hispano communities in the nineteenth century apparently fit with the arguments developed by Said, the paradigm seems less applicable to material from the late twentieth century. A significant part of the thinking about crypto-Jewish identity, even in its retroactive nineteenth-century application, lacks the long historic development and objectification of Said's understanding of orientalism and thus can be only a similar or an analogous phenomenon rather than the same phenomena. Orientalization is a long-term process of objectifying a group, not a short-term process that often or usually has individuals as its primary focus.

One of the significant features of Said's argument is his focus on the basis of the orientalist discourse—that is, power, colonialism, and, more broadly, imperialism. While this element is developed throughout Said's important work, it is perhaps most clearly articulated in a preface written for the anniversary edition of his groundbreaking book (Said 2003:xi–xxiii). In both its nineteenth- and its twentieth-century manifestations, the orientalist discourse is a way of validating and authorizing Western colonial or imperialistic domination of the East.

Carroll's arguments do not provide a compelling demonstration of orientalism in the scholarship on modern crypto-Judaism. While the issue of power and imperialistic expansion is evident in nineteenth-century descriptions of both Pueblo and Hispano culture, the crypto-Jewish hypothesis arose in a very different historical and political context. Crypto-Jewish studies in the United States are a product of the late twentieth century (significant academic interest in crypto-Judaism in New Mexico dates from just before the 1980s), and its proponents lack a clear political motive for "othering" as exotic a portion of the Hispano community.

Those who study or discuss crypto-Judaism (and Carroll and Neulander must be included in this category, as dismissing a subject of study is as much or more of an exercise of power than defining one) come from a range of academic approaches (anthropology, sociology, and folklore), a variety of religious and ethnic groups (practicing and nonpracticing Jews, Catholics, and Hispanics), and a large number of locations (United States, Israel, and Europe). It seems unlikely that there is a common political agenda or exercise of power that unites the players in the development of the crypto-Jewish discourse.

In addition, the study of or interest in crypto-Jews is not restricted to those in New Mexico or the wider American Southwest. Some scholars have turned their attention to the Portuguese diaspora in the northeastern United States as well as the Hispanic communities in many other parts of the country, including Florida and California. Others have discussed crypto-Judaism in relation to communities in Spain and Portugal, Central and South America, and other regions of the Spanish and Portuguese diaspora. Thus the view that the crypto-Jewish hypothesis is essentially about New Mexico is unsupported by the data; in Carroll's terms, it cannot be that New Mexico is "good to think," but that Spanish and Portuguese communities, wherever they are found, are "good to think" and are equally part of an orientalist discourse. It seems unlikely that a common imperialist agenda unites these diverse areas. While some of these areas are in the United States, others are in the perceived imperialist domain of the United States—that is, Latin America—or outside that conceptual structure—for example, Spain and Portugal. Thus, at the most, Carroll can argue for features that appear to be similar to orientalism, yet because of the absence of a common power discourse, they must be accounted for on the basis of a different theoretical paradigm.

Other significant details undermine Carroll's application of orientalism to crypto-Judaism. One aspect of orientalism is its attempt to portray "the other" as monolithically exotic. This feature, however, is weakened by the crypto-Jewish hypothesis. The concept of crypto-Judaism and the associated, although currently unstudied, concept of crypto-Islam present the Hispano community as diverse and thus not subject to a single differentiating discourse. While it is undoubtedly true that in the nineteenth and early twentieth centuries part of the American view of Manifest Destiny led to the orientalizing of both the Native Americans and the Hispanics, arguably the increasing views of diversity within these communities at least in part undermines the concept.

In Carroll's discussion of the orientalization of Hispano New Mexico (and, indeed, most of the sources he cites relate to this broader form of orientalization and are at least in part supportable on the basis of American colonialism and expansion), he picks out the traditions that to an eastern American eye would have appeared exotic. While the art of the *santeros* and the rites of the Penitente brotherhood may have been strange and therefore emphasized in the presentation of New Mexico, they are part of Hispano culture. They may be used by the orientalist, but they were not invented by him; they may be overemphasized in cultural prominence, but they are real. These examples suggest that even were one to agree that crypto-Judaism is utilized in the same way, this would in no way challenge the plausibility of crypto-Jewish authenticity.

After discussing the orientalization of Hispano culture, Carroll turns to crypto-Judaism. In effect, he suggests that the processes of orientalizing crypto-Judaism relate to the Hispano community as a whole, and thus the crypto-Jews represent that community. This argument is problematic, since it presents a nuanced and complex view of Hispano New Mexico that challenges the monolithic nature of orientalism. It also is problematic in relation to the analogy. Much of the depiction of crypto-Judaism is oppositional; that is, it sets the crypto-Jews against not the West, but the Spanish monarchy and, particularly, the Inquisition. But in many respects, these are represented by the Hispano community. Thus crypto-Jews are not a good equivalent for Hispanos, as they are conceptually opposed to them.

Carroll seems to suggest that crypto-Jews were susceptible to even greater orientalization than Hispanos. He makes a link between the crypto-Jews' alleged Middle Eastern origin and therefore the actual "Orient." This argument is problematic on both conceptual and ethnographic grounds. Using Said's approach, the argument cannot be that the orientalist scholars knew that they were orientalizing, as suggested by their conscious or unconscious use of the Middle Eastern origin—this would imply that they were aware that the West had an orientalist view of the Middle East. Rather, for it to stand, his argument must be that the Hispanos in the Southwest were subject to a similar form of imperialism, which led to a discourse of control—that is, orientalism. Thus the Middle Eastern origin is not relevant to the application of the paradigm.

His equation is also problematic because most of the people who study crypto-Judaism are Jews and thus might consider themselves to be of Middle Eastern origin—a historical background that would therefore not be considered exotic and thereby creating difference. In order to deal with this challenge, Carroll introduces the division between Sephardic and Ashkenazic Jews. This, however, relates to settlement in Europe rather than origin in the Middle East.

This is not, however, to say that crypto-Judaism is identical to other forms of Judaism and might not be considered exotic by some. Crypto-Judaism does claim practices that its "adherents" have maintained in secret. Yet in many cases in the literature (rightly or wrongly), these practices are not considered to be distinct and exotic, but similar to mainstream Jewish practices with an overlay of secrecy and a veneer of Catholicism being the only additions.

One of the major points of Carroll's arguments in support of orientalism is the supposed feminization of crypto-Jews and, thereby, Hispanos. It is here that he is able to cite some analyses of crypto-Judaism in the historical and anthropological literature—for example, the work of Renée Melammed (1999) and Janet Jacobs (1996), respectively. This aspect of the orientalist paradigm emphasizes the use of feminization both to distinguish Western (masculine) society from crypto-Jewish (feminine) society and to introduce the element of passivity, which was, in the traditional orientalist thesis, regarded by Westerners to be a part of the identity of the "oriental" woman and, by extension, that of Eastern society in general.

Carroll is correct that the hypotheses of the studies by Melammed and Jacobs have not been fully supported by the evidence. It is, however, a very different matter to group them together, because they deal with very different communities, and to assume that they are orientalist only because they focus on women. Melammed argues that the Inquisition records from sixteenth-century Castile suggest that women played a major role in the preservation and transmission of crypto-Jewish culture. Thus one might ask Carroll if his orientalist thesis extends beyond the scope of America to Spain and if the American orientalist agenda is shared by Melammed, an Israeli historian who would not regard a Sephardic identity as exotic. The fact that she is studying crypto-Jews cannot, in Carroll's terms, necessitate orientalism, as he cites as authoritative a number of scholarly texts that accept the existence of crypto-Judaism in Spain. Thus it is solely because Melammed focuses on women that her work, according to Carroll, is an example of orientalism and relevant to the discourse of crypto-Judaism in New Mexico. It might be suggested that her thesis is potentially valid and thus worth testing; while she may or may not have proved it, the mere fact that she advocates the passage of crypto-Jewish culture through women is not on its own orientalist (rather, it more likely betokens a feminist agenda, one that is also evident in Jacobs's work).

Jacobs, an anthropologist, has tested a hypothesis similar to Melammed's in relation to individuals with crypto-Jewish identity in the American Southwest. In the original presentation of this material, her argument was essentially feminist, seeing crypto-Jewish women as nodes of power and cultural capital in an essentially patriarchal Hispanic society. Jacobs does not make an analogy between crypto-Jewish and Hispanic culture. In a more recent publication, Jacobs (2002) tests her hypothesis in a more extended form. She ultimately concludes, on the basis of the ethnographic data, that there is slightly less support for the idea of women controlling either the preservation or the transmission of crypto-Jewish culture. Nonetheless, Jacobs's work cannot simply be rejected as orientalist. If she had merely presented it as a hypothesis, similar to Carroll's discussion, this characterization might at least be arguable. But Jacobs presents empirical data gathered from ethnographic interviews to support her theory, and it must be on the basis of the data that we accept or reject her argument, not on the basis of assumed motives.

While both Melammed and Jacobs emphasize the role of women in crypto-Jewish society, and thus at least arguably create a "contrast between the culture being studied and a dominant culture" (Carroll 2002:13–16), this does not mean that their hypotheses are incorrect or made for orientalist reasons. As Carroll himself points out, Melammed and Jacobs may be utilizing feminist theory, which argues against the passive view of women that was integral to the orientalist perspective, with its feminization of the cultures to which it was applied. It is clear from their arguments that Melammed and Jacobs do not see the women they are studying as passive (indeed, in crypto-Jewish terms, they are regarded as precisely the opposite). In order to challenge their analyses, one must move outside a pigeonholing enterprise and look at their data. While the sources that Carroll cites on early modern crypto-Jewish culture—Seymour Liebman (1970) and Yitzhak Baer (1961)—may be germane, they do not address the same questions as Melammed and thus do not deal with women as transmitters of crypto-Jewish culture—probably because they were written before the emergence of feminist theory.

Within historical and social scientific analysis, it is necessary to test whether hypotheses that are plausible are in fact supported by documentary or ethnographic data. It is precisely this process that is found in the work of Melammed and Jacobs. Their work might have been regarded as orientalist if they had accepted this paradigm without proper investigation; it is only possibly orientalist if this evidence is present. In a sense, Carroll's own arguments are flawed in this way. He suggests that it is plausible that this "feminization" in Melammed's and Jacobs's studies is a product of orientalism and then purely on the basis of the plausibility, without any detailed evidence, considers them to be orientalist.

In addition to using ethnographic analogy and orientalism to challenge the work of scholars who study crypto-Judaism, Carroll attributes motives to these scholars without providing convincing data to support these charges. His arguments also miss an important aspect of the modern discussions of crypto-Judaism—that individuals from the Hispano community are both claiming and studying this identity. It is clear that his arguments for neither ethnographic analogy nor orientalism can fully account (save on the patronizing notion of false consciousness) for crypto-Jews' self-identification and academic contributions to the subject.

Carroll emphasizes that his article is concerned about not the authenticity of crypto-Jews in New Mexico, but the motives of the academics who support the presence of crypto-Jews in New Mexico. He assumes that the scholars cannot be objectively weighing the evidence, as clearly he is doing, and thus must be motivated by reasons other than scholarly ones. He adds that even if significant material evidence were found to prove them correct, it would not undermine his arguments. But what are these motives? Carroll's introduction of material cultural evidence is not helpful to his discussion or the understanding of material culture in the crypto-Jewish community. He suggests that while it is not crucial to his own arguments, there is the possibility that "artifacts and/or documents which undeniably attest to the presence of a thriving crypto-Jewish tradition" might be found (Carroll 2002:16). While this is possible, Carroll perpetuates a misunderstanding of material culture, assuming that an object, based on particular symbols or the like, can undeniably attest something. It is, however, not the objects or symbols but the use and understanding of those objects and symbols that make them evidence of material culture. Michael Carroll's misunderstanding of the nature of material culture, which has also been discussed in relation to the work of Judith Neulander, is a consistent issue in crypto-Jewish studies.

Barbara Ferry and Debbie Nathan

Although the article by Barbara Ferry and Debbie Nathan (2000) largely derives from the work of Judith Neulander, it is necessary to examine it. It is one of the most substantial critical pieces on crypto-Judaism in the nonacademic press and, more important, is well known and of significance in both the crypto-Jewish community and the wider community, both academic and nonacademic.

As with most popularizations, Ferry and Nathan's article both is sensationalized and focuses on personalities. First among them is Stanley Hordes, who is portrayed as the person who initiated the narrative of Hispanos secretly preserving their Jewish identity and who continues to be one of the primary spokespersons of this hypothesis. Hordes is closely associated in the article with Santa Fe, in which he lived and served as state historian. The article seeks to undermine his credibility by focusing on the city's tourist industry, which is allegedly given added value by the crypto-Jewish hypothesis, and the artificiality of its architecture, which they characterize as "faux adobe." While it may be that both these charges have some truth, Ferry and Nathan use a classic journalistic tactic—guilt by association. The arguments about crypto-Judaism do not relate primarily to Santa Fe and must be examined on their own terms. separate from the suggested artificiality of the city. A contention similar to theirs would be that because of the artificiality of Plimoth Plantation in Massachusetts, no Puritans settled along the east coast of North America. It is also important to note that Hordes is only one of several individuals who observed and argued for the existence of crypto-Judaism and that many of them were not based in Santa Fe and some came from the Hispano community itself. Indeed, the article mentions, among others, Tomás Atencio, a sociologist at the University of New Mexico who was exploring crypto-Judaism in his own family, and Richard Santos from Texas, neither of whom can credibly have the motives hinted at in the opening paragraphs of the article.

Ferry and Nathan's discussion in no way challenges the academic basis of Hordes's research. They focus on two aspects of his work: the way he came to form the hypothesis that crypto-Jews might be present in New Mexico, and the public presentations of his findings. In the first case, the anecdotal material provided by his informants was not the data on which his research was based; it merely led to the research (this mistaken view is directly based on articles by Neulander, who suggests that Hordes's work is based largely on rumor and anonymous sources). Hordes is a historian, and as shown in his publications, his research utilizes documentary evidence to demonstrate that some Hispano families present in New Mexico are of Jewish descent. His work also indicates that many families claiming that they have strong Jewish cultural roots demonstrate clear genealogical descent from Jewish families. The material used by Ferry and Nathan in no way challenges this type of research. As for their second focus, it clearly is a secondary issue, unrelated to the quality of Hordes's research.

Like Neulander and Carroll, Ferry and Nathan hint at hidden motives on the part of those who support the presence of crypto-Jews in New Mexico. To their attacks on the academic and personal integrity of scholars, Ferry and Nathan add questions about the credibility of selectively chosen crypto-Jews. In their discussion of Isabelle Sandoval, for example, they emphasize her use of skin color and facial structure as the bases for her exploration of identity. (It must be noted that Sandoval was interviewed a number of times over several years for this ethnographic study. She used a very wide range of evidence, not just facial characteristics, to support her understanding of herself as being of Jewish origin.) Ferry and Nathan implicitly challenge her identity by hinting at anti-Semitic stereotyping of the Jewish facial type. While it is important to understand how stereotypes of this kind have been used to express prejudice, it is also important to see how it is used by individuals as a means to express an essentialist concept of their own identity—claiming to look like a Jew is ultimately a claim to genetically being a Jew.

Ferry and Nathan's main criticism of Sandoval is that she ultimately expressed aspects of her identity in public in the form of "confrontational" poetry, expressing her feelings (and those of other crypto-Jews) about how she is viewed and judged by the mainstream Jewish community, and thus, in their view, was motivated by the wish for celebrity. (On the basis of their general form of argument, this implies that both academics and crypto-Jews are in some sense artificial, but merely choosing to publicly express one's identity is not sufficient reason to distrust that presentation.)[9] Sandoval has been exploring her identity for a number of years, and her poetry has been a means of doing so. Her writing and presenting it does not mean that her identity is inauthentic.

Unlike Sandoval, most crypto-Jews are very private and do not choose to make their identity or practices public. By focusing on individuals, whose self-identities may or may not be challengeable, Ferry and Nathan seek to challenge all crypto-Jews. This form of argument is clearly unsustainable unless identical motives and identities can be attributed to all those who claim to be crypto-Jews, many of whom remain outside public discussions.

Toward the end of their article, Ferry and Nathan return to their discussion of Sandoval, suggesting that her presentation of self, particularly her memories, have significantly altered—with her original memories focusing on a Protestant–Catholic opposition as shaping a bleak childhood and her reconstructed memories being of crypto-Jewish elements as defining a happy childhood. They imply that Sandoval's original presentation is true and her second is false, related to her wish for celebrity. But they seriously misunderstand the nature of memory and identity. Their discussion suggests that memory and identity are fixed and largely static and that the first recollections are definably more authentic than later presentations. In fact, memory is highly fluid and selective: memories are related to and, to a degree, selected on the basis of how one perceives oneself at a given moment and in a given context. Thus both sets of Sandoval's memories, although apparently contradictory, must be contextualized and recognized as interpretations of the past based on the present; neither has greater authenticity than the other.

Ferry and Nathan then turn to the element of secrecy in crypto-Judaism. They note that in many presentations of research, the subjects' names are changed or are blanked out in photographs of gravestones, attributing this policy to the attempt by crypto-Jews and their supporters to control the presentation of crypto-Judaism and thus maintain their role as the celebrity mediators of crypto-Judaism to the general public. A different interpretation of this practice is suggested by my ethnography and by the explanations of those involved. The respondents, some of whom are mentioned by Ferry and Nathan, expressed a range of views on privacy and secrecy. Some, such as

Sandoval, were happy to talk in public about their explorations of identity and their understanding of their families' histories. Others, however, did not wish to talk in public or have their names mentioned. While some in this group suggested that their desire for anonymity was a result of others in their families rejecting this understanding of the past, many said that secrecy was a part of their identity. Based on these differing views, it is important to be sensitive to the concerns of informants and follow the best ethical practice. Ferry and Nathan misrepresent the causal chain. They imply that the increased secrecy preceded the main attacks on the crypto-Jewish hypothesis; in fact, while some individuals always wished their identities to remain secret, others stopped talking in public and speaking to academics due to the adverse criticism that crypto-Judaism was receiving.[10]

The remaining sections of Ferry and Nathan's article present a biographical hagiography of their protagonist, Judith Neulander, and her critique of the crypto-Jewish hypothesis. I will highlight some issues on which Ferry and Nathan focus that were not examined earlier as well as touch on the aspects of her theory that they pick up and thus have entered the popular discourse on crypto-Judaism.

Their discussion suggests that many of the arguments demonstrating the existence of crypto-Judaism were based on either poor ethnographic practice or false analogy. Thus, for example, they imply that through repeated interviews false memories and understandings of identity were created, which to Neulander's trained eye were the products of the interviewer rather than the interviewee. While interviews are notoriously problematic, and it is possible for interviewers to shape the understandings of interviewees, this is not something that can easily be determined by sitting in on one or more interviews. Thus while Neulander (and Ferry and Nathan) may in part be correct, they do not have sufficient data to support their charge that a significant number of interviews and all the information presented were shaped by the influence of the interviewer.

To support their interpretation, they describe an interview at which Neulander was present in which (in her view) the interviewee had to be prompted to remember what she "had said" in an earlier interview. Given the selectivity of memories, it is apparent that the same memories might not be evoked in different interviews and in different contexts (and in the presence of an individual unknown to the interviewee and, therefore, perhaps not trusted by her). The problem with this interview was that both interviewers (Hordes and Neulander) were expecting the same response as given in the previous interview, and not getting it led to the attempt to retrieve it. Thus the issue is with the expectation, not with the content of the initial interview. (Given that there is no taped transcript of the previous interview, it is impossible to reconstruct whether the type of interview bias alleged by Neulander occurred.) The point does, however, underscore the need for interviews to be conducted by trained ethnographers, a practice that has been followed by both Hordes (who has worked with trained ethnographers) and Atencio (who is himself trained in interviewing) during subsequent periods of research. Subsequent to Neulander's observation of the interview, other trained ethnographers have entered the field and have found cultural understandings and identities similar to those suggested by Hordes's initial work.

The primary aspect of Neulander's analysis utilized by Ferry and Nathan relates to the supposed association between the crypto-Jews of New Mexico and the inhabitants of Venta Prieta, studied by Raphael Patai (1983), whose apparently Jewish practices originated not in Judaism but in Seventh-Day Adventism. Ferry and Nathan go beyond Neulander in contending that individuals who claim to be crypto-Jews must have either forgotten that their families were Adventist or another millenarian denomination or deliberately chosen to lie about their past in order to claim a Jewish present because of their desire for both publicity and economic benefit.

This thesis is supported by neither the history—that is, the number of Adventists and Pentecostals (and converts to these sects)—nor the ethnography. Historically, it significantly overemphasizes the penetration of Judaizing churches in New Mexico. It also patronizingly assumes that those who claim a crypto-Jewish identity are ignorant of their families' relatively recent past, even though some informants were in their seventies or eighties and thus may have lived through that past. Ethnographically, while some informants mentioned family backgrounds in different Protestant denominations, particularly Presbyterianism, with a small minority having recent connections with messianic churches or Mormonism, the majority stated that their families had remained in the Catholic Church. Baptismal and other records support the interviewees' information about their families' religious affiliations.

Thus the burden of proof must be on those who question the credibility of those who support the authenticity of crypto-Judaism in New Mexico. This is particularly true on ethical grounds, since it concerns a living community and the self-perception of its members. The challengers have to demonstrate that all individuals who claim to be crypto-Jews have the motives—for example, celebrity or economic rewards—attributed to them, come from families that were affiliated with or significantly influenced by Seventh-Day Adventism or Pentecostalism, are either forgetful or mendacious about their families' histories and cultural practices, and use Jewish descent to claim whiteness. Even a small group of individuals claiming crypto-Jewish identity who fell outside this characterization would undermine the thesis's viability as generally applicable.

Ferry and Nathan present a rather contradictory version of Neulander's argument about status (in which contradictions are also implicit), according to which would-be crypto-Jews are "racists" who, following the lead of their colonial ancestors, use crypto-Jewish identity as a marker of ethnic purity. This contention not only attributes motives without sufficient empirical evidence, but also is historically inaccurate: *limpieza de sangre* referred particularly to the taint of Jewish (or Muslim) blood. This suggests, without clear evidence, that Jewish blood is indeed a "postmodern marker" for ethnically pure blood, but there is no reason for seeing it in this light in relation to the Hispano community in either New Mexico or the wider American Southwest. Many crypto-Jews emphasize their mixed ethnic heritage, which raises a significant challenge to both the work of Judith Neulander and its popularization by Barbara Ferry and Debbie Nathan.

The theories that reject the authenticity of crypto-Jewish identity in New Mexico are not persuasive. Not only is no empirical data presented in their defense, but there is compelling historical and ethnographic evidence to challenge them. The arguments that come from proponents of the alternative perspective convincingly demonstrate that some ancestors of individuals who claim to be crypto-Jews were of Jewish descent and, in some cases, were called before the Inquisition on charges of Judaizing. While this evidence leaves a significant gap in the record, of perhaps two hundred years, it is highly plausible that traditions of identity could have been passed down and thereby form the basis of the modern expression of crypto-Jewish identity and culture.

THREE

THE CASE FOR THE AUTHENTICITY
OF CRYPTO-JUDAISM IN NEW MEXICO

Countering those who question the authenticity of crypto-Judaism in New Mexico are a wide range of scholars (including me) who argue for its authenticity, both as a historical phenomenon and as a contemporary ethnographic field of study. The two most substantial contributions to this side of the argument have come from Stanley Hordes and Janet Jacobs. Hordes's work focuses primarily on the presence of crypto-Jews among the Spanish colonists who settled New Mexico and the evidence for the persistence of Jewish identity in the community. Jacobs's work is ethnographic, examining the role of women in maintaining crypto-Jewish culture in the Southwest of the United States and in Mexico. Alongside these substantial contributions, a number of academics and nonacademics have published pieces that either implicitly or explicitly address arguments relating to crypto-Jewish authenticity.

Before turning to the contributions of Jacobs and Hordes, a discussion of the work of Renée Levine Melammed (whose work was touched on by Michael Carroll [2002]) and David Gitlitz begins this chapter. Although they study the experiences of crypto-Jews in Spain and thus are not directly involved in the arguments about the authenticity of crypto-Judaism in New Mexico, both address the nature of crypto-Jewish practices, with Melammed focusing on the transmission of these practices. It is important to note that the similarity between historical and present-day practices does not provide a high degree of proof of authenticity, but the issues discussed by these scholars allows us to contextualize modern practices and to determine how they may be understood in relation to the other arguments about authenticity.

Renée Levine Melammed

In *Heretics or Daughters of Israel? The Crypto-Jewish Women of Castile* (1999), Renée Levine Melammed focuses largely on the role of women in the preservation and transmission of crypto-Jewish identity and traditions. One of the points that Melammed emphasizes in her introduction is the complexity of individual responses to the conversion of Spanish Jews to Catholicism. Although she suggests that a community of *conversos* did develop, it was in no sense "monolithic." Some individuals chose to take advantage of the conversion and move into a range of occupations hitherto forbidden—for example, in the church or military. Others, however, could not abandon their Jewish past and thus began the processes that created crypto-Judaism. The community of *conversos* was, she suggests, largely distinct from those of both their former Jewish co-religionists and their new Christian brothers and sisters (Melammed 1999:5).[1] This distinctiveness was exacerbated both by Spanish ideology (for example, the ideology of *limpieza de sangre*) and, even more significantly, by the context of suspicion and fear engendered by the Inquisition. According to Melammed (1999), "Ironically, both those conversos who judaized and those who did not faced lives of fear and insecurity, for they were all suspect in a society unwilling to absorb them" (14).

The context described by Melammed provides a basis for the evolution of an oppositional identity, which may or may not have included the performance of Jewish practices, but in which secrecy would have been a significant component. Interestingly, modern crypto-Jews mirror this cultural situation: the range of identities is equally complex, and crypto-Jews as a "community" are conceptually and culturally distinct from both mainstream Jews and Hispanos. While the fear and insecurity that were part of the historical context are largely absent, to some degree, both the secrecy and the insecurity have been internalized and are key aspects of the identity of many of the individuals interviewed for this and other studies.

Melammed's work focuses specifically on the nature of Jewish culture in fourteenth- to sixteenth-century Spain and on the role of women as the primary agents of transmission of that culture. She argues that Judaism of the fourteenth and fifteenth centuries was largely male-dominated, with most practices associated with the synagogue and thus both institutional and public. With the demise of the Jewish community of Spain in 1492, the nature of the cultural options available to crypto-Jews was significantly transformed. Melammed (1999:32) suggests that within this new context, a significant role for men largely disappeared, while that for women was transformed in the opposite direction. Focused on the home and independent of the public center of Judaism or even of the books and learning that defined the men's role, women became the transmitters of crypto-Jewish culture and the home became the critical center for that culture (Melammed 1999:32).

Melammed's work presents a convincing analysis of the active role played by women in the preservation of Jewish practices and, perhaps, identity among crypto-Jews. She outlines practices associated with the Sabbath, Yom Kippur, Passover, dietary laws, and mourning rituals that were preserved by women (Melammed 1999:93); many of them are characteristic of crypto-Jewish culture as it exists today.

Although Melammed importantly highlights women's role and voice in a historical context that previously been focused on men, and her discussion of the transformation of Jewish culture to crypto-Jewish culture is also convincing, her argument that women were therefore the sole or primary tradents (individuals who preserve and pass traditions from one generation to the next) for crypto-Jewish identity and culture is not sufficiently established. She does not sufficiently contextualize the evidence about women, and the accusations made against them by the Inquisition, in relation to documentary evidence about men. While it is possible that with the move from the public to the private sphere men lost their role in the transmission of culture, it is also possible that they working alongside women in the transmission of the "privatized" crypto-Jewish culture. As we will suggest in our discussion of Jacobs's work, the ethnographic evidence developed for this study suggests that both men and women play important roles in the transmission of modern crypto-Jewish identity and practice—with the majority of the practices being associated with the private sphere of the home.

David Gitlitz

In *Secrecy and Deceit: The Religion of the Crypto-Jews* (1996), David Gitlitz takes a much wider perspective than does Renée Melammed (1999) in her book. While Gitlitz touches on the historical controversies relating to the number and extent of conversions and the maintenance of Jewish identity in Spain and the wider Spanish and Portuguese diasporas, the majority of his book is focused on the nature of crypto-Jewish culture, including practices, beliefs, and communal structures. Both parts of his discussion have implications for authenticity. In the first part, he addresses the arguments for and against the transmission of Jewish culture and practices after the conversions. In the second part, he establishes, at least arguably, both a base line for practices that may have been transmitted to crypto-Jews in the New World and a basis for looking at the processes of cultural transformation already present in the historical documentary evidence.

Gitlitz's chapter "The Major Points of Controversy" is important both for its attempt to address the issues related to the authenticity and extent of crypto-Judaism and for its taxonomy of crypto-Jews, which shares some features with the ideal types of modern crypto-Judaism discussed in this book. In relation to the number of *conversos* and that of Judaizers tried by the Inquisition, Gitlitz mediates among the estimations presented by the main historical schools. He concludes that there probably were up to 225,000 *conversos* in Spain and relatively few in Portugal before 1492 (Gitlitz 1996:74) and that there were between 25,000 and 50,000 Judaizers. Although it is unclear what percentage of the total New Christian population (extended through the seventeenth century) these numbers represent, Gitlitz (1996:76) accepts the general consensus that the majority of New Christians were successfully assimilated into the Catholic community and were not crypto-Jews.

Due to his emphasis on the records of the Inquisition as sources of evidence for crypto-Jewish practice, Gitlitz presents an elaborated discussion of the issues relating to reliability. Although Gitlitz acknowledges that there are some questions about reliability, he argues that we can be confident the records' trustworthiness in some significant respects. The most important area of confidence is in relation to the transcripts of interviews with crypto-Jews. Gitlitz (1996) notes that the scribes were well trained and that the transcripts can be regarded as "generally accurate transcripts of what was actually said" (77). He does, however, concede that although in some senses accurate, a transcript is also in some senses selective, including data that fits with expectations and ignoring or missing information that does not. Gitlitz concludes that while the transcripts of the actual interviews are likely to be essentially true, the summations and conclusions of the documents must be considered more carefully.

Gitlitz's discussion is important, as Inquisition records provide the only evidence of crypto-Jewish identity and practices for much of the period from the fifteenth century to the nineteenth century. His point about transcription bias is also important because it suggests that while the documents may include descriptions of crypto-Jewish culture, they tend to include what the inquisitors expected, leaving out a range of practices that did not conform to the inquisitors' preconceived notions.

Gitlitz highlights some of the issues relating to both statements made by informers and testimony offered by the accused themselves. He suggests that the inquisitors were aware of the possibility that enemies of individuals might falsely accuse them of being crypto-Jews and attempted to reduce this possibility, and he discusses the potential effects of stereotyping in shaping denunciations. Gitlitz (1996:78) concludes that due to the nature of eyewitness accounts, the possibility of multiple substantiation, and the fear of perjury, the statements by informers can be taken seriously as evidence of practice. His discussion about the testimony by the accused recognizes that there may be many motivations for lying, ranging from self-preservation to courting martyrdom (and therefore falsely claiming to perform Jewish practices or adhere to Jewish beliefs as a means to this end). Nonetheless, Gitlitz suggests that when the accused were speaking of their own acts, and naming others involved, their evidence was often corroborated by witnesses. He also notes that many of the accused mentioned "nonstandard events, practices, or details" that could not have been evoked by leading questions or other aspects of the interrogation (Gitlitz 1996:78). While it may be appropriate to take a somewhat more cautious approach to these documents, Gitlitz's arguments suggest that there may be a good deal of factual evidence to be gleaned from them, which could provide at least an outline of the nature of crypto-Jewish practices in the fifteenth to seventeenth centuries.

Gitlitz's discussion of the Edicts of Grace, Inquisition documents that list Judaizing practices, is also significant. Although these records appear to be thorough, Gitlitz warns that they rarely kept abreast of transformations in crypto-Jewish practice. This highlights the fact that even between the fifteenth and seventeenth centuries there were perceptible areas of change in practices, which is important to remember in assessing the arguments for a rather static view of authentic crypto-Jewish culture. Interestingly, Gitlitz suggests that although the edicts were initially rather unreliable as guides to crypto-Jewish practice, by the end of the period they had become more accurate. This, however, was not due to better observation on the part of the inquisitors, but to the use of the edicts by crypto-Jews as a guide for their knowledge about Judaism (Gitlitz 1996:82). If Gitlitz is correct about this process in the seventeenth century and earlier, we should not be surprised that modern crypto-Jews look to a wide range of sources for the same reason. It suggests that to some degree crypto-Judaism, as a culture, because of its origins and development, seeks to look outside itself to gain access to authentic practice; this psychology, as suggested, is consistent with both the historical and the ethnographic evidence.

Gitlitz's taxonomy of New Christians provides an important conceptual link between the historical material that he discusses and the ethnographic material presented in this book. He divides the New Christians into a range of categories, each of which is characterized by a specific relationship to its Jewish past. The first category includes those who thought of themselves as Catholic. He suggests that they related to Catholicism in a number of ways, but Christianity was the main focus of their self-understanding. The second category includes those who considered themselves to be Jews. Again, this group was not monolithic, but ranged from "observant Judaizers" to "accommodationist Judaizers." As in the first category, religion—in this case, Judaism—was the main component of identity. The third category includes those who moved between the two religious identities or had a mixed or ambiguous identity; thus neither Judaism nor Catholicism was the focus of identity. The final category included skeptics—that is, individuals who largely rejected either religion as a part of identity (Gitlitz 1996:85–90). The ideal types of crypto-Jews discussed in chapter 4 share some characteristics with those described by Gitlitz, particularly relating to the first three categories. The key difference between my approach and that of Gitlitz is in the fluidity of these categories: my data suggests that these taxonomies can be seen only as describing general types; individuals constantly fall between them and move between them.

Gitlitz's (1996:82–83) discussion also introduces five "definitional" approaches that have been used to study the relationship between Judaizing and assimilation:

- The biological or racial
- The forms of belief
- The presence of Jewish practices
- Self-conception

- The external environment—that is, the presence of bias or discrimination against New Christians whether or not they were Judaizers

While Gitlitz presents these definitions separately from his taxonomy, many of them are the primary characteristics and differentiators of the four ideal types of modern crypto-Jews. Thus, for example, the strong crypto-Jewish type (which is similar in some respects to Gitlitz's second category) has a significant aspect of genealogical or ethnic self-definition, belief, and practices interpreted as emerging from Judaism, and a strong sense of self-conception as Jewish. The final definition, external environment, is significant in a very different way, although one that was also significant historically. This element is found in the emphasis on secrecy and its role in defining both the way that individuals interact with others and the very construction of their identities.

It is important to emphasize that these definitional factors are not absent from the three other ideal types of modern crypto-Jews. They are present in different proportions in each type. Thus the weak crypto-Jewish type (which overlaps with Gitlitz's second and third categories) displays all the elements, but they are much less developed or of shorter biographical duration than in the strong crypto-Jewish type. The third ideal type (containing aspects of Gitlitz's first and third categories), which might be called assimilationist, as in Gitlitz's taxonomy, includes the characteristics of genealogy and practice, but tends not to have the other three—or, if they are present, they are weaker than those of their Catholic or Protestant counterparts. The final type (having no direct parallel in Gitlitz's taxonomy), which is composed of individuals misidentified as crypto-Jews, seemingly includes the aspects of belief and practice but lacks any of the others. In our discussion, each of these elements is a building block of identity, rather than individually being definitional of identity.

Gitlitz's work also has important implications for understanding the processes of cultural transformation that have characterized the development of crypto-Judaism from the late fourteenth century to the present day. Although it is likely that there were some significant changes in the practices of the *conversos* who retained their Jewish identity between 1391 and 1492, particularly in relation to the need for secrecy, communication of information and transmission of ritual objects continued to be possible between Jews and crypto-Jews. Gitlitz (1996:3–34) provides documentary evidence for this type of interchange. The most significant cultural transformations occurred after the expulsion of the Jews from Spain in 1492. Gitlitz's discussion, based on the work of Yitzhak Baer (1966), indicates that the extent of the changes in practices depended on the location and size of the *converso* communities; thus, for example, Jewish practices and identity tended to remain relatively stable in a large *converso* community, while in areas with sparser settlement, due to the absence of communal support, practices tended to change more significantly.

Gitlitz's (1996:39–43) discussion of the years between 1492 and 1540 highlights some of the key issues in the process of transformation, including fear and self-doubt, to which could be added secrecy. Like Melammed, he notes the loss of the public institutional aspects of Jewish culture after the expulsion and the substantial danger incurred through retaining specifically Jewish material cultural objects, especially ritual objects and books. A key point of Gitlitz's (1996) analysis is that due to the loss of the Jewish literary culture, "the entire post-Biblical rabbinic tradition became inaccessible" (40). This observation is particularly important because some scholars consider the absence of substantial postbiblical knowledge to suggest that modern crypto-Judaism is historically inauthentic.

Based on his reading of Inquisition documents, Gitlitz highlights both the main sources of knowledge retained by crypto-Jews and the related areas of cultural transformation. He suggests that crypto-Judaism was largely an oral tradition, with only those prayers and practices that were frequently repeated and thus easily memorized being retained. In the late fifteenth and early sixteenth centuries, the Hebrew Bible was accessible, thereby providing a biblical rather than a rabbinic basis for crypto-Jewish traditions. This availability, however, ceased by the mid-sixteenth century, returning only in New Mexico with the arrival of Protestant missionaries in the nineteenth century. Finally, as suggested earlier, the Edicts of Grace also provided a source of knowledge, both framing and narrowing the range of crypto-Jewish practice. It is important to note that the processes outlined by Gitlitz were variable, depending on location and context, and likely were progressive over time. An additional element of transformation that he does not mention is cross-cultural influence. His work, however, emphasizes the fact that all crypto-Jewish identities were in part syncretistic—that is, bringing together a range of cultural forms. This syncretism probably increased over time, particularly as *conversos* became more integrated into non-*converso* contexts and came into contact with new cultural forms. While some degree of cultural compartmentalization might have been possible, particularly in the early generations, it seems likely that it broke down as cultural information was passed along and integrated by generations more remote from their Jewish ancestors.

Janet Jacobs

Although Janet Jacobs's book *Hidden Heritage: The Legacy of the Crypto-Jews* (2002) is based largely on an ethnographic study of crypto-Jews living in the American Southwest, her main argument is about the persistence and transmission of culture, primarily through the agency of women, and it thus relies on a clear assumption that the practices and self-identities that she identifies have an authentic basis in a historical tradition. Although Jacobs's work indicates that she is clearly aware of Judith Neulander's (1994, 1996, 2001) critiques of crypto-Judaism, and she at least in part deals with some of them in her ethnography,[2] her discussion about how she determined or dealt with the general question of authenticity is relatively brief. Jacobs (2002:12) utilized three indicators of authenticity:

- The performance of crypto-Jewish practices in the immediate family
- The presence of the family name in Inquisition documents
- The oral transmission of Jewish traditions in the family

Each of these elements has a somewhat different nature from the others. The first, the performance of rituals, is perhaps the most precarious in terms of arguments about authenticity—and is, indeed, the most important contribution of Neulander's work. Practices on their own, or even in the context of other indicators, are theoretically problematic as evidence of authenticity because it is difficult not only to be absolutely sure that a particular ritual is necessarily of Jewish origin but also to determine when it was adopted by a family or an individual. As Neulander suggests, and as borne out in my research, people can adopt "Jewish" practices in relation to the increasing importance of the crypto-Jewish element of their identity. Thus although it often is an independent factor, it can depend on crypto-Jewish identity, which is the third of Jacobs's markers of crypto-Jewish authenticity. Practices are, however, essential to Jacobs's work, as much of her argument rests on the role of women as the primary agents for preserving and transmitting both crypto-Jewish identity and, perhaps even more important, crypto-Jewish rituals.

Jacobs's second marker, the presence of the family name in Inquisition records, has two interrelated aspects: it provides a proxy for genealogical research, and it indicates, alongside the genealogical evidence, at least accusations of crypto-Jewish practices and/or identity in historical documents. Presence of a name in Inquisition or other archives, however, is not unproblematic. Many surnames taken up by *conversos* were common in the wider population (and also were adopted by Native Americans). Thus without detailed genealogical research tying present-day crypto-Jews to fifteenth-century *conversos*, the mere identity of names may purely be coincidental. There are also potential problems with the use of accusations of Judaizing (or related accusations) as proof of actually having Judaized or of having had a crypto-Jewish identity. There may be many reasons why this accusation was leveled at a particular individual or family, ranging from a malicious attempt to undermine political or economic prominence to a mistaken denunciation. It is clearly essential to examine the nature of the accusations and their context before determining their value as evidence of crypto-Judaism.

The third indicator used by Jacobs, the transmission of Jewish traditions, is the key marker used in our ethnographic research. It relies on the internal point of view—that is, the self-understanding of the individual or family. To an extent, this factor can be emphasized in two ways. In Jacobs's work, it is used to suggest a long-standing tradition of self-understanding, with less emphasis on its role in the construction of crypto-Jewish culture today. In my work, it is used to focus on of self-understanding and its role in the construction of present-day meaning and value, with less emphasis on the passage of this self-identity through time. Nonetheless, I agree with Jacobs that self-identity must be taken seriously and is the most important evidence of the persistence and transmission of crypto-Judaism—indeed, may be the most significant element transmitted.

Each of these markers relies on a specific form of evidence and, in some respects at least, is problematic as proof of authenticity. Jacobs seems to utilize all three to provide a preponderance of evidence for historical authenticity rather than absolute evidence of authenticity. In some sense, each of the markers limits the pool of interviewees to those in whom there is a reasonably strong current (or recent level) of crypto-Jewish identity and practice, combined with some historical evidence that an individual with the same family name was considered a Judaizer by the Inquisition. It is important, in light of the arguments made by Neulander and others, to ask whether Jacobs's three makers together are proof in the strong sense of historical authenticity. While the second indicator has the potential for demonstrating a historical connection with Jewish ancestors or Judaizers, its use by Jacobs does not provide this evidence. There is no suggestion that she examined the historical records to determine if there is a genealogical connection between the modern individuals and those brought before the Inquisition and if the veracity of the accusations was tested. Thus the potential evidence for authenticity is not in fact verified. The other two factors are, as we have suggested and as indicated by Neulander, primarily evidence of current identity and identity construction, rather than of a crypto-Jewish past. I am not challenging the quality of Jacobs's ethnography, which provides an important insight into the understanding and experience of modern crypto-Jews, but arguing that her work provides no unequivocal evidence of the historical authenticity of crypto-Judaism.

Jacobs, however, directly addresses the alternative theories proposed by Neulander and clearly indicates that while they may be true for a proportion of her interviewees, they do not provide a convincing basis for explaining the existence of the phenomenon of crypto-Judaism as a whole. As discussed in chapter 2, one of the fundamental aspects of Neulander's explanation for the origins of crypto-Jewish identity and practice is acknowledged or, more often, unacknowledged Pentecostal or Adventist roots in the immediate family. Of the fifty people whom Jacobs interviewed, only six had converted from Catholicism to Protestantism. While it is possible that some were from families that had experienced some degree of conversion from and reversion to Catholicism, there is no evidence that this might be so in the majority of cases studied by Jacobs (2002:13). Thus Jacobs's ethnography directly challenges Neulander's unsubstantiated assertion, since only 12 percent of her sample had any involvement with Protestantism (and, in all likelihood, only a minimal number of them were outside the mainstream Protestant denominations).

It is important to emphasize, in light of these statistics, that none of the studies of crypto-Judaism in New Mexico (including Jacobs's, Neulander's, and mine) employed random samples. Thus any statistics introduced here or elsewhere can be used only in relation to the specific ethnographic sample from which they emerged. The extension of the findings to the broader community can only be taken as suggestive. Clearly, the size of the sample must be considered, and it is important to note that Neulander's sample (although never directly stated in her work) appears to be the smallest, with that included in this book being the largest.

Jacobs also addresses Neulander's second alternative theory—that the word "Jew" is being used in place of the term "white European." This suggests that the claim of crypto-Jewish heritage is a way to raise one's ethic or "racial" status to be white rather than mestizo. Jacobs's sample included a range of variation that does not support Neulander's hypothesis. She notes that "close to half" of her interviewees claimed to have Native Americans among their ancestors. While many of the remainder did assert a Spanish background, the significant proportion claiming a mestizo heritage challenges Neulander's view of racial status as a general explanation for the existence or claims of crypto-Jewish ancestry. Jacobs's (2002:13) discussion also indicates that there was ambivalence in some of her interviewees' families about their Jewish background, which suggests that Jewish descent is not a straightforward symbolic replacement for white European descent.

Jacobs (2002) takes up these issues in detail in her chapter "Jewish Ancestry and Ethnic Identity" (125–148), which examines the complexity of her respondents' feelings about Jewish identity and ethnicity. One of her key findings relates to the sense of otherness created by crypto-Jewish identity, which emerged from differences between the interviewees and others in the Hispano community in terms of identity and origin (which at times was related to overt anti-Semitism) as well as practices. Countering Neulander's argument, Jacobs (2002:128) makes it clear that some of her respondents regarded their Jewish heritage as separating them from the mainstream Spanish Catholic tradition, rather than as being a clear link with pure Spanish heritage.

Adding to the complexity of this issue is Jacobs's (2002) finding— discussed in her chapter "Ethnic Identity and the Idealization of Jewish Culture" (140–146)—that some of her respondents did consider Judaism to be a trope for whiteness. Indeed, one interviewee admitted to utilizing Jewish identity in opposition to Mexican and Chicano identity (Jacobs 2002:131). Her argument suggests that this racial bias may have been inculcated in some by a sense of self-hatred engendered by American racism. While these individuals and her theory suggest that Neulander's argument may be correct in some cases, Jacobs (2002) emphasizes that "a sizable number of descendents have taken a more multicultural view of their Jewish heritage"

(145). Her work shows that many crypto-Jews embrace both mestizo and Hispano identity and see their Judaism as part of that identity. Individuals interviewed for both Jacobs's and this study specifically stated that they are not claiming an elitist white identity and reject the Eurocentrism that underlies Neulander's argument.

In chapter 2, we touched on Michael Carroll's (2002) suggestion that Jacobs's arguments about the central role of women in crypto-Judaism was a result of an orientalist perspective. But her work seems to rest on a feminist, rather than an orientalist, paradigm. Her analysis is both highly complex and nuanced, presenting a much more heterogeneous cultural context than would normally be found in discussions influenced by an orientalist framework. As her introduction indicates, her initial and, indeed, ongoing focus was on the role of women in the preservation and transmission of Jewish culture within the framework of the household. Following other forms of feminist scholarship, Jacobs is attempting to recover the active role and voices of women in the processes relating to culture.

Regardless of motivation, either orientalist or feminist, the significant questions are, first, whether the hypothesis examined by Jacobs is coherent, and second, whether the evidence that she presents, and that which is available from other studies, supports or challenges her hypothesis. There are good historical and cultural reasons that lend credence to the hypothesis. As mentioned earlier in this chapter, Judaism at the time of the conversions—that is between 1391 and 1492 (and, indeed, in both previous and subsequent periods)—contained two significant spheres of religious practice: the public and the private. The public sphere, which focused on the community and synagogue, was predominantly male. The private sphere, which focused on the home, was largely familial, with the responsibility for religious practice vested primarily in women. If we take into account the historical events, which largely removed the public sphere, including the processes connected with the transmission of Jewish knowledge through the study of texts, the main aspect of Jewish tradition and practice that remained was the domestic sphere. This historical inference is supported by the work of Renée Melammed (1999), who demonstrates the important role historically of women in the transmission of crypto-Jewish culture (Jacobs 2002:42–47). The importance of the home and the potential role of women as tradents are also suggested by the cultural practices that have been reported by modern crypto-Jews (Jacobs 2002:42–66). While some informants speak of practices that are commonly associated with men—for example, *shechita* (ritual slaughter of animals)—or public ceremonies, such as weddings and funerals, the majority of crypto-Jewish traditions mentioned are associated with the private sphere and, more particularly, with women—for example, lighting candles on Friday nights and maintaining forms of *kashrut* (food rules) (Jacobs 2002:48–50). Jacobs's hypothesis also utilizes a more general ethnographic view of the role of women as tradents in Hispano families; thus she argues (based on the work of other ethnographers) that "in keeping with the cultural norms of Latina family life, it was primarily the women in [the] family who provided a tie to crypto-Judaism" (Jacobs 2002:27). The dominance of women, she suggests, has shaped the nature of crypto-Jewish culture and spirituality as it has been experienced by crypto-Jews who are exploring their identity and spirituality (Jacobs 2002:66).

The historical and cultural data, as well as the evidence collected for this book, suggests that Jacobs's hypothesis is plausible and not merely the product of either orientalist or feminist arguments. But, in relation to the second question, it must be examined in light of her own and other ethnographic studies. This issue is addressed by Jacobs in only one chapter of her book. Where the evidence provided by Jacobs and my own data raise a significant question is in relation to the preservation and transmission of culture. Jacobs argues that the predominance of rituals associated with women, and the relative absence of those associated with men, demonstrates that women were the primary agents of crypto-Jewish cultural transmission and persistence. Historically, the fact that home-based rituals were the main survivors of Judaism in *converso* families may indicate only that they were most amenable to secret preservation. Public rituals, by their nature, required significant knowledge and a community. The latter was under threat in fifteenth-century Spain, so it was difficult to preserve the former. While we can postulate that women preserved and transmitted the private practices, the male members of a family could equally have participated in this process. Similarly, while Inquisition records demonstrate the role of women in the perpetuation of Jewish identity and practice, other documents show a similar role by men. Thus while the historical data indicates that women had a role in the preservation and transmission of culture, it does not clearly demonstrate that women had the primary role in this process.

Ethnographically, it is very difficult to determine from Jacobs's book the relative significance of women and men as tradents. She interviewed twenty-five women and a similar number of men, indicating that current-day crypto-Jewish identity is expressed by both women and men. In order to maintain confidentiality, Jacobs does not identify her interviewees; thus it is almost impossible to disentangle different individuals in her text and to determine whether crypto-Jewish practices were passed down by men or women. When Jacobs's respondents mention the sources of their traditions, it does appear that the majority were women; a significant minority, however, cite men as the source of their identity. Thus, at the most, Jacobs's work illustrates the significance of women in preserving and transmitting culture, but it also indicates that men had a significant role in this process as well.

My research also presents a very mixed picture. Among the more than one hundred interviewees, just over 50 percent were women. When individuals spoke about the sources of their identity, a slight, although insignificant, majority suggested that women played an important role. In most cases (including those that favored the role of women), however, the respondents mentioned both men and women, with different roles on the paternal and maternal sides of the family and in different generations. Thus, for example, one informant from Albuquerque spoke of her father as the main preserver of crypto-Judaism in the previous generation and of her paternal grandfather and grandmother in the generation before that. Although the data collected by Jacobs and for this study do not provide convincing support for women playing the more significant role in the transmission of crypto-Jewish culture, both studies demonstrate that women played and continue to play an important role.

Despite this disagreement in emphasis in relation to the role of women, Jacobs's book is an important contribution to the ethnography of crypto-Judaism. While it does not make a significant contribution to the issue of historical authenticity, as an ethnography of a present-day community and its process of self-interpretation, Jacob's study adds an important level of theoretical sophistication: it provides a basis for the understanding of a conflicted community trying to find its way through issues of memory, tradition, identity, and race.

Stanley Hordes

One of the key features of Janet Jacobs's arguments relating to the authenticity of crypto-Judaism in the Southwest relies on the use of either historical materials or other forms of historical evidence. Unfortunately, her work does not develop this line of argument and thus does not adequately provide data for historical authenticity. The most substantial contribution that utilizes historical sources as the basis for a discussion of authenticity is Stanley Hordes's *To the End of the Earth: A History of the Crypto-Jews of New Mexico* (2005). While we have explored some aspects of this book in relation to the arguments presented by both Judith Neulander and Michael Carroll, their critiques of crypto-Judaism do not relate to the main historical contribution of this work. As suggested, Carroll's (2002) concern is essentially about the motives of the scholarly community, and he addresses the historical aspects of Hordes's (1982, 1993) (and others') work only briefly—and in one case, in a very positive sense.

Neulander focuses specifically on the identity and practices of modern individuals who claim to be crypto-Jews as well as on issues that relate to the potential misinterpretation of their practices by external observers. While these analyses may have had some impact on Hordes's (2005:215–295) discussions of the modern crypto-Jewish community and perhaps on his initial research methods in interviewing crypto-Jews in New Mexico, Hordes, as a historian, is interested primarily in examining the documentary evidence for the origins in Spain and the settlement in New Mexico of the families that claim to be crypto-Jewish. This aspect of historical inquiry is not challenged by any substantial arguments by the critics of the crypto-Jewish hypothesis.

Genealogical research has been an important aspect of study both by crypto-Jews as a means of both exploring the past and establishing self-authenticity and by professional scholars. Nonetheless, Hordes's book is the first substantial study that provides detailed genealogical research with historical contextualization. He both examines the links between present-day families in New Mexico and their Judaizing and Jewish ancestors in New Mexico, Mexico, and Spain, and provides a historical argument for why crypto-Jews may have moved to New Mexico and the basis on which their cultural practices were preserved.

For the sake of clarity, Hordes's historical discussion can be divided into three sections: the experience of Jews in Iberia, which includes the process of conversion and the origins of crypto-Judaism, which concluded with the expulsion of Jews from Spain in 1492 and from Portugal in 1496; the experience of crypto-Jews in New Spain (Mexico); and, finally, the origins and experiences of crypto-Jews in New Mexico. It is important to emphasize that Hordes is not suggesting that most crypto-Jews moved from Spain to Mexico and that the resultant population of New Mexico was predominantly crypto-Jewish; rather, he is demonstrating the evidence for the presence of crypto-Judaism in both Mexico and New Mexico and suggesting that some crypto-Jews may have chosen to settle in New Mexico because of its remoteness from the centers of Spanish colonial authority—and that this distance may have enabled them to preserve aspects of practice and identity.

Jews in Spain

In order to develop a strong argument in support of the authenticity of crypto-Judaism in New Mexico, Hordes highlights the origins of the Jewish community in Spain and the historical developments within that community until its expulsion in 1492 and the related rise of crypto-Judaism in the fifteenth and sixteenth centuries in both Spain and Portugal. The historical evidence for the existence of a significant Jewish community in Spain and for its flourishing, particularly under Islamic rule, are not contentious. The arguments among historians are focused on issues relating to the existence and nature of crypto-Judaism in Spain in the period following the *reconquista*, particularly between 1391 and 1492. They relate particularly to the fate of a very large segment of the Spanish Jewish population, perhaps as many as 100,000, who were converted to Catholicism either by force or by choice in 1391 (Hordes 2005:18). Hordes (2005:18–19) outlines the positions of the proponents, with one group, centered around Yizhak Baer (1961, 1966) and his students, arguing that these *conversos* maintained a very strong connection to Judaism and continued to perform a wide range of Jewish ritual practices, and another group, characterized by Benzion Netanyahu (1966, 1995), arguing that the majority of *conversos*, at least within one generation, were authentically converted to Catholicism, with no remnants of their Jewish past.

Hordes also discusses a third group, of "less dogmatic" historians—including Jane Gerber (1992), Michael Alpert (2001), and himself—who consider the situation to have been less monolithic than that espoused by Baer and Netanyahu. This approach focuses on the variability of human responses to historical events and contexts. It attempts to take seriously both the extensive documentary evidence for the continuation of Jewish practices among the *conversos* and Netanyahu's important challenges to the nature of this evidence—for example that the accusations of Judaizing were anonymous or extracted under torture (Hordes 2005:19). Gerber (1992:123, quoted in Hordes 2005:19) particularly emphasizes the liminal nature of the *converso* living between two cultures, with his or her identity in flux. Interestingly, this depiction of the fluid identity of crypto-Jews in the fifteenth century is similar to that in the modern ethnographic context. Alpert's (2001:16–17) arguments are particularly compelling, highlighting the nature of the documentary evidence as well as the existence of many individuals who, after fleeing Spain, returned to Judaism (and, indeed, the rabbinic discussion of how to deal with such returnees). Hordes's discussion highlights both prejudice and violence against *conversos* well into the fifteenth century, which supports the view that the *conversos* may have developed an identity in opposition to their oppressors and were identifiable as a separate community in the years leading up to the expulsion of the remaining Jews from Spain.

While all these historical arguments agree that a substantial number of Jews became *conversos*, there is some significant scholarly debate about whether a large number of them retained connections to Jewish identity and practice. The "less dogmatic" position is the most likely of the three; it seems highly implausible that an expensive institution like the Inquisition would have been established to deal with a chimera or that the issue of the connection between *conversos* and Jews would have been one of the justifications for the expulsion of the Jews had not some degree of crypto-Judaism existed. Thus it is likely that some portion of *conversos*, perhaps a minority, retained aspects of Jewish identity and practice and, at least until 1492, some degree of connection with the remaining Jewish community. Out of this group came both those individuals who, after fleeing to Amsterdam or the Ottoman Empire, returned to Judaism and, potentially, those individuals in many parts of the Spanish diaspora who continue to adhere to traditions of Jewish identity. Those *conversos* support an argument for the historical authenticity of this community.

Crypto-Jews in New Spain

The second stage of Hordes's (2005:30–71) discussion relates to the presence and experience of crypto-Jews in New Spain. The primary evidence for the existence of crypto-Judaism in New Spain relies on Inquisition documents and is found in the very early stages of the colonial conquest of

Mexico. For example, in 1528 one of Hernán Cortez's associates, Hernando Alonso, was penanced by the Inquisition (Hordes 2005:30). It is important to note that Hordes (2005:31) is keenly aware of the potential political uses of such accusations and punishments, citing Richard E. Greenleaf's (1969) view that the harsh punishment of Alonso, who was burned at the stake, may have been a political act rather than the penancing of a "confirmed *judaizante.*"

The caution expressed by Hordes in this case is important and indicative of his approach. While Inquisition documents are perhaps the most important historical evidence for the presence of crypto-Judaism (and often the only record), they must be contextualized. As noted, Netanyahu (and many others) have challenged their use because of the anonymity or distress of the accusers. Greenleaf and Hordes highlight their potential political utility, as a means to gain advantage in the infighting among different factions in colonial society. This should not debar the use of Inquisition documents, but force the historian to both contextualize the events and exercise caution. Hordes maps out the social, religious, and economic life of individuals identified by the Inquisition as crypto-Jews. His analysis provides an insight into their cultural practices, particularly those that may have facilitated cultural and social cohesiveness, and therefore their preservation of crypto-Jewish identity. Thus, for example, he examines the business and social networks and the patterns of endogamy that bound the members of the community (Hordes 2005:46).

Religious practice is one of the areas of Hordes's discussion that is of particular relevance to the analysis of modern crypto-Jews. The Inquisition documents reveal an emphasis on endogamy—that is, marrying within the group—with, in at least one case, conversion to Judaism being sufficient to fulfill this requirement. A preference for endogamy continues to be expressed by many crypto-Jews, even if the actuality of their marriage patterns suggests that it is practiced inconsistently. Hordes (2005:48) also suggests that the fast on Yom Kippur and the observance of the Sabbath were emphasized in Inquisition documents. While the practice of fasting in the autumn, associated by some crypto-Jews with Yom Kippur, has been reported by a small number of families, the performance of traditions associated with the Sabbath, particularly lighting candles, continues to be the most reported set of rituals among the crypto-Jews interviewed for this study.

Hordes (2005:49) also mentions male circumcision as a significant practice among crypto-Jews in New Spain, and, indeed, it was regarded by inquisitors as proof positive of Judaizing. Circumcision continues to be important in New Mexico, with individuals from across the state (many of whom were sixty years of age and older when interviewed) claiming that they and their fathers had been circumcised. Many informants also stated that the practice was uncommon and clearly distinguished them from their non-crypto-Jewish neighbors.

While the details of the social and cultural lives of the crypto-Jews of New Spain are of great interest and historical importance, and are crucial to understanding the practices and social patterns of modern crypto-Jews, the key issue in relation to the arguments about authenticity is the presence of these and similar practices in records from throughout the period between the settlement of New Spain and the seventeenth century. This documentary evidence, as presented by Hordes, makes a compelling case for the presence of crypto-Jews in New Spain and thus establishes the basis for their inclusion among the colonial settlers of New Mexico. The information compiled by Hordes also argues for the existence of significant crypto-Jewish identity and practices in New Spain; even if a proportion of these documents were compiled as a result of political or economic motives, the quantity and quality of detail offers very strong support for the persistence of crypto-Jewish culture after 1492. The records also provide, in part, a link in a chain of evidence that takes us both forward and backward. Individuals and families that were accused of Judaizing in New Spain can, through genealogical research, be tied to *conversos* in Spain. This connection suggests a presumption, due to the practices reported in the Inquisition documents, that the genealogical link was more than merely genetic, but also included the transmission of Jewish cultural traditions, practices, and identity from Spain to New Spain.

Crypto-Jews in New Mexico

The final stage of Hordes's discussion, relating to the presence and experiences of crypto-Jews in New Mexico, is clearly the linchpin of the argument in support of the authenticity of crypto-Judaism in New Mexico. It has three aspects:

- The participation of crypto-Jews in the colonial settlement of New Mexico
- The motivations of crypto-Jews for moving into New Mexico

- The historical and genealogical evidence that links families claiming crypto-Jewish identity with identifiable crypto-Jews in New Spain and *conversos* and Jews in Spain and Portugal

While these aspects of Hordes's argument are clearly related, they can also stand on their own and to some extent rely on different forms of evidence. The arguments about the settlement of New Mexico and the genealogies of families rely on historical documentary evidence. While in some cases this evidence may be linked, with modern families being historically connected to original settlers, the two arguments are distinct. The argument about motivations—that is, that crypto-Jews chose to move to the periphery of the Spanish colonial empire in order to escape from the centers of inquisitional power—may ultimately be plausible but not demonstrable. Even if this is the case, the other two arguments do not depend on this one for their historical plausibility or, indeed, demonstration.

In discussing the participation of crypto-Jews in the settlement of New Mexico, Hordes is not suggesting that the enterprise was motivated by crypto-Jewish sentiment or, indeed, that the majority of the colonists were crypto-Jews. He ties the settlement of New Mexico to the earlier attempt to establish a new colony, Nuevo León, in northern Mexico. The leader of the Nuevo León project was Luis de Carvajal y de la Cueva, who although of *converso* descent was not necessarily a crypto-Jew. Some of Carvajal's Portuguese associates, however—particularly Alberto del Canto, Manuel de Mederos, Diego de Montemayor, and Gaspar Castaño de Sosa—had been viewed by the Inquisition as practicing Judaism (Hordes 2005:73). Equally significant, Carvajal's nephew, also Luis, is documented as openly practicing Judaism and as Judaizing and was ultimately one of the causes of his uncle's downfall (Hordes 2005:72). Hordes also points out that the edict establishing the colony, promulgated in 1579 by Felipe II of Spain, included a clause stating that no inquiry should be made into the background of the colonists; that is, the usual requirement for the ethnic purity of the colonists would not be enforced. Hordes (2005:75–76) views this clause as originating with Carvajal and implicitly allowing individuals of *converso* descent to legally participate in this new colonial enterprise. Hordes (2005:76) quotes figures from the historian Eugenio del Hoyo (1972), which suggest that as many as 68 percent of the settlers of Nuevo León were New Christians. Although Carvajal was ultimately deposed as governor of the new province due to his treatment of the Native American population, the

Judaizing practices of his nephew led to both the arrest of Carvajal and the persecution of the *conversos* of Nuevo León (Hordes 2005:78).

Hordes argues that the wave of persecutions in 1590 was instrumental to the move of crypto-Jews into the hitherto unexplored regions that are now the parts of the southwestern United States. The initial illegal exploration, or "flight north," was led by Castaño, Carvajal's lieutenant governor. According to Hordes (2005), the evidence suggests that Castaño was of *converso* origin and "even a practicing crypto-Jew" (86). He believes that the flight was precipitated by Carvajal's conviction by the Inquisition and thus was an expression of fear of further persecution of crypto-Jews (Hordes 2005:86–87). Although there is only minimal evidence of the ethnic backgrounds of the members of this expedition, Hordes (2005:89) states that some crypto-Jews (that is, individuals accused of Judaizing by the Inquisition) were included. The expedition explored New Mexico as far north as Santa Fe before Castaño was arrested and returned to Mexico City. While many of the participants in the expedition settled back in Nuevo León, Hordes suggests that some of them subsequently were involved in the colonization of New Mexico.

The ultimate settlement of New Mexico was led by Juan de Oñate. Although historians have found that Oñate had prominent Jews among his ancestors, there is no direct evidence that he either was aware of these ancestors or was a crypto-Jew himself (Hordes 2005:106–110). Some of the members of Castaño's expedition who were of *converso* origin were included in Oñate's group, as were other individuals of *converso* origin who had not taken part in the earlier endeavor (Hordes 2005:111). It is important to emphasize that Hordes is not suggesting that the second expedition was motivated by crypto-Jews' fears of persecution, although some individuals may have participated for that reason. The *converso* contingent in the expedition and among subsequent reinforcements probably was a minority. This has implications for Hordes's views of the settlement of New Mexico— that is, that it included crypto-Jews, in some key positions, but they were in all likelihood a minority of the settlers. Hordes presents strong documentary evidence that some of the participants in the ultimate settlement of New Mexico were of *converso* origin and, based on the Inquisition records, that some may have been practicing crypto-Jews. Thus, at the very least, his analysis provides a historical basis for demonstrating the presence of *conversos* in New Mexico and the potential for a tradition of Jewish identity and perhaps traditions to be passed to descendents living in New Mexico.

Hordes (2005:133–214) takes this argument one step further, examining the evidence in relation to the periods of the establishment of the colony both before and after the Pueblo Revolt (1680–1692). His analysis of genealogical data and documents from the Inquisition suggests that both individuals of *converso* origin and those accused of Judaizing continued to arrive and were present in New Mexico. A key aspect of the evidence presented by Hordes is the association of individuals and families with Inquisition documents and, more specifically, the testimony by the individuals or, in some cases, accusers that they had retained some aspects of Jewish identity and performed a range of practices associated with Judaism. Although this evidence presents some problems, as noted earlier, in association with genealogical evidence, it provides reasonable grounds for assuming at least some degree of Jewish identity and practice among settlers in New Mexico. With the end of Judaizing as a central concern of the Inquisition in the latter half of the seventeenth century and, finally, the annexation of New Mexico by the United States in 1848, this form of relatively direct evidence disappeared—until the modern period.

In suggesting the reasons for some of the historical events just outlined, Hordes turns to the motivations of the crypto-Jews who participated in the settlement of New Mexico. Northern Mexico and later New Mexico, according to him, were chosen as places of refuge by some individuals due either to fear of persecution or to actual periods of extreme persecution of *conversos* or crypto-Jews. Hordes cites the work of Solange Alberro (1988), who argued in her study of Zacatecas that the northern frontier of New Spain served as an important sanctuary. Her work particularly highlights the significance of the separation of the frontier from the centers of political and, most important, inquisitional power (Hordes 2005:81). Her discussion also extends this concept to New Mexico, regarding it as potentially an even more significant place of refuge.

This line of argument is a key part of Hordes's discussion, providing the motivation for Castaño's expedition into New Mexico, for the settlement of other individuals of *converso* origin in New Mexico, and perhaps for the movement into northern New Mexico in search of locations even more remote from colonial centers of power. Of Hordes's arguments, this is the most conjectural. While the other two offer different types of documentary evidence, there appears to be no direct evidence for this one. Thus while this line of argument is tantalizing and seems to provide a reasonable explanation for behavior, it is not subject to proof.

Even with such reservations, this hypothesis does make an important contribution to the understanding of crypto-Jewish culture as it existed in the early modern period and as it has developed. The material cited by both Hordes and Alberro indicates, aside from issues of motivation, that in the areas remote from colonial power, many practices that would have been impossible to maintain in more central locations were ignored or tolerated. Thus we might find different levels of crypto-Jewish practice and perhaps identity in these areas than in the centers of political and religious power. Both the historical and the ethnographic evidence supports this line of argument. As noted in chapter 1, the patterns of crypto-Jewish practice vary in New Mexico in relation to geography and remoteness from the established centers of power. Thus in the mountains around Taos, we find a stronger narrative of a community-based form of practice, while in Albuquerque and Santa Fe the narrative tends to be restricted to family- or individually based traditions.

Genealogical data provides a link between settlers of *converso* origin and New Mexicans who claim crypto-Jewish identity today. Hordes provides evidence that some participants in the settlement of New Mexico, both in the initial colonization and during the subsequent period of colonial rule, were descended from Jews. The analysis of the genealogies of New Mexicans whose families have a tradition of crypto-Judaism (or who exhibit genetic diseases statistically associated with Jewish ethnicity)[3] and their links with *converso* ancestors is the most important aspect of Hordes's third line of argument. He presents evidence about nine families that are diverse in relation to expression of identity, "age, gender and geographic origin" (Hordes 2005:273–281). Hordes's research on these families demonstrates that each family includes in its genealogy settlers who have been identified as being of *converso* origin. The average number of ancestors fitting this profile is twenty-three. His work also indicates that members of the families intermarried within a small range of families, suggesting a pattern or preference for endogamy (Hordes 2005:278).

The first and the third elements of Hordes's argument—that individuals who were considered to be crypto-Jews participated in the exploration and settlement of New Mexico, and that New Mexicans who either claim to be crypto-Jews or have genetic diseases statistically associated with Jewish ethnicity may have *converso* ancestors—provide both direct documentary proof and an explanation for the presence of crypto-Jews in New Mexico that does not require either the attribution of unstated economic or social motivations or the patronizing assumption of forgetting or lying about a supposed Pentecostal past. They are simpler reasons that fit the internal understanding and expression of meaning of those who consider themselves to be crypto-Jews. Hordes's second argument—that the settlers hoped to find a place of refuge in New Mexico—is suggestive and, indeed, helpful in conceptualizing patterns of practice, but is only conjectural and thus does not provide the same level of evidence as do his other arguments.

Hordes's historical discussion of crypto-Judaism continues into the period between the late seventeenth century, with the end of direct evidence from Inquisition documents, and the mid- to late twentieth century, when individuals in the Hispano community began to claim crypto-Jewish heritage. The nature of the data for these three hundred years is qualitatively different from that for the preceding period. With the absence of records, such as those of the Inquisition, that provide evidence for the persistence and transmission of a crypto-Jewish cultural tradition from one generation to the next, genealogical data remains important. But such evidence proves only the historical authenticity of claims of Jewish ancestry. It does not demonstrate that the individuals with that genealogy were crypto-Jews: descent relates to genes, not culture or identity. Given the number of Jews whom historians believe converted to Catholicism between 1391 and 1492, and taking Netanyahu's arguments seriously, it is likely that many who had Jewish ancestors were not crypto-Jews and, indeed, may have had no knowledge of this aspect of their families' history. Thus indirect evidence becomes important, and an important line of such data is naming patterns. Hordes (2005:222–228) presents evidence, which is supported by the individuals interviewed for this study, that in families of *converso* origin or, indeed, claiming crypto-Jewish heritage there is a pattern of using given names from the Hebrew Bible. This tradition is, significantly, distinct from that in Mexico (Hordes 2005:225). Hordes (2005:226) suggests that the choice of names cannot be the result of Protestant missionary influence, as significant inroads in that direction were not made until the 1870s, while this pattern of naming began almost immediately after the annexation of New Mexico by the United States in 1848.

This pattern of naming is perhaps the most significant data for the interim period; it appears to provide a distinctive association with the Hebrew Bible and thus a possible statement of crypto-Jewish identity. According to Hordes, early crypto-Jews had a secret "Jewish" name and a public "Catholic" name. The evidence presented suggests that with the end of the

Inquisition, the secret name began to be used openly. Although Hordes's arguments provide support for this interpretation, no direct historical statements associate this change in practice with crypto-Judaism (although in interviews conducted for this study as well as in the context of Hordes's study, modern crypto-Jews stated that these naming patterns were associated with an expression of identity). A broader comparative analysis of naming patterns in New Mexico would lend strong support to Hordes's contention if it can be demonstrated that this change in pattern is statistically associated with individuals of *converso* descent and evidence of current-day or historical crypto-Jewish identity and/or practices.

Hordes also includes a discussion of modern ethnographic evidence. While much of it is compelling and important to understanding crypto-Jewish culture, it must be viewed as separate from his demonstration of historical authenticity. The existence of practices, material culture, or even identity on their own would merely be suggestive or, at the most, indicative of a historical connection; individually, they might have alternative explanations, such as those suggested by Neulander (2001). The importance of Hordes's work is that it provides the crucial link between the historical genealogical data and the ethnographic data. He clearly establishes that the settlers of New Mexico included individuals of Jewish descent and individuals who were regarded as crypto-Jews. Hordes thus demonstrates that there is a strong basis for arguing that New Mexicans who express crypto-Jewish identity may have an authentic line of historical evidence for claiming that identity. It is important to note that due to the lacunae in the data, many individuals with an authentic historical tradition of crypto-Judaism may not be able to demonstrate it; and, conversely, individuals without a historical basis for that identity may, for personal reasons, claim it.

It is essential to be clear about the nature of the data and the type of evidence it provides. Due to the absence of Inquisition documents in this interim period and thus direct statements of identity or attributions of identity, statements about identity or about the persistence of cultural forms are somewhat problematic. The lacunae in the data suggest two possible interpretations: while *converso* descent is present in New Mexico, crypto-Jewish identity and traditions vanished since the time of settlement and thus any present-day traditions and identity are inventions or re-creations; or, although there is no direct documentary evidence for crypto-Jewish identity, it and perhaps practices persisted and are now openly expressed by crypto-Jews in New Mexico.

The indirect evidence presented by Hordes and the ethnographic evidence discussed both in this book and by Hordes (particularly the tradition of circumcision prior to its common use in the United States) are strongly suggestive of the continuation of crypto-Jewish practices and identity, but they cannot be taken as proof. The genealogical evidence establishes that *conversos* were present in colonial New Mexico, and the ethnographic data shows that some of their descendants who claim this identity adhere to a range of traditions and practices associated with it. Hordes's arguments and evidence provide the most convincing explanation for the presence of crypto-Judaism in New Mexico, offering a more comprehensive coverage of the data than do Neulander's explanations, while not discounting the possibility that some of the individuals who claim that identity (even possibly including individuals with *converso* ancestry) are doing so for the reasons suggested by Neulander. The ethnography presented in this book suggests that authenticity of tradition and processes of cultural construction are not mutually exclusive; individuals who have a strong and authentic family tradition of crypto-Judaism and, indeed, a range of practices associated with that identity reinterpret and explain aspects of their past on the basis of their present understanding of self as crypto-Jews (and thereby bring into play some of the processes suggested by Neulander). Thus the strong argumentative opposition of the two views of authenticity is unhelpful; both positions are necessary to understand the complex cultural phenomenon that is crypto-Judaism today.

Shulamith Halevy

Shulamith Halevy's article "Jewish Practices Among Contemporary Anusim" (1999) provides a synthesis of crypto-Jewish practices from a wide range of crypto-Jewish communities (based on three hundred informants). While some of her research was direct, either participant observation or interview, much was indirect, based on correspondence or published material. She provides a comprehensive list of crypto-Jewish practices, many of which are similar to those discussed in this book. Halevy's work does not, in general, deal with the issue of authenticity. She does, however, argue that specific customs that link with "obscure rabbinic practices" offer convincing evidence for historic authenticity (Halevy 1999:82), a point that was a key aspect of her earlier article "Manifestations of Crypto-Judaism in the American Southwest" (1996). She suggests that these obscure practices include fasting on Mondays and Thursdays, orientation of beds, sweeping to the center of the room, and burning or burying nail clippings (Halevy 1999:82). While we have encountered a number of these traditions in New Mexico, particularly sweeping and disposing of nail clippings, and it is possible that they have rabbinic roots, it is also possible that they come from alternative sources and thus are only suggestive rather than compelling evidence. It is also important to note that many of these practices are not currently performed but are part of memories, which in the process of self-understanding can be subject to reinterpretation. Where Halevy's material is especially compelling is in her evidence of the similarity of practices in wide-ranging communities, and in this respect it is important to observe the differing locations for the testimony she provides. Many of the practices she lists are also found in New Mexico and thus, as a set of traditions compared with others, offer a compelling case for a "shared" crypto-Jewish cultural tradition.

In her earlier article, Halevy focused more directly on the crypto-Jews discussed in this book. Her argument directly addresses Judith Neulander's (2001) attack on authenticity and thus emphasizes the presence of rabbinic customs as markers of authenticity (Halevy 1996:69). Although in general terms we agree with the tenor of Halevy's arguments, it is necessary to look at each set of practices on its own terms. Halevy, however, falls into the genetic fallacy. Even if some of the practices have a particular origin, that does not indicate either why people continue to perform them or how they choose to understand them.

Halevy also provides some important challenges to Neulander's assertion that crypto-Judaism is largely due to forgotten Adventist antecedents. First, she argues that the crypto-Jewish aspect could have been the reason why individuals chose to become Adventists rather than the reverse (Halevy 1996:72). This suggestion is supported by Halevy's research and indirectly by the interviews conducted for this book. A number of respondents stated that they had chosen to become messianic Jews because of their crypto-Jewish identity; they saw messianism as a form of Christianity that allowed them to express aspects of their Jewish identity. Second, Halevy (1996:72) contends that if crypto-Judaism emerged from Adventism, it would be associated with abstention from wine and tobacco. But neither Halevy nor I found disavowal of alcohol and tobacco among the subjects of our studies.

Tomás Atencio's article "Crypto-Jewish Remnants in *Manito* Society and Culture" (1996) provides a much more narrow focus than do Shulamith Halevy's (1996, 1999) studies, specifically on the New Mexican context. The title of his article is significant to his argument. He uses the term *manito*, which refers to Indohispanos—that is, individuals with a variety of ethnic roots—to describe the Hispano community. This term emphasizes a common thread through many crypto-Jewish self-narratives: that the Jewish aspect of their identity is only one part of their background (Atencio 1996:59). The word "remnants" is also significant. Atencio does not regard crypto-Judaism as a living culture and thus focuses on the pieces of tradition that have been passed down. While he assumes that the crypto-Jewish heritage is present, he makes it clear that he is not seeking to prove its authenticity, which he suggests may be "lost behind the veil of history."

Atencio's paper brings together a number of important issues. It highlights the experience of the *manito* community in both the Spanish/Mexican and the American contexts. It also provides a basis in early modern crypto-Jewish practices for those that were retained in New Mexico. One aspect of his argument that is especially noteworthy is his discussion of marginality and secrecy. Utilizing the work of the German sociologist Georg Simmel (1906), he develops an important theoretical understanding of the development and effects of secrecy in the past and its retention by crypto-Jews in the present.

Crypto-Jews' Arguments for Authenticity

Although to a great extent the way in which crypto-Jews respond to the arguments about authenticity are touched on in chapters 4 and 5, it is important to include a discussion of the general issues here, as authenticity has become one of the most important features of crypto-Jewish discussions of self, particularly with the popularization of Judith Neulander's work in the *Atlantic Monthly* (Ferry and Nathan 2000) and other popular media outlets. As discussed in chapter 1, many papers presented by crypto-Jews at the conference of the Society for Crypto-Judaic Studies are shaped almost entirely by the challenges to their historical authenticity and the need to provide evidence validating that authenticity.

During the course of the research for this study, a range of forms of argument were used by crypto-Jews to demonstrate or assert their historical authenticity. Some arguments have changed due to academic challenges to their veracity as evidence—for example, the use of symbols particularly on gravestones. In other cases, the dominant tropes of Western society influenced the choice of evidence. Thus, with the increased availability of genetic testing, the dominant scientific mode of evidence has become the preferred form of demonstrating authenticity at both the individual and the communal level.

Outlining some of the forms of argumentation that exemplify these different approaches, my goal is to indicate how these arguments have shaped crypto-Jews' self-understanding and presentation of self, particularly in the public sphere, not to suggest that they are either historically or sociologically supportable. It should be noted that some of the approaches have come under academic scrutiny, and the challenges are discussed either here or elsewhere in this book.

In the 1990s, the early stages of historical and social scientific study of crypto-Judaism, individuals who claimed crypto-Jewish identity could rarely produce more than their family traditions of identity, genealogy, and practices (or often only their own perception of these) as evidence of authenticity. Thus, for example, the relatively easy access to verifiable genealogical information on the Internet and through other computerized resources became available to nonprofessional historians only at the turn of the twenty-first century. While for many this level of authentication was sufficient, challenges to the authenticity of crypto-Judaism by Neulander and others were already threatening these individuals' perception of self (and their interrelated need for both public and often private validation).

Evidence of material culture was regarded by many as a strong indicator of crypto-Jewish presence and identity. Some individuals who identified themselves as crypto-Jews (as well as some scholars, both lay and academic, from outside the community) explored cemeteries in New Mexico to see if they could find evidence in stone to back up their family traditions. Symbolic material was the most common evidence attested to. This initially focused on symbols commonly associated with Judaism—for example, the six-pointed star, interpreted as the Star of David. Other symbols included seven-branched candelabra and hands. Some individuals extended their search for symbols beyond this narrow range, looking at symbols on gravestones in Anglo Jewish cemeteries and seeking the same symbols in Hispano cemeteries in New Mexico. This larger range included, for example, books, candlesticks, and symbols taken from texts on Jewish art.[4]

Alongside the symbols on gravestones, occasional use was made of other forms of material evidence. Some individuals pointed, for example, to crucifixes that they believed contained secret compartments in which Hebrew scrolls had been hidden. To this date, however, none of the scrolls has been produced. Other individuals owned handmade items identified as crypto-Jewish ritual objects, including candlesticks and tops often identified as dreidels. The final category of material culture that was occasionally alluded to included ritual items that had been hidden or buried. There are many long-standing traditions in New Mexico of objects or treasures buried for safekeeping. Among the crypto-Jews, these hidden objects include Torah scrolls or other ritual items. Although many respondents suggested that they had seen these objects, none of them appear to be publically available.

Names were seen by crypto-Jews as a second avenue of proving authenticity. Some read published records of Inquisition trials, seeking the family names of those accused of Judaizing and associating them with those in their own genealogies. Others looked to the use in their families of particular given names from the Bible, such as Avram, Moisés, and David, a tradition that Stanley Hordes (2005) has argued is characteristic of many families of *converso* descent. Many other crypto-Jews utilized lists of names or forms of names that were assumed to be restricted to *converso* families as a means to demonstrate the authenticity of their traditions.[5] And others even visited cemeteries to investigate the names—in Hebrew or associated with biblical characters—on gravestones.

Genetic testing is the final and the most significant method used by crypto-Jews to demonstrate authenticity. A number of kinds of tests are used. Some individuals who believe that their families descend from the *kohen*, or priestly, line have undergone tests to look for genetic markers that might connect them to that line of descent. More general testing has been used to determine if an individual's DNA contains markers that are statistically more common in the Jewish than in the general population. The importance of genetic tests as proof of authenticity is clearly tied to the popular perception that, unlike historical and social scientific evidence, genetic data is unchallengeable and provides definitive answers to counter the arguments presented by those who challenge the authenticity of crypto-Jews' traditions and sense of self.

Some might suggest that this focus on genetic testing serves the purpose of strengthening a claim of European, white identity. Although a small number of people may have this motive, none of the respondents in this study or interviewees quoted in other published research regarded genetic tests as proving that they were of pure European or, indeed, Jewish descent; they hoped to prove only that there was evidence of some Jewish descent. It is also important to note that most of these individuals underwent the test in order to confront the challenges to authenticity on any level, not to express a form of inverted racism.

Different aspects of essentialism come into play in genetic and, occasionally, other forms of argumentation. They imply that the genes carry not only biological information, but also cultural or, at times, spiritual content. Thus some see genetic inheritance as sufficient proof of crypto-Judaism, contending that individuals inherit Jewish cultural traits along with biological traits. (Some arguments utilize phenotypes stereotypically assigned to European Jews as part of this aspect of inheritance and evidence of Jewish background.) On occasion, individuals draw on Jewish mystical resources to make these essentialist arguments. Some suggest that accompanying the "Jewish" genetic inheritance is a "Jewish soul" that carries with it Jewish culture and, more significantly, "Jewish spirituality."

The efforts of crypto-Jews to validate their (in Western scientific or academic terms) culturally less privileged forms of identification—family history, traditions, and self-interpretation—have been supported by historical, ethnographic, genealogical, and genetic evidence. As analyses and understanding of crypto-Judaism both historically and ethnographically have moved on, some of these modes of evidence, both internally and externally, have been recognized to be less authoritative than others; this is particularly true of symbols and names. In contrast, new forms of technology have made some evidence, such as that derived from genetic testing and genealogical and census data found on the Internet, more authoritative. The work of non-crypto-Jewish scholars, particularly Stanley Hordes, is also used by crypto-Jews to support their claims of authenticity, particularly at the communal rather the individual level. The challenges to the authenticity of crypto-Judaism raised by some scholars and, to some degree, by mainstream Jews have become central concerns for many crypto-Jews, for whom authenticity has become a matter of their sense of self.

FOUR

IDEAL TYPES OF CRYPTO-JEWISH IDENTITY

Both historically and currently, crypto-Jewish identities are very complex. There is no single crypto-Jewish identity, and, as David Gitlitz's (1996) discussion and taxonomy suggest, it is likely that there never was. In the main period of conversion, from 1391 to 1492, Jews converted to Catholicism for a wide range of reasons. Some were forced to convert at the point of a sword, while others chose to convert for social or economic reasons; these various motives potentially led to different relations with the ancestral religion. The response of the *conversos* to subsequent conversion was equally complex, with some moving wholeheartedly to the new religion and others attempting in different ways to maintain some aspects of Jewish tradition and identity. The journey from Spain to the various parts of the Spanish diaspora, including New Mexico, added an additional degree of complexity. Communities, families, and individuals had different relations with the Inquisition, and those who became crypto-Jews idiosyncratically retained or lost different elements of Jewish tradition. This complexity has increased even further in the (post)modern period, with individuals perhaps having a greater opportunity to define themselves and, at different times and in different contexts, to redefine themselves.

This chapter explores the historical processes that may have led to the types of crypto-Jewish practices that are currently found. As Judith Neulander (2001) has suggested, a (perhaps the) fundamental aspect of interpretation of a cultural practice rests in present understanding rather than exclusively in historical genesis. Thus the possible origin of a practice provides one horizon of interpretation, while present understanding and context provide the second horizon, which can seem to be incompatible with the first. This level of complexity is also present in relation to identity. Although a historical connection to their ancestors is part of what makes up the identity of crypto-Jews, it is only one horizon. An equally important horizon is self-definition, which may at times be separate from or even entirely divorced from objective historical considerations.

Crypto-Jews in New Mexico are the product of this very complex pattern of transmission of identity and culture. Individuals interviewed for this study form a continuum, ranging from those with a very strong consciousness of their Jewish heritage to those with no consciousness at all. Although the ethnographic reality is both complex and fluid, with the continuum including a wide range of variation, it is necessary to create a heuristic taxonomy in order to analyze the processes of identity construction and the ways that individuals transform their constructions of self over time and in context. The four categories used here are the strong crypto-Jewish identity, the weak crypto-Jewish identity, the Christian identity with *converso* elements, and the Christian identity without *converso* elements (but with Judaizing practices).

These four ideal types should be understood in the sense used by Max Weber. Thus they should not be regarded as corresponding directly with ethnographic reality. Rather, they somewhat artificially divide individuals and groups in order to allow us to both compare and contrast the ways that these individuals relate to different aspects of their self-identity. These categories are ideal in two senses. First, no individual fits precisely into one category, but is along a continuum and has been placed in the type that most approximates his or construction of identity. Second, the model suggests that particular identities are fixed, belonging to one category or another, but the ethnographic evidence suggests that identity is highly fluid and that individuals can move among the categories depending on a wide range of contextual features.

On one level, the four ideal types presented here are similar to those outlined by Gitlitz (1996:85–90). His taxonomy focuses on religious self-perception; his type one is characterized by a Catholic self-definition and type two, by a Jewish self-definition. Although his type three is more fluid, moving between the two religions, Gitlitz considers religion to be the defining element of identity. The classification presented here also utilizes religious identification, but differs from Gitlitz's in at least two respects. First, religious identification is only one aspect of identity, which also includes genealogy, practices, and belief. While all four elements are discussed by Gitlitz, only religious identification played a key role in the construction of his taxonomy. Second, religious identification is defined in a very broad sense. While it includes the common definition of religion (that is, adherence to a tradition that has a shared theology), it also contains a cultural dimension (that is, affiliation with a community of either Christians or Jews). It can also include a view of shared history. Thus crypto-Jewish identity does not lead to any particular choice of religious affiliation; a crypto-Jew may join a synagogue or a church or be an atheist or an agnostic.

Elements of the Taxonomy

In order to establish a basis of comparison among the ideal types of crypto-Jewish identity, four factors are used: self-identification, genealogy, practice, and belief. In each category, some or all of these elements are present, albeit with a differing level or quality. It is important to note that while these elements emerge from an external process of definition, they are also significant to those individuals who identify themselves as crypto-Jews. Each forms part of the narratives and oral histories of crypto-Jews. This is true in relation to both the public presentation of self and the private narratives addressed to ethnographers and other crypto-Jews (albeit in the presence of an ethnographer).

Self-Identification

Self-identification or -definition is the most significant constituent in the context of this research, since identification of oneself as a crypto-Jew is, for our purposes, sufficient for cultural authenticity. Self-identification, however, is not simple. For different individuals, this element can be of greater or lesser duration. Thus some people have considered themselves to be Jews or crypto-Jews throughout their lives. Others have identified themselves as such relatively recently, perhaps as a result of conducting research or being informed by a family member. There are also different qualities in the way self-identification is expressed. Some individuals express it in a clearly oppositional way; that is, self-identification as a Jew or a crypto-Jew is a clear rejection of any other form of religious or cultural affiliation. For others, the identification expresses only part of their identity, with other elements—perhaps Catholic or Hispanic—playing an equally important role. Finally, this aspect can be more or less fluid. Some individuals, for example, are exploring different ways of thinking about themselves, with a Jewish identity being one among which they move. One of the theoretical issues that arises from this discussion, which is specifically addressed in chapter 6, suggests that all crypto-Jewish identities and, perhaps, all identities, particularly in the postmodern world, are characterized by relative degrees of fluidity—both conscious and unconscious.

Genealogy

Genealogy, like identity, includes a range of possible levels and aspects. There are two main forms: academic genealogy and traditional genealogy. Academic genealogy refers to historically documented heritage. While it has only recently become relatively available to nonhistorians with the advent of the Internet, documented genealogy (or at least the concept of it) has played an important role in both crypto-Jewish and Hispano society; in a different respect, it also plays an important role in Jewish identity—that is, the genealogical definition of Judaism as descent through a line of Jewish women. In Spanish society, the importance of a concept of genealogy is expressed in the myth of *limpieza de sangre*—that a single drop of non-Christian blood was sufficient to taint a family line. Today, crypto-Jews of all categories use genealogical information as a means to validate different aspects of their identity.

Traditional genealogy refers to a family tradition of descent from Jewish ancestors. It is closely associated with self-identification and can be more or less developed. In some families, it is very detailed and thus is indistinguishable from academic genealogy. In other families, it may be merely a tradition of descent from an individual identified as a Jew or a crypto-Jew, or, indeed, only a tradition of descent from Jews. This is occasionally expressed in the words passed from one generation to the next: "Somos judíos."

Different marriage patterns or expressed preferences for particular forms of marriage are also part of this element. Some crypto-Jews state that their family had a preference for or a practice of endogamy—that is, marrying only within a bounded group. Thus members of these families married into only other families that they knew were of Jewish origin or that formed crypto-Jewish communities in particular villages. While the ethnographic evidence suggests that there was a wide variation of marriage patterns, and some families express no preference for endogamy, both the historical record and recent genealogical analysis suggest that some families did practice a form of endogamy with other families that also have documented *converso* ancestors. Tomás Atencio touches on this issue, highlighting that endogamy historically was a crypto-Jewish practice. Due perhaps to his focus on the *manito*, and thus by definition mestizo, aspect of the New Mexican community, he does not find an ongoing pattern of crypto-Jewish endogamy. Atencio (1996:63) also suggests, however, that in some villages were families that traditionally married only among themselves. This last aspect is consistent with the evidence provided by crypto-Jews from northern New Mexico.

Increasingly, information provided by genetic testing also shapes this aspect of identity. In response to challenges to the authenticity of their self-definition as crypto-Jews, some individuals choose to have their DNA tested to prove that they have Jewish ancestors. Others learn of the possibility of Jewish descent as a result of being diagnosed with particular genetic diseases that are more prevalent in the Jewish than in the general population. Doctors and other scientists are finding evidence in the Hispano community of genetic mutations that lead to various diseases—for example, breast cancer and pemphigus vulgaris—that usually are statistically associated with Jewish populations (Hordes 2005:289–295). While many of these conditions were originally found primarily in Ashkenazic Jews, there is some evidence to suggest that the mutations may have emerged prior to the split between the Sephardim and the Ashkenazim. Whereas Janet Jacobs (2002) and David Gitlitz (1996) use genealogical and genetic evidence to define "who is or who isn't a crypto-Jew," I consider identity to be cultural rather than biological. What is important is how genealogical and genetic information is used to create meaning and self-understanding. Ancestry is important in communities—such as Hispano and Jewish—that value both continuity with the past and some aspect of ethnic purity. Some individuals, including an interviewee who had been unaware of the crypto-Jewish history of his family, have used the discovery of a Jewish ancestor revealed through genealogical research to build an understanding of their crypto-Jewish heritage and rethink their identity. The discovery of DNA markers associated with Judaism had a similar transformational effect on the identity of some respondents. Other informants, though, expressed interest in the idea of a crypto-Jewish past but chose to retain their Christian understanding of self.

It is, however, important to note the limitations of the genealogical model. If we take into account the number of Jews who became *conversos* between 1391 and 1492, even with the conservative figure of 225,000 estimated by Gitlitz (1996:74), the number of their descendents in the wider Hispanic population is huge. It is therefore likely that most families in Spain and in the Spanish diaspora could find at least one Jewish ancestor on their family tree. Given that most of these families embrace no aspect of crypto-Jewish identity or heritage, it is clear that descent from Jewish ancestors is not a sufficient defining feature of crypto-Judaism.

The definitional aspect of genealogy, however, is occasionally used by crypto-Jews as a means to establish boundaries. One crypto-Jew, interviewed in Albuquerque, said that he regarded evidence of descent from Jews or crypto-Jews as being perhaps the most significant factor in crypto-Jewish identity. His statement and its context implied that he considered those individuals who were unable to provide such evidence as inauthentic.

Practice

Within the four types of crypto-Jewish identity, the element of practice may or may not be present, although by definition it is found in very different ways among those with a strong crypto-Jewish identity and those with a Christian identity without *converso* elements. The first key issue in relation to practice is its interpretation. Some individuals state that a particular practice performed by their families has always been regarded as being of Jewish origin and different from those traditions followed by their neighbors. Others do not have a tradition of interpretation, but may have considered some practices as being of Jewish origin on the basis of different sources of knowledge. Yet others describe a range of family traditions without interpreting any of them as being of Jewish origin, but merely as the way they lived, which was different from those around them. In some of these cases, either outside scholars or other crypto-Jews identify a practice as being Jewish. Although from the external perspective we are aware of the issues raised by Judith Neulander (2001) and others in regard to the interpretation of practices, particularly that of false analogy, the main concern in this discussion is not the genesis of practices, but the way individuals and/or communities use them to construct identity.

Categorization is a key aspect of the perception and interpretation of practices by crypto-Jews and others. Thus some rituals can be interpreted in a range of ways, each of which may be expressive of a different construction of identity. For example, members of an extended family that lit candles on Friday nights while reciting the Rosary interpreted the ritual in at least two ways: as a practice that emphasized Jewish identity and as a tradition that allowed for both Jewish and Christian identity. Although we have not found these interpretations, it is possible to project a range of others— for example, as a Christian ritual that looks to a family connection with a *converso* past, or as a messianic or Sabbatarian Christian ritual that consciously includes Jewish elements but has no link to a Jewish past. The key aspect, therefore, is not the ritual itself or even its historical genesis, but the way it is understood and used by an individual, a family, or a community.

Belief

Belief is the element in the taxonomy that perhaps is the most difficult to pin down. In many respects, beliefs tend to be negative—that is, what crypto-Jews do not believe rather than what they do. Interestingly, Gitlitz (1996) suggests that this negative aspect is also found historically; indeed, many of the elements that he identifies as significant to early crypto-Jewish beliefs continue to be expressed by crypto-Jews. The negative beliefs are usually expressed in somewhat oppositional terms—for example, "We do not believe that Jesus was God, as our neighbors do."

A range of positive beliefs are also found. They appear to be related to the strength of identity. For example, individuals with a strong crypto-Jewish identity often make use of biblical narratives as a model for understanding crypto-Jewish experience. Thus several respondents used the Exodus story as a model for the journey of their ancestors from Spain to the New World. This narrative is also associated positively with a range of ritual practices that unite both the biblical and the more recent journeys, such as the use of a harvest booth (sukkah) and the celebration of Passover. The use of the name Dio as opposed to Dios is also interpreted by some crypto-Jews as a positive statement of belief; that is, they consider the singular form to express belief in one God rather than in the Trinity, which they think is implied by the apparently plural form.

The importance of belief—like that of self-identification, genealogy and genetics, and practice—is related not to its historical bases, but to whether it is expressive of Jewish or crypto-Jewish identity. Beliefs about what Jews are like, and the internalization of those beliefs, emphasize this point. Many crypto-Jews utilize a range of prevailing stereotypes as a means to express what being Jewish means or as evidence that they are Jews. Thus they may use physical characteristics, such as size of nose or color of skin, or social factors, such as being good in business or having an interest in education, as a way to distinguish themselves from their neighbors. Jacobs's (2002) explanation of the processes by which members of an oppressed minority internalizes the stereotypes used against them in part explains this process. Gitlitz's (1996:82) discussion of the Edicts of Grace is also helpful. He highlights the role the edicts played in defining what it meant to be a Jew for a community that was increasingly distant from other forms or sources of knowledge. In a similar way, crypto-Jews in the twentieth century, in trying to define the parameters of their identity, accepted and internalized the stereotypes about Jews that were prevalent in the wider society.

The four elements out of which crypto-Jewish identity is constructed and the identity that is built from them are conceptually distinct from the types of historical analysis performed by Neulander and others. Identity is not objective or based on historical fact. It is subjective and arises from the interpretation of and the meanings attributed to the four elements. This subjectivity is fundamental. If we were to focus on objective fact, we would essentialize the identity and present a static view, defined from the external perspective. This static view, however, does not correspond with the ethnographic evidence, which suggests that identity is highly fluid and has little or no relation to the factuality of the elements from which it is constructed.

The Four Ideal Types

Strong Crypto-Jewish Identity

Individuals who manifest the strong crypto-Jewish identity consistently emphasize the Jewish aspect of their identity and exhibit the other elements of the taxonomy in a strong sense. Twenty-one respondents were primarily in this category. Due to the fluidity of identity, particular individuals cannot be specifically located along the continuum. Their backgrounds are very wide-ranging. They come from all parts of New Mexico and from different socioeconomic classes. It is also important to note that they include all aspects of the public or private expression of crypto-Judaism. Three of the interviewees, including *Marta*,[1] play an active role in the public expression and communication of crypto-Judaism. Others, approximately ten, have participated to different degrees in various conferences and other public presentations, as observers and speakers. Their participation is usually occasional rather than consistent. While some of these individuals had been interviewed before, most were first interviewed in the context of this study. The remaining eight respondents were not connected in any way with the public exploration of crypto-Judaism, and none of them had been interviewed outside the context of this study.

The Jewish religion (in a broad sense) is the defining aspect of their identity and is expressed as consistently present. Many of these individuals suggested that Judaism was something they were always aware of; others stated that it was something they learned about in early childhood. The following statement, by a crypto-Jew who, although living in Albuquerque at the time of interview, was born in the 1930s in a small village near Taos, is characteristic of this category.

> I've always known [that we were Jews] because my grandfather told us early in life. We were told from the time we were very little, but you see we didn't know what it was. . . . Cause you see we had a language translation here. . . . It wasn't until I became an adult that I knew what a Jew was, even though I know that we were. We were Ladino. And the thing you have to remember is I knew we were different, but I didn't know how we were different. We weren't allowed to do a lot of things that other children would. And it wasn't until I came back to New Mexico that I started listening to these things that people would say. . . . [W]e are crypto-Jews . . . and I said wait a minute, we were not hidden. It was an open thing. Everybody knew we were Jews, but I didn't know what a Jew was. (*Marta*, July 1999)

This statement highlights several interesting issues. *Marta* makes it clear that she was aware of the Jewish aspect of her identity from very early in her childhood. This information was passed down through her grandfather, who (other parts of the interview make clear) was the primary source of crypto-Jewish knowledge in the family. The statement suggests that to the child *Marta*, the idea of being a Jew was undefined; it was associated with practices and beliefs, but they were seen as "what our family did." *Marta* makes interesting use of the term "Ladino," which in the course of the interview she emphasized was used in her village to refer only to those identified as Jews. There is, however, no corresponding evidence that the word "Ladino" was used historically to refer to Jews or crypto-Jews. In recent popular usage, it has come to refer to the language Judeo-Spanish, which was spoken by many Jews of Iberian descent. *Marta*'s statement also highlights her perception of the relationship between the crypto-Jews in her community and the non-crypto-Jewish majority. Crypto-Judaism was not something hidden or secret: "Everybody knew we were Jews."

Exclusivity is the second key aspect of self-identification, alongside an ongoing family identification as Jews. Many of the interviewees emphasized that they were Jews, not Christians. They regarded the Christian parts of their identity as merely a public cover for the secret Jewish part, which was the more important. The significance of this exclusivity is highlighted by the story told by a man from Albuquerque who was born in the 1960s:

> When I was young, my uncle told us that we were Jews—we did a lot of Jewish things—we never ate pork or blood. When I became a priest, I was rejected by my family; they considered me dead. I visited my brother once; he gave me a cup of coffee; after I drank, he threw the cup away because I had used it. (*Pablo*, August 1998)

This narrative, whether or not it presents an actual event, indicates that in *Pablo*'s view the two religions—Judaism and Catholicism—were mutually exclusive. Even though his family was publically Catholic, his decision to become a priest out of conviction alienated him from his family. In some families, it is said that individuals became priests as a means to help maintain the public Catholic identity; this was not true of *Pablo*, who stated that he had become a priest against his family's wishes and did not consider himself to be a crypto-Jew, although regarding his crypto-Jewish heritage to be important.

This concept of exclusivity is also expressed by *Marta* in a much less dramatic way:

Number one, we were educated, a lot of my family was educated in the church. The Catholic Church we were not allowed to take catechism. My uncle had wanted to become a Penitente. He was not allowed, even a grown man, and my grandfather said no, you are not going to. Little things that I knew later on. (*Marta*, July 1999)

Marta indicates that although members of her family were educated in Catholic schools (and in other interviews adds that many in her family were educated in Presbyterian schools), they were not allowed to take catechism classes. This suggests that in her family there was a conscious rejection of the "religious" aspects of Catholic education as being incompatible with the Jewish aspects of her identity. It is possible that while *Marta* may have had to take these classes, her perception of them is incompatible with her self-identity and thus excluded from her memory. The power of her grandfather in shaping familial practice, particularly in relation to forbidding her adult uncle from becoming a Penitente, is characteristic of *Marta's* account as a whole.

The opposition between the Catholic and Jewish aspects of identity also shapes the way that history and folklore, both familial and communal, are structured. In the course of interviews over several years, *Maria*, a crypto-Jew from Albuquerque who was born in the 1940s, told a number of stories: one was about her own childhood; the second, about a great-grandmother; and the third, about crypto-Jews or *conversos* in Spain or Portugal. The interesting aspect of the three stories is that they share a structural pattern of exclusivity:

This is about a special herb my mother gave us. When I was little we lived in Albuquerque, and we had to go to church. We did not want anyone to know we were Jews. Before we went to church on Sunday, our mother gave us some of this herb from a bag; I don't know what it was. We went in the church, but just before the father gave the bread and wine we all became violently sick and had to go out. I guess my mother did not want us to eat that bread. (*Maria*, June 1997)

This narrative highlights the nature of *Maria's* experience of crypto-Jewish identity; it is an identity in conflict, with the public sphere being incompatible with the private. The story emphasizes that although the family had to attend church, and *Maria* does not wish to deny that fact, they never actually took communion and thus were never really Catholic. It is important to note that this story is contextualized in an oral history in which *Maria* was consistently aware of her Jewish roots.

The second story recounts a family tradition about *Maria*'s great-grandmother as a baby:

> When my great-grandmother Isabelle was born, her family lived in the mountains—there was no church near by. They had to take her to Santa Fe to be baptized. They got into a wagon and started the journey. On the way, they hit a bump and my grandmother fell out—no one knew it. They got to the church and could not find my grandmother. They had come so far, so the priest put her in the book anyway. They started back, and there on the side of the trail was my great grandmother, as happy as could be. So they went home. (*Maria*, August 2001)

This narrative has the same structure as the first. It recognizes the tension between the two religious identities and the fact that *Maria*'s family had to be at least publicly Catholic. But it narratively subverts this public avowal of Catholic faith by having the baby absent from her own baptism. The story suggests that although *Maria*'s family publicly had to conform to the requirements of the church and seemed to be Catholic, even being listed in baptismal records, the public identity and church records were false.

The third story concerns *Maria*'s earlier forebears:

> My grandmother told us many stories about our ancestors in Spain that had to flee to the mountains and stay there. They were hiding from the *inquisatores* and that there was a rule that they had to come down from the mountain and attend Mass. It was a rule. And it had been over a month since these two men had not been to a church. Of course, one of the situations they found it very hard to attend a Catholic service. But these two men, who were sheep-herders, that's what they could be in those days, decided not to take the bath on Sunday. And they would smell just like Mother Nature would, the smells of the sheep and the horses, whatever they had up there—donkeys. So they were going to church to obey what had to be obeyed in that village. And as they went into the church, they saw the two plates held by the angels, one on each side of the aisle as they were looking at the altar. And they had holy water in that, in the plates, but these . . . or sheep-herders decided they were going to act as [if] they were not too smart, as if they were locos, they were crazy. So they said ooh, . . . here's the washing place. So, they took off their shirts and they started scrubbing their elbows, scrubbing their necks, scrubbing behind their ears. And the sacristan

said, "Oh my goodness, it's almost time for Mass; we came out to light the candles on the altar; you're disturbing us; you get out of here, you crazy men." And that's how they got out of attending Mass that day. (*Maria*, July 1996)

Although this narrative is initially presented as a family story, in its content and elaboration it can be considered to be a folk narrative. This characterization is supported by the fact that many other informants told stories that were almost identical in structure and content. This narrative has the same structural form as the other two told by *Maria*. All three set up both an opposition, between crypto-Jews and the church, and potential mediating acts between the two: taking Communion, being baptized, and attending Mass. The reconciling element creates the possibility that the two primary structural threads are not mutually exclusive. In each narrative, a conscious or an unconscious event occurs to derail the mediation. In the first story, *Maria*'s mother acts consciously to prevent the taking of Communion. The third story also includes a conscious rejection of Catholicism. In the second narrative, the avoidance of mediation is unconscious; the baby falls out of the wagon accidently rather than purposefully. Nonetheless, all three narratives provide a structural rejection for the possibility of mediation between the Jewish and Catholic aspects of self, with the Catholic being strongly rejected in each.

It seems very unlikely that *Maria* was consciously structuring these stories. They were told in very different contexts in different years. Thus the structural relations that characterize the three stories are, minimally, the unconscious pattern that shapes the way *Maria* constructs narratives. It is likely that the oppositional structure is more generally shared, as other interviewees with strong crypto-Jewish identity told stories that were structurally similar to *Maria*'s. *Pablo*'s story of rejection, for example, shows the same pattern of opposition.

The tale "The Padre and the Jew," cited by Judith Neulander (2001:321–324; see chap. 2), is also interpreted by many crypto-Jews as having the same oppositional quality as *Maria*'s three narratives. This story was told to me by several individuals. All of them recounted the story without mentioning the issue of marriage. They explained the story as emphasizing the difference between Christians and crypto-Jews, with the conclusion—associating the Christian traditions with toilet paper—clearly making a negative statement about Catholicism and thereby a positive statement about Judaism. The possible mediation between Christianity and Judaism is suggested by the plant–cactus metaphor, but the opposition is clearly established by the concluding sentiment.

Genealogy is important on many levels to the strength of self-identification. All the interviewees with strong crypto-Jewish identity had a clear tradition of being descended from Jewish ancestors. This genealogy often was associated with particular individuals, often backed up by different degrees of research. Thus some individuals either had trained themselves to do documentary research or worked with professional genealogists; others relied on Web sites to gather data. One common feature of most of these individuals was a family knowledge of genealogy going back a significant number of generations. The importance of knowing their heritage was seen by many as a fundamental part of their identity.

A stated preference for marrying into only other families with a crypto-Jewish background was also characteristic of this category. Thus *Leah*, a woman from a small town to the south of Taos, stated:

> In my village we all knew each other, who was one of us and who was not. We had fourteen families who were all Jews. We only married people from those families, never from the others. (*Leah*, August 2001)

Other informants—for example, *Martin*, whose family was originally from the northern part of New Mexico but who was born in Albuquerque around 1935—echoed *Leah*'s statement. *Martin* mentioned thirty-two families in the area from which his family originated:

> My family were related to the Perezes; the Perezes were related to the Espinosas and the Bravos; the Bravos, to the Castillos and Naranjos . . . so that all these families were related, but you married only into these thirty-two families. (*Martin*, August 1999)

More communal structures of crypto-Judaism seem to have characterized the villages in the mountains that were remote from Santa Fe and Albuquerque. All the respondents who mentioned a large number of families with which their families married came originally from this northern part of the state.

It should not be thought, however, that the strong crypto-Jewish identity was associated solely with these more remote regions. Several of the individuals who fit into this category came from Albuquerque, Santa Fe, or other more established centers. Although they almost never spoke of a communal aspect to their crypto-Jewish practices, most did mention a small set of closely connected families, many of which were closely related to them. All these informants, whether from the mountains or the cities, stated that their families usually intermarried with other families that shared a crypto-Jewish heritage and were well known to them. It should be noted that in addition to their preference for endogamy, most of these families were aware of marriages with Native Americans or with individuals from other ethnic groups and largely considered themselves to be mestizo.

The significant role of endogamy in this category is also clearly indicated by some of the professional historical and genealogical work done by Stanley Hordes (2005:273–281). He specifically examined individuals and families included in this category and demonstrated that the stated preference for marrying within a small range of families that had *converso* ancestors was in fact the most common marriage pattern. His work does not suggest that this was absolute, but that it was a strong preference that shaped the marriage choices over many generations.

Practices that are interpreted as being of Jewish or crypto-Jewish origin, particularly by the individuals who perform them, are the third component of the strong crypto-Jewish identity. The ethnographic evidence suggests that each family was highly idiosyncratic in relation to practices, which were performed privately in the home, often not even in conjunction with other families known to be of *converso* origin. Thus each family would retain a subset of the possible rituals based on the vagaries of oral transmission. The important shared aspect of this category is not the particular practices, but the acknowledgment by the individuals and families that some of their practices were performed as an expression of their Jewish identity and distinguished them from their neighbors.

The following description of a game by *Maria* is told in a way that emphasizes its association with Judaism and with an ongoing tradition of crypto-Judaism:

There is a game that we played as children during the time of Passover. We were told the story of the tribes. And this game is played with stones in a circular fashion, like a clock. Except we use thirteen stones because we include Moses in it. [On] each stone we would write the name of a tribe with pencil. We would put them on the ground and make a little circle of thirteen stones. We counted around this little circle of stones. We would count up to twelve, but you must remember that there are thirteen stones in the circle, one representing Moses. If your count of twelve should land on the stone of Moses, you couldn't get any more tribes out of this circular game, for the tribes were traveling to get to the promised land and Moses never made it to the promised land. Now I could start anywhere in the clock circle; I could start above the stone that was Moses, which would be vertically up, would be the count of twelve on our clock. And I would count one, two, three, four, five, six, seven, eight, nine, ten, eleven, twelve. So maybe my count would be on the stone that represented Simeon. Simeon would come to the center of the circle, and he has made it to the promised land. I could count backward from Simeon and go backward one, two, three, four, five, six, seven, eight, nine, ten, eleven, twelve. Maybe I landed on the tribe of Ben. I would take that stone representing the tribe of Ben and put it in the circle, and then I would count again. Maybe this time I wanted to start with Moses, for Moses was very important in our storytelling. And we could go round the circle counting with Moses. One, two, three, four, five, six, seven, eight, nine, ten, eleven, twelve. Oh, I didn't make it on Moses, and therefore I can still continue the game to see how many stones I can get into the promised land, which is in the center of the circle. However, if my count of twelve would land on Moses, that would stop my game. And maybe I would get four points for getting four tribes into the promised land and so forth. But Moses could not be moved from that spot. for he never made it to the promised land. This was a story that was told to us during Passover. (*Maria*, August 2002)

This game was also described by *David*, a man born in the 1930s who lived north of Santa Fe, as well as by *Pablo*. It is similar to a wide range of other folk children's games that do not have the same connection with the biblical text; this version seems to be found solely among individuals who claim crypto-Jewish identity.

Although the conscious interpretation of practices as being of Jewish origin or expressing crypto-Jewish identity is important, some experiences, especially those of childhood, may have been taken for granted and thus not interpreted until well after they happened. This is indicated in *Marta*'s statement that she knew that her family was Jewish, but "didn't know what a Jew was." Other sections of her interview also show that *Marta* understood many practices as being Jewish—for example, in connection with lighting candles on Friday nights or during Hanukkah—but others, such as not eating pork, as being just done by her family. This aspect is highlighted by the following statement:

I thought that everybody did things that we did. It wasn't until later . . . I didn't know that people didn't wash meat. You don't wash meat? We washed meat. You had to get rid of the blood. (*Marta*, August 1999)

While the interview indicates that the food practices prevented *Marta*'s family from eating in other people's houses, the rules were never specifically interpreted as being connected with Jewish identity.

The process of retrospective reinterpretation by an individual is indicated in a section from an interview with *Isabel*, who was born in the 1930s and lived in Albuquerque:

Actually, you started in the corners, and you swept it all to the middle and the reason you had to go to the corners first was because there were *duendes* that were hidden there, and the *duendes* you had to get rid of them and put them in the center and then kick them out. I didn't find out till later. . . . That's what we were told: *duendes*. (*Isabel*, August 2003)[2]

Isabel stated that she had found out that crypto-Jews did not sweep through the door because the mezuzah was there, but as a child she did not know this. While this aspect of retrospective reinterpretation is conscious, it is also likely that individuals utilize their current knowledge to interpret their past and may unconsciously substitute present explanation for past understanding.

Some practices, though, originated in non-Jewish cultural and religious traditions. They offer a range of interpretations and emphases. A consistent feature of the strong crypto-Jewish identity is the emphasis on the aspects of a practice that are interpreted as being of Jewish origin, associated with the rejection of those elements that are seen as being of Christian origin. Many interviewees regarded the Christian aspects to be either unimportant or, indeed, not even Christian. Other respondents considered the Christian elements to be merely a cover for the hidden Jewish ones. None of the individuals included in this category considered the Christian aspects to have cultural significance or religious meaning for them.

The association of reciting the Rosary and lighting candles on Friday nights was mentioned by several individuals with strong or weak crypto-Jewish identity. One informant, *Paulo*, a man born in the 1960s, stated:

The Rosary was just words; it did not mean anything to me. We lit the candles; that was important. The Rosary was just a cover up. (*Paulo*, July 2002)

While for other crypto-Jews the Catholic aspect of the ritual was significant, only the Jewish aspect was meaningful for *Paulo*.

The area of belief is perhaps the most difficult to isolate. To some extent,
it is the least important of the four elements of the taxonomy. As noted,
beliefs tended to be expressed in negative terms; thus most of the respondents with strong crypto-Jewish identity rejected Christian beliefs, particularly that Jesus was either the Messiah or God. While some dismissed him
entirely, others saw him as a Jewish prophet, but certainly not divine. To an
extent, this rejection of Jesus is complemented by the positive belief in one
God, as opposed to the Trinity. Other beliefs included an emphasis on the
Hebrew Bible or the Ten Commandments.

Some individuals with strong or weak crypto-Jewish identity have joined
mainstream Jewish congregations. They have taken on a range of other
ideas that emerge from these different Jewish communities. Interestingly,
when speaking of their childhoods, they tend not to project back many of
their current crypto-Jewish beliefs, but still emphasize their rejection of
Christian beliefs. Belief is also a somewhat problematic element, as it has a
built-in assumption that crypto-Judaism is a religion. For some crypto-
Jews, their crypto-Jewish identity is not religious. Thus while they reject
Christianity, they do not necessarily embrace Judaism. They speak about
crypto-Judaism as a cultural tradition, with the practices being cultural
rather than religious. Some set their crypto-Jewish identity in opposition to
Hispano rather than Catholic identity. One individual, *Sarah*, stated that
she saw her crypto-Judaism as preventing her from being involved in Hispanic politics: the two, she thought, were mutually exclusive.

The only extended set of beliefs expressed during this study associated
different aspects of the crypto-Jewish historical experience with biblical
narratives. Many of the interviewees made this connection, particularly
linking the story of the Exodus to the journey from Spain to New Mexico,
with Ferdinand and Isabella being given the role of Pharaoh. While it often
was unclear whether the association was being made by the respondent or
had been traditional in his or her family, this second aspect was emphasized by both *Marta* and *Maria* in very different ways.

Marta described a very detailed story that was retold in the spring and
made a direct association between the crypto-Jewish and Exodus narratives:

When they had to put the blood to save the children, he said that the heavenly,
the angel couldn't get his feet wet, his heavenly feet wet on the blood of the lamb

because they were heavenly. He skipped not to get his heavenly feet dirty. I do have that one written. He would say that. Now, the funniest thing, the water, the Rio Grande, turned into blood.

The Nile, everything was the Rio Grande. Everything was the Rio Grande. And also you had Queen Isabella and Pharaoh. They were cruel people who did not like Ladinos. And, oh, by the way, every time that Pharaoh would break his promise to Moses, well I've got to tell you, God got angrier and angrier. (*Marta*, August 1999)

In the context of the interview, *Marta* recounted a much more extended version that tied specific aspects of the journey to New Mexico with the Exodus.[3] *Maria* made similar connections and attributed them to long-standing family traditions. She described booths used during the autumn harvest as associated with the Jewish festival of Sukkoth and thus the trek of the Israelites as well as the journey of her ancestors through the desert in southern New Mexico.

The four elements of the strong crypto-Jewish identity are based on a similar pattern. An opposition is set up between two categories, usually Jewish (crypto-Jewish) and Christian (Catholic) but occasionally Jewish and Hispanic. The two categories are perceived as being mutually exclusive, with the Jewish category being seen as positive and the Catholic category as negative. This negativity is emphasized by both its rejection as having no meaning or importance and its association with persecution by the Inquisition. Individuals in this category identify strongly as Jewish and privilege that aspect of their identity in their self-definition, genealogy, practices, and belief.

Weak Crypto-Jewish Identity

Individuals who manifest the weak crypto-Jewish identity share many traits with those in the strong category, but often in a mediated sense. They tend to be more consciously fluid in their self-understanding, often coming to a crypto-Jewish identification relatively late in life. Each of the elements out of which their identities are constructed brings out this fluid or mediated aspect. This category was the largest, comprising sixty-eight individuals. They come from all parts of New Mexico and from all levels of socioeconomic background and education.

The aspect of self-identification has a range of variations in this category: family declaration, self-discovery, or self-attachment. Each of these has different implications. The first subcategory includes those individuals who did not grow up with a consciousness of Judaism or crypto-Judaism, but at some point, often around the time of puberty (but occasionally much later), were informed either that their family is Jewish or that they had Jewish ancestors. Up to the point at which they were told, these informants considered themselves to be Christian (usually Catholic), and their attachment to Christian traditions tends to remain as part of their identity. The following is taken from *Manuel*'s narrative of how he learned of the Jewish aspect of his heritage:

> I was I think fifteen or sixteen, or something like that. My uncle came and took me to the mountains. We got there and he said, "I have something important to pass to you—Somos judíos." I was really shocked. (*Manuel*, August 2003)

This form of narrative is highly characteristic. Many individuals report similar stories. They include going to a secluded place, often with an elderly uncle or another older relative, who informs them that they are Jews. Although most of the interviewees were told at around the time of puberty, this varies from narrative to narrative. While many of the individuals (both men and women) state that they were surprised by this news, they also present it as a transformative event. Secrecy is part of the usual explanation for this process. Their families feared that if they had been told when they were young children, they may not have been able to keep their identity secret.

Other crypto-Jews in this category express a degree of ambivalence about learning of their Jewish heritage. This is illustrated in the following section from an interview with *Joseph*, a resident of Albuquerque who was born in the 1930s:

> She said I can't tell you why or how you're different, but go ask your great-grandfather. And my grandfather lived not too far away from us, and well he was there and I asked him and he sat me down by the tree and said "Somos judíos." And I was angry; I used to wear a medal around my neck. I grabbed it, tore it off, and threw it way. Because you live, and all of a sudden you're told something. Because the Spanish mentality blames Jews as God killers. And that does influence you. But in our family once we grew up, we're finally told at about that time [puberty]. (*Joseph*, August 1999)

While *Joseph* experienced a degree of ambivalence, this information was assimilated and became a positive part of his life. Similar ambivalence is expressed in this statement by *Julio*:

> They don't want to know how Jewish they are. They're too shocked. It's too difficult. You can't just go up to one another and say: hey—Jew—you have to be very sensitive. Because as shocking as it was for me, it's going to be just as shocking for them. When I first found out, I was in denial for several years. I couldn't face up to it. I couldn't reconcile being Hispanic and a Jew. It took me a while. And the reason I did this . . . how I kind of corrected this was, was by reading more about Sephardic history and customs and Jewish customs and being able to identify with them, do it that way. It is a difficult situation, and I'm in my mid-50s now. It's not a place I'd like to be in. (*Julio*, August 2003)

This statement is interesting because it reflects both the original ambivalence of the informant and that of individuals (including members of his family) to whom he reveals this identity. It also indicates a perception of conflict between being Hispanic and being Jewish. For others, the information and the identification remain ambivalent. This is particularly true when one person in a family learns of this identity and shares it with other members. Many interviewees reported that their siblings are often hostile to this information and just do not want to know about it.

A transformational effect is occasionally found among individuals who learn of this identity from a relative when they are adults. This often occurs right before the death of an elderly relative who transmits the information in almost his or her final words; it sometimes occurs after they have considered the possibility of Jewish origins as a result of genealogical or other research. The following is a description from *Rosa*, a resident of Albuquerque born in the 1930s, of the tradition of deathbed transmission in her family:

> When my mother's oldest sister, Tía [Aunt] Maria, was dying, my mother was very ill. She was an epileptic, and she was in a coma; she had had a grand mal. And my *tía* was there; it was a ritual at the deathbed that somebody was elected to remind the families of the lighting of the Sabbath candles. My *tía* was crying, where's [inaudible]? Bring her to me; I must give her the message; and then she held her oldest daughter's hand and said, "Tell her, light the candles." . . . [S]he called her daughter's first name. . . . She named her first daughter. . . .

[S]he immediately came to see Mother, who was in a coma, and she couldn't talk to her about the death, so, ah, it had to be told to her later. (*Rosa*, July 2003)

Many respondents suggested that this new knowledge forced them to re-look at themselves and the practices from their families' past with a new consciousness of being in some sense Jewish.

In some cases, self-discovery is equally transformative. By self-discovery, I am referring to either individuals who engage in genealogical research and discover *converso* or Jewish ancestry or those who explore the strange practices found in their families' traditions and find them to be similar to those of Jewish or crypto-Jewish origin. There is an important difference between these two subgroups. Those who do genealogical research may or may not be looking for Jewish ancestors. In many cases, as that of *Lawrence*, a man from Santa Fe born in the 1950s, there was no expectation of Jewish ancestry. Like many in the Hispano community, *Lawrence* had an interest in his family's origins. It was only in the context of the research that he discovered *converso* ancestors, a discovery that led him to rethink his identity and ultimately to speak with elderly relatives who confirmed both a tradition of Jewish descent and a range of Jewish practices. Those who investigate their families' practices often include a parallel exploration of Judaism with that of family traditions, and it is this simultaneous exploration that leads to the discovery. A good example of this second type is found in the following statement by *Julio*:

Or "Why did Grandma wash the meat before she cooked it; was there any reason for that?" "Well, no, because we thought it tasted better that way." You know, questions like that. Never at any time did I say, "Do you think we were Jewish?" Because first of all we wouldn't know what a Jew was; we'd never seen a Jew in New Mexico.

And the discovery has been wonderful. The analogies, the tying in of a lot of things I remember. One of things we had a big laugh about was in mourning, when somebody dies: when my grandmother died, dad's sisters were sitting in a darkened room and covered themselves, and they removed the springs from the beds, and the springs in those days were coil springs, so they were not allowed to sit on anything soft with cushions. They had to sit on something hard. So they were all sitting on the top of the bed, and the coils and the bed broke, and all the sisters wound up on the floor. I said, "Mom, why did people sit on the coils?" And she said, "Because that's what we did." You know, when somebody died, first of all, we'd cover the mirrors, and second we'd remove the springs, and people would sit in this hard room on the hard surface and this is where you'd go in and express your condolences. (*Julio*, August 2004)

The context of this statement suggests that *Julio* and other members of his family were attracted to Judaism at the same time that they began to rethink their past traditions. Today, an additional element has come into play: increased public knowledge about crypto-Judaism and crypto-Jewish practices. This knowledge has led individuals to explore their family traditions and come to a new understanding of their past. In some cases, like that of *Lawrence*, they then validate this discovery through discussion with family members; in other cases, the identity rests solely on the process of discovery and the interpretation of family practices.

An additional form of this subcategory includes individuals who have particular genetic diseases that are statistically associated with Jewish ancestry. This diagnosis has led some of them to develop a self-identification as crypto-Jews and begin a process of family and historical research. It should be noted, however, that this type of discovery—and, indeed, the other types of discovery just mentioned—do not necessarily lead to the development of a crypto-Jewish self-identification. The individuals may consider the information to be interesting but not relevant to their sense of self or their religious choice.

The third variation, self-attachment, is relatively rare in the context of this study, but may in reality be common. This category includes individuals who have no evidence, in terms of either genealogical information or family practices commonly identified as crypto-Jewish, of Jewish ancestry, but due to social or almost mystical attachment believe themselves to be of Jewish origin. This is illustrated by the words of *Luke*, a man born in the 1970s who lived in Santa Fe:

> When I was a small boy I used to dream of a building, night after night. I looked in a book and realized it was the Temple; I knew then that I was a Jew. (*Luke*, July 1996)

Luke did not find any heritage or practices of Judaism in his family (or even claim that there were, although not yet discovered), but based on this experience, which he interpreted as mystical, came to this self-understanding.

As with self-discovery, many individuals who initially come to a Jewish self-understanding through self-attachment begin to search genealogical

records or reinterpret family traditions to see if they can find Jewish validation. This process was evidenced by three individuals from a messianic
synagogue who spoke at a recent conference of the Society for Crypto-
Judaic Studies. All three stated that their initial association was with the
synagogue and only on the basis of messianic Christianity's connection
with Judaism did they begin to explore their genealogies. They found *converso* ancestors, which allowed them to validate their sense of self.

The sense of identity found in this category is thus highly complex. Individuals in the different subcategories come to the identity through very
different processes: family declaration, genealogical research or interpretation of family practices, and desire to find connection or perhaps a sense of
connection. All three lead to a process of interpretation and reinterpretation. It should be emphasized that that this is not necessarily a process of
invention. The ethnographic evidence of crypto-Judaism in other parts of
the world suggests that rituals and practices can be passed down uninterpreted; thus it is possible that some of the practices that are interpreted as
Jewish by individuals with weak crypto-Jewish identity are part of a historical tradition. It is likely, however, that alongside these potentially historical
traditions the process of reinterpretation serves to give content, originally
unconnected, to the growing sense of Jewish identity.

Self-identification has in part merged into genealogy. Each of the subcategories initially starts with a different relationship to the role of genealogy.
Within the family declaration and the genealogical aspects of the self-
discovery subcategory, genealogy is implicit. In the first, the sentence "Somos judíos" is often included in the wider statement that either ancestors
in general or a particular set of ancestors were of Jewish origin; in the second, it is the discovery of genealogical information that is operative. While
the other subcategories initially include no genealogical information or
family tradition, a common feature of how individuals develop a crypto-
Jewish identity is through an ongoing process of research. Thus an individual, as I have suggested, may see the evidence of his or her identity as
being associated purely with practice, but may add genealogical information through either family knowledge or genealogical research.

Marriage patterns (in actuality or as stated preferences) tend to be more
varied among those with weak rather than strong crypto-Jewish identity.
The research conducted by Stanley Hordes (2005) suggests that some families, especially those in which the identification is consciously passed from
one generation to the next, follow the pattern of marrying into other families

identified as being of crypto-Jewish origin. But while many individuals with strong crypto-Jewish identity consciously expressed the preference in their families for endogamy, those with weak crypto-Jewish identity, even those whose families tended to practice endogamy, did not express a strong preference for that form of marriage. Many instead emphasized the fact that their families included a wide range of ethnic backgrounds. Thus, for example, *Manuel* suggested that his genealogy included Hispanic, Native American, African American, and Mexican as well as Jewish ancestors. *Ruth*, an artist from near Taos, was equally clear on this issue:

> My mother was Cherokee Indian, and she was adopted by Spanish people. Her father was part Indian and part French, and there was a Spanish couple that would go by and see this little boy and girl all dirty and looking out the window, and they couldn't have children so they thought maybe they could adopt this little girl and little boy. So they went to my grandfather, which was my real grandfather, and asked if they could adopt that little girl and little boy. (*Ruth*, August 2003)

The Jewish contribution to her family came on her father's side. Of the individuals in this category, more than 60 percent discussed their genealogies in terms similar to those used by *Manuel* and *Ruth*.

Due to the complexity of identity and sources of identity, the range of practices that characterize the weak category are more variable in both form and interpretation than those found in the strong category. There are, however, two main characteristics of the practices found in all the variants: they were never specifically identified as being Jewish, and many of them tend to have syncretistic aspects—that is, a mix of cultural forms.

Julio's statement about mourning rituals is characteristic. He cites a range of practices that he seems to have been aware were different from those of neighboring families, but were never identified as being of Jewish origin. This feature is often associated with food. Many respondents mentioned that their families followed a number of food rules about the preparation and consumption of food with no explanation. Thus *Manuel* suggested that he had thought that his family was allergic to pork. He discovered that it was a Jewish practice not to eat pork only after he was told of his Jewish heritage and learned more about Jewish and crypto-Jewish practices.

One interesting aspect of practices and their reinterpretation arises when there is a perceived conflict between knowledge gained through research and family traditions and actual practice. *Flavio*, a man born in the 1940s who lived near Española, came from a family that claimed descent from the *kohenim*, the Jewish priestly caste. Upon researching the restrictions on this group, he learned that they were not allowed to go into cemeteries. In the context of an interview discussing funerals, he stated that "we went into cemeteries but we did not like to." This or similar phrases have come up in many interviews about this type of conflict between knowledge and practice. It suggests that while the respondent does not wish to lie about what he and his family did, he must reconcile past practices and present understanding. Syncretistic form and content is the second key aspect of many practices strongly associated with weak crypto-Jewish identity. Many individuals speak of purification rituals that bring together what they perceive to be Jewish elements and Christian elements. Thus *Frank*, a resident of Albuquerque born in the 1940s, described a practice performed by his mother and grandmother:

> My mother had a bowl in her bedroom; it had water in it and some green herbs; I do not know which. She had a *retablo* of a saint, a woman above the bowl; I do not know who it was. My mother and grandmother used the bowl each month. (*Frank*, August 1996)

Frank associated the ritual with the traditional Jewish practice of *mikveh*, particularly in connection with purification after menstruation.[4]

A second example that has the same structural elements is found in some communities in northern New Mexico and was reported by informants with either strong or week crypto-Jewish identity. Families that had a Jewish identity placed two pieces of metal in the shape of a cross on the doorposts of their houses. When asked about the practice, the interviewees said, "We did this to fulfill the biblical commandment to Jews; but we used a cross to hide the fact from the priests." Many individuals, however, also indicate that the cross was a powerful symbol.

The important aspect of these syncretistic practices for our understanding of the weak crypto-Jewish identity lies in the nature of the interpretation. Most individuals in this category emphasized the Jewish element of the practice: the role of the water for purification and the association of the cross on the door with a mezuzah. They did not, however, completely reject the power or meaning of the Christian symbol. If we return to the ritual of candle lighting accompanied by the recitation of the Rosary, some of the individuals in this category said that lighting the candles on Friday night was the more important part of the practice, but they included the Rosary not merely to hide the Jewish aspects but also because it was powerful.

Belief is much weaker in this than in the strong category. Very few individuals reported their families' as having any strong positive beliefs or narratives. The most common beliefs were negative—that is, a rejection of Catholic doctrine about Jesus and the Virgin Mary. As did those with strong crypto-Jewish identity, some families replaced adherence to Christian tenets with the belief in one God. Others spoke of a clear emphasis on the Hebrew Bible:

> We always read from the Old Testament, never the Christian Bible. (*Frank*, August 1996)

Some respondents noted additional emphasis on the Ten Commandments and some use of stereotyping of Jewish behavior. Although a significant minority of the individuals in this category rejected Jesus as God, many of them considered him to have been a very important prophet.

Belief, however, is not the defining element in crypto-Jewish identification. Many individuals in this category believe in Jesus (in some way, not necessarily as the son of God) but also consider themselves to be crypto-Jews. They tend to express this seeming contradiction as a connection with Jewish and *converso* history and culture, which they do not regard as mutually exclusive from continuing to believe in Jesus. Over the course of this study, several interviewees moved from being nonpracticing Catholics, with a crypto-Jewish identity, to joining messianic churches or synagogues, because they felt that those communities allowed them to express both the Jewish and Christian aspects of their identities.

The four elements of the weak crypto-Jewish identity are shaped by the same underlying structure or pattern. While this identity is much more complex and variable than the strong. Like those with strong crypto-Jewish identity, the individuals in the weak category primarily organize the elements of their experience into two categories: Jewish and Christian. But the opposition of Jewish and Christian elements and the rejection of the latter are not found to the same degree in the weak category as in the strong. The elements tend to overlap, with value being placed on both. This is seen with genealogy, in which the mixed nature of the family line is at times a source of pride, and with practices, in which the Christian elements are valued and considered to have power apart from their role as screens behind which the Jewish rituals can be performed in secret.

Despite the varied level of mediation of the Jewish and Christian elements, with some informants giving the Christian aspects of their experience more meaning and value than others, it is the Jewish element that is considered to be of primary meaning and value. Individuals who fall into this category identify themselves as crypto-Jews, which makes them crypto-Jews.

Christian Identity with Converso *Elements*

Individuals who manifest the Christian identity with *converso* elements are descended from Spanish Jews who converted to Catholicism and often are included in accounts of crypto-Judaism by other scholars. Thus it is important to address how they fit into the context of crypto-Judaism in New Mexico. Although this category was smaller than the first two categories in the sample, comprising thirteen individuals, it probably represents a larger number of individuals than the first two categories. Evidence from other ethnographic contexts suggests that a significant number of descendants of *conversos* retain vestiges of practices that are neither interpreted nor historically contextualized. It seems likely, therefore, that a similar balance may be found in New Mexico. These individuals are not highly represented in the sample, however, as they do not consider themselves to be crypto-Jews, are not exploring the role of Judaism in their lives, and thus fell outside the networking process used to find subjects for this study.

The original discussion of this category (Kunin 2001:50) included only those individuals who performed practices regarded as being of Jewish origin, excluding those who also had Jewish or crypto-Jewish ancestors. We now consider this to have been confusing genealogy with self-identification. Some of the individuals included in this category have both a genealogical tradition and practices associated with it, but regard crypto-Judaism as part of their past rather than their present.

The identification of these individuals as being connected to crypto-Judaism has several variations. Some of them make this association themselves, based on the genealogical tradition of their families, or occasionally the connection is triggered by information they have read. Thus *Margaret*, a resident of Albuquerque born in the 1940s, had a strong tradition of *converso* genealogy in her family and was aware of a range of practices associated with that genealogy, concerning food and the Sabbath. This led her to have a strong association with and, indeed, interest in the crypto-Jewish aspects of Hispano culture. Nonetheless, she and her family as a whole had a very strong Catholic identity and rejected any idea that they might be crypto-Jews.

Identification can also be made by an observer, from inside or outside the crypto-Jewish community. A form of archaic Spanish is spoken by crypto-Jews in parts of New Mexico. It has been associated both by these crypto-Jews and by some scholars with Judeo-Spanish, popularly called Ladino. The following extract from an interview indicates how language is used to identify individuals who hitherto had no sense of crypto-Jewish identity:

> Now when we meet here, like this lady that has the hereditary blood disease, and we started talking Ladino . . . her eyes went big. You already speak our Ladino. She was very moved by her discovery; she comes to us when we have our meetings. (*Maria*, August 1999)

While this woman, who was identified by both her speech and her hereditary disease, began to explore crypto-Judaism, others who speak Ladino and have been diagnosed with diseases prevalent among Jews do not.

Within the small group of Christians with *converso* ancestors interviewed for this study, a wide range of practices were retained, including those associated with Sukkoth, food, and the Sabbath. The practices were idiosyncratic, with little or no pattern of retention among families. In part, the individuals depended on a source of outside knowledge to select practices that may have had a Jewish connection.

The structural features of the Christian identity with *converso* elements are related to those of the strong and weak crypto-Jewish identity. The individuals tended to see an opposition between Judaism and Christianity. As in the weak category, the two were not regarded as mutually exclusive. All the interviewees considered the vestiges of crypto-Judaism and, if present, the fact of Jewish or *converso* ancestors to be positive but not decisive in their self-identification. Thus the structural pattern is the inversion of that found in the weak category. Christianity and Judaism are seen to overlap, and each is acknowledged as having value, but the Christian elements are privileged.

Christian Identity Without Converso Elements

Individuals who manifest Christian identity without *converso* elements are identified by others as crypto-Jews due to their practices, but clearly regard them as coming from a non-Jewish, usually Adventist or messianic, source. This category was the smallest in the study and, in a certain sense, has the least importance for understanding crypto-Judaism in New Mexico. Ironically, it is the only group that reflects the comprehensive explanation for the presence of crypto-Jews in the state offered by Judith Neulander (2001). These individuals do not consider themselves to be crypto-Jews and have no tradition or documented evidence of a crypto-Jewish past. All either come from Albuquerque and have recent associations with Judaizing messianic churches or live in the southern part of the state and have historical associations with Seventh-Day Adventist churches.

The following is a good example of how the individuals in this category are identified by others and identify themselves. I was given the names of two people in southern New Mexico who had been identified as potential crypto-Jews because they had expressed interest in Jewish festivals at a public lecture. I drove for about three hours to their home to interview them. They made it very clear that they did not consider themselves to be crypto-Jews. In fact, they said, "Our great-grandfather was Adventist; he started us on Saturday rather than Sunday." They emphasized that he had disliked the Catholic Church and had decided to become an Adventist due to reading the Bible—but he had no Jewish roots. Thus they were aware of the origin of their family tradition and considered it important to remember it. They recently had joined a messianic church in Albuquerque so they could retain the Judaized aspects of their Christian beliefs.

While this evidence seems in part to support Neulander's thesis, it is the exception that proves the rule. These interviewees, far from forgetting or wishing to forget their origin, remembered it over several generations. The family is from a region in which there are active Seventh-Day Adventist churches. The majority of the informants were from northern New Mexico, a region with very little historical penetration of Judaizing churches, and all were asked about the religious traditions in their families. Only a tiny minority adhered to a sect other than Catholicism or mainstream Protestant denominations that did not have Judaizing practices. Thus while this suggests that some individuals and practices can be associated with Adventism or other Sabbatarian traditions, there is little evidence to view this as generalizable.

The structural pattern found of the Christian identity with no *converso* elements is almost the inverse of that of the strong crypto-Jewish identity. The individuals expressed an oppositional relation between Judaism and Christianity. In their description and interpretation of practice, they strongly emphasized the Christian elements. Nonetheless, there was a slightly mediated aspect, with Jewish practice—particularly that which could be associated with Jesus—being regarded as relatively positive.

Despite the rather static depiction of crypto-Jewish identity, the discussion of ideal types provides a basis for exploring the different ways that crypto-Jews conceptualize and organize the elements out of which they construct meaning. Thus each type is associated with a pattern of identification: strongly oppositional, with an emphasis on Judaism; mediated, with an emphasis on Judaism; mediated, with an emphasis on Christianity; and strongly oppositional, with an emphasis on Christianity. Like the types themselves, these patterns should be seen as fluid, flowing one into the next.

The element of self-identification is the most significant for crypto-Jewish identity. It is important to emphasize that the approach taken in this study privileges internal understanding of self. Thus individuals, who fall into the first two categories, whatever the source of their self identification, are considered to be crypto-Jews because they consider themselves to be. Those who fall into the last two categories are not considered to be crypto-Jews because they do not consider themselves to be.

While this chapter has not considered issues of authenticity—and, indeed, the concept of fluidity of identity suggests that any such discussion should be undertaken with caution—the ethnographic evidence indicates the basis for some conclusions about authenticity. The evidence presented in relation to those respondents with strong crypto-Jewish identity indicated that there was a strong association among self-identification, genealogy, and practice. The genealogical evidence is particularly significant because it demonstrates not only *converso* ancestry, but also endogamy. Thus the strong crypto-Jewish identity expressed by many of these informants has authentic historical roots in an ongoing crypto-Jewish tradition. The respondents with weak crypto-Jewish identity can be divided on the basis of the source of their self-identification. The transmission of information from one generation to the next most likely reflects an ongoing tradition. Evidence presented by Stanley Hordes (2005) indicates that families with weak crypto-Jewish identity practice endogamy, but not as consistently as those with strong crypto-Jewish identity. The association among self-identification, genealogy, and practices that are identified as crypto-Jewish suggests that there is a strong plausibility of authenticity for some individuals with weak crypto-Jewish identity.

The element of practice in relation to the groups discussed is less clear-cut, however, since some rituals may be of more recent vintage than others. Some practices are more widespread than others, and many have exemplars in Inquisition documents. Thus it is possible that they represent the vestiges of a historical crypto-Jewish tradition.

FIVE

CRYPTO-JEWISH PRACTICE

MEMORY AND BRICOLAGE

Although some aspects of crypto-Jewish practice continue to be part of lived experience, many of the rituals and traditions are now part of cultural memory. Thus, unlike many ethnographies that describe practice on the basis of participant observation, this study considers many of the practices on the basis of information provided in interviews and conversations. This approach is important to emphasize from the outset, as it has implications for interpretation. While being interviewed or discussing their crypto-Jewish heritage, individuals select from their memories, both consciously and unconsciously, practices and experiences that conform to their expectations of what a crypto-Jewish practice might be. Perhaps, if they have a weak crypto-Jewish identity, they may describe traditions that they think might be interesting for the ethnographer or other people listening to them.

This process of selection and interpretation creates a number of potential problems:

1. Respondents may interpret certain practices as being Jewish due to false analogy.[1]
2. Interviewees may include only material that fits their understanding of crypto-Jewish practice, thus disregarding information that they do not consider relevant.

3. Due to the contingent nature of memory, different recollections and, indeed, interpretations may be evoked in different contexts.
4. Informants may add a significant aspect of interpretation that may shape their descriptions or may suggest that a practice was understood as they interpret it when it was originally performed.

Given these pitfalls, the discussion of practice has a different focus than might often be found. While I am interested in the practices that people actually followed and the way they understood them, and where possible (particularly when the practices are still performed) will explore these aspects, my main interest is how practices are understood by individuals today. Thus, I consider them as elements out of which individuals construct meaning, rather than as ways of acting. Many of the individuals were interviewed on multiple occasions in order to allow for the contingencies of memory and to look at the different interpretations offered. This approach transforms the drawbacks into assets, because each involves a process of constructing meaning out of experience and memory. This being said, I limit the material discussed to those practices that respondents stated they had either performed themselves or observed directly, rather than including the wide range of practices that they were told about as having occurred in the remote past.

In considering the breadth of traditions described by crypto-Jews, it immediately becomes apparent that they look to a broad range of cultural sources. This syncretistic approach seems, as suggested by David Gitlitz (1996), to have been characteristic of crypto-Jewish culture since its origins in fourteenth- and fifteenth-century Spain. The practices include elements taken from Spanish, Mexican, Native American, and Euro-American culture, as well as, arguably, Anglo-Jewish culture. Other elements specific to crypto-Jewish society, particularly secrecy, also play a significant role in shaping these practices.

Bricolage: Construction of Crypto-Jewish Practice

The word "bricolage" was coined by Claude Lévi-Strauss (1966:16–36) to describe the process by which cultural objects—including myth and ritual—were created. The French term *bricoleur* is similar to the English concept of tinker, and bricolage is the process of taking a variety of elements that happen to be available and reusing them for a new purpose. The difference between bricolage and the work of a tinker is that bricolage is unconscious. The tinker creates an airplane out of bits and pieces of a car, a sewing machine, and a sofa; the pattern and the goal of the process are conscious. The *bricoleur* creates cultural objects out of bits and pieces of heterogeneous cultural contexts; the pattern by (and the goal for) which these pieces are put together is unconscious. It is this pattern or structure that makes the cultural item work.

The context out of which the crypto-Jews create their practices is relatively large, due to the overlapping cultures of which they have been part. The way that the elements are put together (that is, structured) is constrained by the patterns and variations associated with the ideal types of crypto-Jewish identity. The interesting aspect of crypto-Jewish ethnography is the presence of both variations on these patterns (for example, the emphasis on the Jewish or the Christian elements of a cultural object) and differences in structure (for example, the oppositional pattern of the strong crypto-Jewish identity and the mediated pattern of the weak one). The cultural objects created through this unconscious process often are able to fit in with these differing structural models.

Bricolage, particularly in a context in which many rituals exist in memory and story rather than in current practice, occurs on several complex levels. The main aspect, which is the primary focus of this chapter, is the creation of a cultural object. This level is also the focus of most discussions of these practices that argue about whether they have Jewish origins. Are they syncretistic, or is the Jewish association based on a false analogy? There is, however, and in relation to a culture of memory, a more important level on which bricolage occurs—in the process of telling and retelling, remembering and re-remembering. As an informant describes a practice from his or her past, a process of reconstruction occurs: the practice is shaped and interpreted by current knowledge. Thus if an interviewee has learned about mainstream Jewish ideas, he may unconsciously bring them into the construction of the memory. This is not, however, an argument for ignoring the memories and stories of crypto-Jews. It merely indicates that the process of cultural creation and re-creation did not occur only in the past, but occurs with each new instantiation of a practice—whether it is performed physically or narratively.

Some scholars have used the concept of compartmentalization to examine how individuals or communities can hold two different and, perhaps, mutually exclusive cultural or religious traditions at the same time. The approach suggests that the material can be placed in separate categories and thus remain largely discrete (see, for example, Dozier 1961, 1970). On the basis of this approach, we might expect that crypto-Jews would have two sets of traditions: a public Christian set and a private Jewish set that is largely untouched by the Christian cultural forms. The compartmentalization theory assumes that these traditions are based largely on content and do not include different ways of structuring or conceptualizing the world. If culture is more than merely content, it seems unlikely that two ways of structuring material could be maintained over an extended period of time. The evidence from crypto-Judaism suggests that such compartmentalization may be possible only in the short term. Both historically and currently, the material from different cultural contexts has been brought together in new forms that reflect in part a synthesis of different ways of thinking about and structuring reality. The complex means by which crypto-Jews relate the different aspects of their experience—outlined in the discussion of the four ideal types—involve a synthesis of Jewish and Catholic models of relating categories—that is, in a strongly oppositional way for the strong type and a more mediated or overlapping way for the weak type. In this sense, both the models of thinking and the content of those models, whether Christian or Jewish, are combined to create both new models and new content that is characteristic of crypto-Jewish culture rather than either Jewish or Catholic culture (or, indeed, any of the other cultures that come into the crypto-Jewish mix).

The nature of crypto-Jewish culture and practice is perhaps more complex than many other cultural contexts, both religious and secular, although perhaps it has close relations with the way that postmodern cultures are developing, due its focus on the idiosyncratic history of particular families. Unlike other models of culture, which through constructs reflect a degree of boundedness often in relation to geography, that of crypto-Judaism does not have a basis in common geography or—until recently in a significant sense—in bounded identity. Although there were some connections between families, practices and identity were focused largely on the individual (perhaps extended) family rather than on a larger community. Thus each family has its own history of movement; its own set of practices, which may or may not be interpreted; and its own engagement with the different elements out of which its cultural identity is constructed. Unlike many other cultural contexts, in which the process of enculturation both occurs in the family and is supported and enhanced by larger social processes, crypto-Jewish enculturation was restricted and thus was both idiosyncratic and precarious.

The general absence of compartmentalization and the particularized family historical journeys are significant factors in the development of crypto-Jewish identities, emphasizing that the practices we find today are likely to be both individualized and based on cultural synthesis. It is also important to reiterate some of the issues raised in chapter 3 relating to the effects of conversion and expulsion on the maintenance and transmission of Jewish knowledge. As both David Gitlitz (1996) and Renée Melammed (1999) observed, much of the public sphere (and, indeed, the private sphere) of Jewish practice was based on a complex system of textual knowledge and a core of authorities, the rabbis, who were trained to interpret and explain those texts. With the expulsion of the Jews from Spain in 1492, both the texts and the authorities became unavailable to crypto-Jews. Gitlitz's analysis suggests that this led to significant transformations in the content of crypto-Jewish practice. Based on this historical evidence, it seems equally likely that this process of simplification based on memory and oral tradition would continue, with different families preserving different aspects of the tradition and different levels of content. Although I disagree with Melammed on the extent of the move of power from men to women, her discussion indicates that women took on a much more significant role than they traditionally had played in Jewish practice, which had a potentially transformative effect on the nature and content of crypto-Jewish practice.

It is unlikely, therefore, that crypto-Jewish practices remained largely unchanged between the late fourteenth and the early twenty-first century. The community as a whole and each family interacted with a range of cultural contexts, each of which transformed the content and shape of crypto-Jewish culture. Minimally, I would expect that elements that relied on complex knowledge might be lost or simplified; maximally, I might expect that elements merged with those of the various cultures with which crypto-Jews interacted, potentially, significantly transforming the way that the practices are structured.

Bricolage: Types of Crypto-Jewish Practice

Contemporary crypto-Jewish practices combine Jewish and Christian, primarily Catholic, elements; reshape Jewish rituals to accommodate to new conditions; include secrecy as a key component; and incorporate aspects of mainstream Judaism.

Practices with Jewish and Catholic Elements

In exploring the relationship between crypto-Jewish history and practice, it is clear that the most important overlap was between Jewish and Catholic culture. This was largely true whatever the individual response was to either religion. Thus even Jews who truly converted to Catholicism likely retained aspects of their previous cultural and religious forms and, to a large extent, Catholicism in relation to Judaism. This process would have been even more significant among those *conversos* who retained a strong sense of Jewish—now crypto-Jewish—identification. From the other perspective, the need to publicly espouse Catholicism, the penetration of that religion into the homes of all *conversos*, and the resultant enculturation into Spanish (Hispanic) Catholic culture progressively affected the cultural forms created and used by crypto-Jews. Thus it is not surprising that many practices described by crypto-Jews include apparently Catholic influences.

It is important to emphasize that I am not suggesting that these practices were consciously constructed; indeed, bricolage is largely an unconscious process. Rather, elements of practice, or ritemes, that were available in the larger Catholic and Jewish cultural environment were used to create and re-create syncretistic cultural practices. It is also likely that, due to the nature of crypto-Jewish identity, the mixture of ritemes facilitated the development of these forms of practice, as they could be reinterpreted and differently emphasized by individuals or groups with different ways of viewing the relation between the Catholic and Jewish aspects of identity.

Rituals associated with Friday night, the start of the Jewish Sabbath, are some of the most widely reported that exhibit this form of bricolage. The kiddush, or blessing over wine, is part of traditional Jewish practice. On Friday night, a particular blessing is recited, associating the wine with the celebration of Shabbat. The kiddush is traditionally associated with a second blessing, the motzi, which is recited before eating bread. On Friday night and Saturday, to emphasize the significance of the practice on the Sabbath, a special bread is eaten—the egg-rich, braided challah.

Although I have not found any evidence of a general practice concerned with drinking wine or eating bread, many crypto-Jews describe rituals related to bread and wine associated with Friday night. *Emma*, a resident of

Taos who was born in the 1950s in a small village to the south of Taos, described a practice that she and her family continue to perform on Friday night:

> On Friday we clean the house, and come together at night. I take a cup of wine and some bread. We dip the bread in the wine and then eat it. We do not say any words, but my mother told me we do it because we were Jews. (*Emma*, July 1999)

Similar practices have been reported by other crypto-Jews from Santa Fe and Albuquerque. In some cases, their ritual is identical to that described by *Emma*; in others, they mention words being said before the bread and wine are eaten. *Maria* was observed to recite a blessing before eating and drinking; her blessing thanked god for the bread and wine. It was relatively simple; she translated it as "Blessed is God for giving us this wine.'" It is perhaps notable that *Maria* used Dio in place of the name Dios. Dio is used (ungrammatically) instead of Dios to indicate the belief in one god rather than the three persons of the Trinity. None of the interviewees claimed a tradition in their families of saying blessings in Hebrew. Some suggested that they did have blessings in archaic Spanish, which they associated with Judeo-Spanish, or Ladino. (None, however, shared the words of these blessings with me or continued to use them themselves, even if they maintained the practice of drinking wine on Friday night.)

The practice is understood by many crypto-Jews to relate to the Jewish rituals performed on Friday night. Some individuals who are now associated with synagogues in Albuquerque made a direct association between their practice and the rituals they have seen, particularly in the Reform temple. Others, from parts of New Mexico more remote from organized Jewish communities or less aware of mainstream Jewish practice, may have a family tradition that the practice is related to their crypto-Jewish identity but do not associate it with current Jewish ritual. Still other respondents, as with all the practices described in this chapter, may have no explanation or interpretation of the practice, regarding it as merely a family tradition.

The most significant difference between the crypto-Jewish and mainstream Jewish traditions is found in the act of dipping the bread into the wine and then eating the bread, rather than consuming them separately. The way that the ritual is described by many crypto-Jews, connecting the bread and wine, is similar to the way they describe taking Communion during the Catholic Mass—although none of the interviewees made this link consciously. It is possible that this ritual is the outcome of a process of bricolage, bringing together the Jewish ritemes associated with Friday night—the blessings over the wine and bread—and the Catholic riteme associated with the Mass.

A second practice associated with Friday night, lighting candles, highlights this form of bricolage. Within mainstream Jewish practice, it is traditional to light two candles on Friday evening to bring in the Sabbath. This ritual is performed by most Orthodox and Conservative Jews and many Reform Jews. It has also been reported as being practiced by crypto-Jews in both New Mexico and other parts of the Spanish diaspora, many of whom light the candles without reciting a blessing or offering an explanation for the practice. But some do give a reason. Fay Blake (1997) reported the following statement by a crypto-Jew she interviewed:

We are Catholic now, but my family was once Jewish—back in Spain. I light candles in their memory. It's good to know who you come from. The Jewish people are smart people; I like the thought that I have Jewish blood. . . . I don't want to forget who my people were, so I light candles on Friday night. (18)

This explanation is similar to many that I have heard. Many individuals also emphasize that these traditions have been passed down from previous generations; for example, several said, "I saw our mother and grandmother do this on Friday night."

Five families in New Mexico, however, perform a ritual connected with lighting candles on Friday night that is distinctive. They enter a back room or close the curtains, and sit at a table. As a woman lights the candles, she recites the Rosary. Members of the families offered three main explanations. Several said they knew that it was different from what their neighbors did, but they did not know why they did it and assumed it was for some Catholic reason. Others, who knew about crypto-Jewish traditions in their families past, stated that they knew that lighting candles on Friday night is a Jewish practice, but they also considered the Rosary to be important and powerful words. A small number of respondents, from one part of the family with strong crypto-Jewish identity, acknowledged that they said the Rosary only to cover up the fact that they were performing a Jewish ritual.

This practice provides strong evidence for the process of bricolage. The Jewish and Catholic elements are brought together in a way that creates a novel ritual, distinct from the components from which it was constructed.

Perhaps the most interesting aspect of this example is the variation of interpretations by individuals with different self-identifications, which seems to be facilitated by the composite nature of the ritual.

Other practices unconnected with Friday night also contain a similar mix of Catholic and Jewish elements. One practice associated with ritual purity presents a variation on the theme. It was described by *Frank*, a resident of Albuquerque born in the 1940s, who stated that his mother and grandmother kept a bowl of water and herbs in their rooms, under a picture (*retablo*) of a female saint. They used the water to purify themselves after menstruation. He associated the practice with the biblical requirement and the Jewish practices relating to *nidah*. In his view, it was Jewish, although the picture of the saint was also an important part of it. A second version of this ritual was described by *Martin*:

> Why do the women have a cup of water and piece of bread near a *retablo* of saints, and why do they put a coin every month and why do they pray before it. It's the purification . . . the coin, the circle for the cleaning, and the water's the purification and the bread [*inaudible*]—so that's left over from centuries ago when in Spain you'd go to the rabbi and pay your shekel . . . if you purified the woman. My mother did it; my sister did it and everything else. Finally, it wasn't until many years later that I was told. Because you had to grow up in a Catholic environment, my mother would always say "Well, it's for, because women in [*inaudible*] communities have a different heart . . . a woman becomes a lioness. (*Martin*, August 1998)

This excerpt clearly associates this variation on the practice with Jewish purification rituals.

This practice is particularly interesting because its "Jewish" element is different from the traditional Jewish form, which involves going to a ritual bath (*mikveh*) and immersing oneself. The ritual, however, is similar to crypto-Jewish practices in seventeenth-century Spain (Gitlitz 1996:273–274). It also fits into the wider context of rituals of purification described by other crypto-Jews in New Mexico.

A second practice unconnected with the Sabbath that brings together a reshaped Jewish element and Catholic aspects is found in northern New Mexico. It involves the placement of two pieces of metal in the shape of a cross on the doorpost of houses. One informant said that his village was divided into two groups: one with and the other without crypto-Jewish identity. The identity, although kept quiet, was common knowledge. Only individuals who came from the crypto-Jewish part of the village placed these crosses on their doors. Residents of other villages also described this practice; all of them explained it in the same way.[2] According to them, the cross was not a sign of Christianity, but of Judaism. Some used the word "Ladino" to refer to Jews. The cross was meant to fulfill the biblical precept of having God's word on the doorpost of a Jewish house. Some, who were aware of the practices of modern Judaism, associated these crosses with mezuzahs.

The metal cross, like the herbs and water, alludes to a Jewish practice but is in many respects an innovation. The traditional mezuzah is a parchment scroll, inscribed with verses written in Hebrew from Deuteronomy 6:4–9 and 11:13–21, that is placed in a decorative case affixed to a doorpost. While many Orthodox and Conservative Jews place mezuzahs on the jambs of most doors in the house, some attach them to only the external doorposts. The object used in crypto-Jewish practice is significantly different in that it does not include the parchment scroll. Nonetheless, all the interviewees clearly associated the metal cross with the biblical text or used the term "mezuzah." The Christian element, the crucifix shape, is interpreted by most crypto-Jews whose families followed this tradition as being a form of cover to hide a Jewish practice. Some individuals also added words to the effect that "It's a powerful object, and it's good to play it safe."

Some discussions of crypto-Judaism have suggested that the scroll from a mezuzah might be hidden in the doorpost, perhaps under an image of a saint. While this may be true in other contexts, none of the respondents suggested that the crosses marked the spot of secret mezuzah scrolls. Some traditional mezuzahs have been found in the walls of houses in Albuquerque (Hordes 2005:267). There is, however, significant difficulty in contextualizing these examples, and they are a very different phenomenon than that discussed here.

The use of more formal crucifixes as a means to hide Jewish parchments and, occasionally, to function as mezuzahs has been mentioned by crypto-Jews from all parts of New Mexico. Many have described crucifixes with cavities in the back, in which, they suggest, parchments or other religious items were hidden. Most informants did not suggest that they had seen these parchments, but that there was a tradition in their families that the scrolls were in the crucifixes. One individual from Taos, who had a strong interest in New Mexican folklore, owned such a crucifix, which was sealed. He stated that the parchment in the cross had Hebrew words on it, but it is impossible to confirm his claim. Thus, although I have seen a number of these crucifixes, I have never seen any actual parchments.

Many of these crucifixes fit, in one sense, within Catholic Hispano material culture, with the cavity in the back being to hold either holy water or a stand for the cross. Thus their use and origin is distinct from any aspect of historical crypto-Judaism. This, however, does not mean that they have no authentic meaning or value to crypto-Jews today. While it is possible that some were used to hide Jewish objects, even if this were not the case, the family tradition that they were used in that way allows these objects to be expressive of crypto-Jewish identity. Thus although they do not necessarily speak to historical crypto-Jewish authenticity, they do play an important role in current crypto-Jewish cultural authenticity.

One additional example in this category is the tradition of venerating Saint Esther. It has led to some specific challenges by Judith Neulander (2001) and thus it is worthwhile examining in some detail. Many individuals, including several crypto-Jews interviewed for this study, indicated that their families venerated Saint Esther because they considered her to represent the biblical Esther. Several also said that their mothers or grandmothers had *retablos* of this saint in their houses, even though no other statues or paintings of saints were permitted. This practice utilizes a clearly Catholic object, attaching to it an additional level of Jewish meaning. For different individuals, Saint Esther can express either Jewish or Christian identity— or, indeed, a syncretistic aspect of both.

Some of the initial discussion of this saint suggested that no such saint existed and thus the practice represented a crypto-Jewish innovation— inventing a saint as a connection with a biblical Jewish past. Neulander argued that in the Catholic list of saints there is a Saint Esther, who has nothing to do with the biblical Esther. Thus families that displayed images of Saint Esther were not necessarily crypto-Jews, but Catholics who venerated a rather unpopular saint.

While Neulander's arguments are technically correct, I am not convinced that they are decisive. It is important to take seriously the internal point of view. The individuals interviewed for this study believed that Saint Esther was an authentic saint, not invented by crypto-Jews, and was the biblical character. They claimed that their mothers and grandmothers had chosen to venerate Saint Esther, not because she was a saint, but specifically because it allowed them to express their crypto-Jewish identity. Other crypto-Jews have interpreted other images as depicting biblical characters, like Saint Job and Saint Moses (Tobias 1990:19); they, too, suggested that they had a connection to them as Jewish figures, not Catholic saints.

The veneration of Saint Esther by crypto-Jews in New Mexico can be contextualized within the larger crypto-Jewish and *converso* experience. Simon Schama's (1999:430–431) description of Jews and *conversos* in seventeenth-century Amsterdam provides evidence for the existence of a similar practice. He describes the experience of Portuguese "New Christians" in Amsterdam: "Most of the first generation of the Sepharadim were hardly recognizable as Jews at all. As 'New Christian' Marranos [*sic*] in Iberia, they had to walk a fine line between self-protecting conformity and oblivion. . . . Some of the festivals—Passover especially—were surreptitiously observed. . . . The heroine of an older persecution was invoked as 'St. Esther'" (Schama 1999:431). Schama's work indicates that the veneration of Saint Esther was not limited to New Mexico and provides support for seeing it as an authentic crypto-Jewish practice.

The process that I see in relation to these saints fits in with the model of bricolage. The riteme of the saint is taken out of its Catholic context and restructured to be expressive of Jewish identity. The significant feature that allows this to occur is the coincidence of names or other means of interpretation. The crypto-Jews are thus utilizing elements that are superficially Catholic, but due to their possible association with Judaism or Jews become private means of expressing crypto-Jewish identity.

This process of identification on the surface seems similar to Neulander's concept of false analogy. In one sense it is a false analogy: the object or practice being given Jewish significance originally was not Jewish. In another sense, however, this argument misses the point. Objects and practices do not have intrinsic meanings. Even if they originate with one meaning, as in the case of Saint Esther, processes including bricolage can move them into a new cultural context, where they can take on a different meaning. Thus any argument that focuses on the genesis of an object or a practice and on "original" meaning is likely to miss the inherent possibility of fluidity as the object or practice is taken into new contexts and cultures.

Additional examples of this category of bricolage share a structural pattern, although applied to very different life-cycle events: birth and marriage. In both these examples (and possibly in relation to death as well), the Catholic element is retained through a public ceremony—that is, baptism or marriage—and subverted by a private crypto-Jewish ceremony.

Several individuals from the small villages to the south of Taos reported the following practice associated with baptism, as described in the version presented by *Marta*:

> I was little when I saw this. When a child was born, he had to be baptized in the church. We would take him to the church to baptize him and give him a name. Afterward, when the priest was gone, we would all get together . . . all of the crypto-Jews. We washed the baby with perfume and gave it a new name, his real name. (*Marta*, August 1999)

Informants from Albuquerque described similar practices, many of them using water instead of perfume. Interestingly, analogous practices have been reported in Portugal, and I heard about an identical practice from an interviewee in Puerto Rico in 2006.[3] This practice is particularly interesting. While it brings together Catholic and Jewish elements, the former is not included in an ambiguous way—potentially positive or negative. The opposition between the two traditions is strongly maintained, and the rejection of the Catholic practice is accomplished by both washing the baby and changing his or her name. Both baptism and a Catholic name are clearly understood as required merely to fit into the public Catholic world.

The practice associated with marriage occurred prior to the public wedding. On the night before, a formal meeting was held between the two families; this was regarded as either the betrothal ceremony or, by some, the actual marriage ceremony. The key events included drinking wine and sometimes exchanging gifts. While this type of practice may have been found in the larger Hispano community, the significant aspect was how the ceremony was perceived. The crypto-Jews, from towns near Taos, who described this ceremony, which included only the ceremonial drinking of wine by the bride and groom, said that it was the real wedding, with the Catholic or Protestant wedding being performed only to keep the church happy.

A similar practice, although much more elaborated, was described by *Martin*:

> And so when it comes time for the marriage . . . they get married in a Catholic church, but the night before all the families meet together. We go through the same thing . . . then the father of the groom and his mother come and stand in the middle of the room, and [*inaudible*] and they formally ask each other if they

still want to be married; they have to anyway, in our family. It's not a democracy. It's just a courtesy. And they say yes. You know, they're going to get married in the church in the morning. But what happens, and it's very, very beautiful, because they agreed, the oldest person in the room [*inaudible*], the man first and then the woman. Then he must present her [with] a *rebozo*—a covering for Spanish women—a white one. He covers her. She must give him a belt with a silver buckle. She puts it around him. Symbolically, it means now he is betrothed to her, and she basically got the fattened calf. But he covers her up, and I found out that it means [*inaudible*] that he has chosen her and he is legally, basically, married to her. (*Martin*, August 1998)

This variant has the same elements as that described by the crypto-Jews from near Taos, with the added element of the exchange of gifts.

One informant described a wedding ceremony that was more distinctive, performed after the church wedding. The bride and groom exchanged glasses of wine (other respondents mentioned two glasses). He also mentioned a written or, more often, an oral contract stating that the new family would live under the laws of Moses. This description has clear similarities to the rabbinic form of marriage ceremony used by all branches of mainstream Judaism. Although this particular practice was mentioned by only one individual, from northern New Mexico, some elements of it were described by other interviewees from the same region.

The baptism and wedding rituals are structurally similar. They include both Christian and Jewish elements (or elements perceived as being Jewish), which are understood to be in an oppositional relationship. The ultimate conclusion of each is a structural rejection of the Christian half of the practice, emphasizing that the two halves are mutually exclusive. Unlike other examples of Christian–Jewish bricolage, these practices are reported only by individuals with a strong crypto-Jewish identity, in which the Jewish aspect is emphasized in relation to the Christian.

Alongside these rituals, which represent the subversion of Christian practice through its association with the alternative crypto-Jewish practice, many individuals report patterns of more direct conscious or unconscious subversion. Images and statues of saints, Jesus, and the Holy Family are a common feature of Hispano households in New Mexico. While some crypto-Jews have indicated that they never had these objects of veneration in their houses, others do mention their presence. A woman from Taos said that her family put all its *santos* in a public room, in which the family entertained the priest; thus publicly, they seemed to be good practicing Catholics. In all the other rooms of the house, they had no *santos* at all; it was in these rooms, she suggested, that they expressed their secret identity as crypto-Jews.

Other individuals' descriptions suggest a more oppositional use of these Catholic images. Several interviewees described their grandmothers' or grandfathers' practices associated with Friday night, such as lighting candles. Before these rituals were performed, the images were turned to the wall. Some interviewees thought that their grandparents may have known about their Jewish heritage, while others believed that they did not, and the turning of the pictures was just a family tradition.[4]

An interesting tradition will provide the final example of this form of bricolage: a stated aversion to the color yellow. Although its exact origins are unclear, I have chosen to include it here as it may have reflected an aspect of Hispano culture, but has been reinterpreted by crypto-Jews in light of both knowledge and experience. The following statement was made by *Maria* and is matched by similar statements by *Roland*, a resident of Albuquerque who was born in the 1950s, and his wife, *Josephina*, both of whom were closely related to *Maria*:

> Yellow, we didn't wear yellow. No, yellow was the sign of the Inquisition. No yellow. There was this cousin of mine by the name of Sarah. And they had given us our allowance. We were, I was already driving a car; Sarah was young. Everybody's younger than me. [*Laughter*] Younger than me, about two years, and we went downtown because we were going to buy blouses. And I bought a blue one, because I knew better than to buy yellow. She bought a yellow, and when we got home and, well, we showed our blouses. And Mother looked at Sarah and said, "You'd better return that before you show it to your mother." "Why?" she said. "I look nice in yellow." She had very pretty golden hair. Longish hair, and she was a beautiful girl. So she says, "I don't think my mother would object." So the next place we went, I had to take Sarah home, and Tía R . . . was there and we showed her our blouses and . . . her eyes grew angry. Her hands grew tense, and she stretched that blouse in a mean way, as though she wanted to kill it, crush it, and she said, "Sarah, sit down. I'll tell you why I don't want you to wear yellow." And then she told us the story, how in Spain they either had to wear a yellow ribbon or some sign that they were Jews, and they used yellow. This is what is so interesting to me that during the Holocaust they also used the yellow star. (*Maria*, August 2000)

The rejection of yellow was restated in several interviews with other crypto-Jews. While the origins of this practice are ambiguous, the levels of interpretation that have been added to it have transformed it into a practice that retains its power for these individuals and is expressive of their understanding of past and present crypto-Jewish identity.

Practices with Jewish and Local Elements

Perhaps the classic form of bricolage includes a range of rituals that largely retain aspects of traditional Jewish form but transform practices due to a change in context, both cultural and environmental. Some of the practices that combine Jewish and Catholic elements also fit into this category. Thus, for example, the purification ritual can be regarded as one that takes the Jewish practices associated with *nidah* and reshapes them in the new context in which the ritual bath (*mikveh*) is no longer available. The retelling of the story of the journey of the Israelites through the desert associated with Sukkot and, for some crypto-Jews, with Passover is also an example of this, with elements of the crypto-Jewish experience replacing or joining the original biblical narrative. The key aspect of this group of practices is that although the elements are replaced, the cultural role and meaning of the practices remain unchanged, although the conscious association of the practices with their Jewish roots may be absent or lost.

This is one area in which Judith Neulander's (2001) discussion of false analogy is relevant. Some of the rituals highlighted by crypto-Jews as being reformulated traditional Jewish practices may, in fact, have non-Jewish cultural origins and merely be similar to Jewish practices. This is, however, an argument about historical authenticity. Thus although the direct association of some rituals with historical Jewish practices may be absent or not provable, crypto-Jews interpret these practices as expressive of both Jewish past and crypto-Jewish present, and thus they are culturally authentic, expressing a real crypto-Jewish identity.

One of the most complex set of rituals that exemplified this type of bricolage was described by *Hannah*, a resident of Albuquerque who was born in the 1940s. They were performed in the autumn, and *Hannah* associated them with the festival of Sukkoth. The key component of the practice, the sukkah, or harvest booth, was similar to that found in the traditional Jewish celebration of the holiday (and also similar to harvest booths used in other folk traditions). It was a temporary booth, with walls made from branches and decorated with items associated with the harvest. She called this booth a *jacal*, equating it with the Hebrew word for "temple."[5] The family ate in the *jacal*, which *Hannah* suggested remained up for several days.

The second aspect of the practice, relating to the *lulov* and *etrog*, however, evidenced significant aspects of bricolage. *Hannah* used these traditional Hebrew words to describe a related set of ritual objects used during Sukkoth in all mainstream Jewish communities. The *lulav* (bundle composed of the branches of palm, willow, and myrtle) and the *etrog* (citron) perhaps are associated with rain. *Hannah* said that her *lulav* was composed of branches from trees other than the traditional species, including sweet or lemon grass; she could not remember which others were used, although she thought that one might have been willow. Other individuals stated that they used only willow for the *lulav*. The citron was replaced by a quince. Although other respondents mentioned a range of fruits, the quince seems to be the most consistently used. The quince appears to have an important symbolic resonance for many families, with some seeing it as symbolizing the crypto-Jew.

Hannah described the way these objects were used:

> We took the quince and the grass—and some other branches, which we call now the *lulav* and *etrog*. We held them and shook them in four directions. We then touched piles of food from our harvest. These were given to each person in my family. (*Hannah*, August 1997)

Her description indicates that she did not use the Hebrew terms for these objects in the past. It also presents a practice that is similar to that of traditional Judaism, with the addition of touching the piles of harvested produce. *Hannah* also explained that, as a child, she had understood this ritual as being connected to the journey of her Jewish ancestors to New Mexico, especially through the desert in the southern part of the state:

> The *jacal* was a very humble shelter that they built in the desert. As they were walking, they would get these branches from trees and tie them with the, whatever they could find. Ah, that would be a stem of something of a plant and put the branches over that. That was their shelter, but it was also their prayer room and a *jacal*. (*Hannah*, August 1997)

She added that today she knew that it was also connected to the trek of the Israelites through the desert. Other crypto-Jews made a more direct association of the practice to the biblical journey of the Israelites following the Exodus from Egypt.

This practice includes a significant number of elements that are similar to those of traditional Jewish celebration of the festival. The process of bricolage is found in relation to objects not easily available in New Mexico— for example, the replacement of the citron by the quince. In spite of these substitutions, the ritual is largely unchanged. *Hannah* and several other crypto-Jews who discussed this practice indicated that they understood it as part of their Jewish inheritance. Others stated that they performed these practices but had no explanation or interpretation.

A second example of this form of bricolage is described by *George*, currently resident in Colorado but whose family originated in the northern part of New Mexico. He remembered foods that were eaten in his grandmother's house in the spring and associated them with Passover. The primary food was wheat tortillas, which his family usually did not eat. The key difference, however, was that his grandmother made the tortillas herself and specifically burned them. He believed that they were meant to be matzo. Similar practices have been mentioned by other crypto-Jews and were reported by David Gitlitz (1996:57, 386). Both *George* and other crypto-Jews added that when the tortillas were made, a small amount of the dough was fashioned into a tiny tortilla. In some families, it was eaten; in others, it was burned to ashes in a fire or an oven. Tomás Atencio (1996:64) describes a similar practice, with a pinch of dough being thrown into a fire. This ritual and that described by *George* is similar to the traditional Jewish practice of bread making.[6]

Different practices relating to circumcision have also been described by many crypto-Jews from all parts of New Mexico. In northern New Mexico, the procedure is usually full circumcision, physically identical to the Jewish practice. Some might suggest that this is not a crypto-Jewish practice, as circumcision is routinely performed in the United States. The regularization of this operation, however, occurred just before World War II and on babies who were born in hospitals. A number of men from northern New Mexico who were born before the war indicated that both they and their fathers had been circumcised.[7] They also suggested that the procedure was very uncommon and that they were teased by other boys because they were circumcised. *Fidel*, born in the 1920s, from outside Española, said that both he and his father had been circumcised, but his three brothers were not. He thought his circumcision had been done by an itinerant healer.

Other individuals indicated that circumcisions were performed by some midwives. The role of the midwife in circumcision has also been reported by Stanley Hordes (2005:230), in relation to individuals not included in this study. Additionally, *Rosa*, a resident of Albuquerque, stated that in her childhood circumcisions were performed by a local man who was also the slaughterer. *Fidel* stated that only he, not his brothers, was told of their Jewish heritage; his father said to him, "No somos cristianos; somos judíos." *Fidel* believed that the decision to circumcise him was connected to choosing him to continue the Jewish traditions in his family.

The following section from an interview with *Vera*, a seventy-four-year-old resident of the Albuquerque area whose family had come from Las Vegas, New Mexico, discusses the attitudes toward circumcision both in her grandparents' and in her generation:

> VERA: As far as I know from my grandmother down, all her brothers were circumcised.
>
> INTERVIEWER: How would you have known that?
>
> V: My grandmother told me.
>
> I: And did she say why they were circumcised?
>
> V: It's cleaner.
>
> I: When would they have been born—your grandmother's brothers?
>
> V: In the 1870s.
>
> I: Would you have any idea where they would have had them done? Who would have done them?
>
> V: I have no idea.
>
> I: But this was when you (they?) were still living in Vallecitos?
>
> V: No. This was when they moved over to Las Vegas.
>
> I: So they were done in Las Vegas?
>
> V: Yes.
>
> I: So that's your grandmother's generation. And your father's generation?
>
> V: My father was circumcised. All her boys were circumcised.
>
> I: And how old was your father . . . ?
>
> V: Three days
>
> I: When was he born?
>
> V: Oh, boy. 1905.
>
> I: They were all three days?
>
> V: Three to five days. My brother was circumcised. My father insisted . . . it was cleaner.

I: When was your brother born?

V: 1932 or '33.

I: And he was born in Las Vegas?

V: My brothers and sisters were all born in California. I was the only one born in New Mexico.

I: So in your generation, do you have any idea who did the circumcisions? Was it done in the hospital?

V: My brother was done by the doctor. And my boys were done by the doctor, when they were born, as soon as they were born.

I: Did you have the sense that was something only done in your family or was it done by other people around?

V: I didn't have any sense of that.

I: Was there any sense that it was done against the wishes of the larger society?

V: He [the priest] just berated them for circumcising.

I: Who did he berate?

V: My grandmother.

This interview is interesting in several respects. Although *Vera* had learned of her Jewish heritage from the same grandmother mentioned in this part of the interview (on a trip to New Mexico), her grandmother did not connect circumcision to Jewish heritage. Nonetheless, the interview reveals that the practice was continued, despite the opposition of the priest, and over several generations, two of which preceded the introduction of circumcision as a public-health measure.

The practice of circumcision discussed to this point is largely similar to that followed by mainstream Jews. There are two minor differences: the operation does not conform to the legal details of Jewish circumcisions, and it does not seem to necessarily have been performed on the eighth day. Interviewees from the southern part of New Mexico described a variation on the practice that may have its roots in the early modern period.[8] Several individuals from Santa Fe and Albuquerque, including *Martin*, said that although they were not fully circumcised, they had a slit cut in their foreskin that was meant to be a symbolic circumcision. They suggested that this tradition persisted in their families because it was too dangerous to be fully circumcised. According to *Martin*,

Some were. But I'll tell you why a lot were not. What they would do is they pulled the foreskin over and cut a slit into it. That's the way that would be. But with me, they found out I was a bleeder, and that could be very disastrous, so I had to take coagulation. . . . But it was done then. Why? Because Spanish people when they had a suspicion of something . . . now when you're young . . . and you have water . . . what do boys do? They strip themselves totally naked and go into the water. In those times, say fifty years ago, the majority of the gentiles did not circumcise, so it was a dead giveaway. So with us, having that scar we knew, but we were basically like the other ones; they couldn't judge you by that. But there were families that did circumcise; I remember one family. There were always risks because it was hot, kids would jump in the water, and you see this and they get hit, punched around. . . . This young man that I was telling you about, thirty-two years old, that's exactly what happened to him when he was nine or ten. They went swimming . . . by the river . . . and he literally got beaten within an inch of his life. (*Martin*, August 1999)

Martin's statement is interesting for both its description of the operation and its acknowledgment of the fear associated with being publicly differentiated. It also indicates, in support of statements by other informants, that some families in the Albuquerque area appear to have practiced full circumcision on their sons.

Several respondents, including *Martin* and *Maria*, described practices associated with the period in early autumn coinciding, according to them, with Yom Kippur. This is taken from an interview with *Martin*:

The other thing was that we always did this great fast that came out about the time now that regular Jews celebrated Yom Kippur. We would all go out into the open fields and get wild spinach. . . . [W]e were not allowed, even if it was hot, to take water or eat anything. . . . Why were we picking food and we can't eat? Toward the evening, we were given water . . . in little clay jars . . . and then we were washed, and we drank the water after we washed our hands. (*Martin*, August 1999)

Martin did not interpret the practice, which had not been explained to him, and made the connection with Yom Kippur only after learning that Jews fast on that High Holy Day. But other interviewees said that the spinach was collected to prevent anyone from realizing that they were fasting. They also stated that they ate the spinach as part of the ritual, although they did not know if the spinach represented anything.

Various food rules are among the most common forms of practice described by crypto-Jews. While in a sense they are similar to those found in early modern Judaism and in contemporary Orthodox and Conservative Judaism, there is an important area of transformation—that is, their complexity and extent. While on the surface traditional Jewish food rules appear relatively simple—for example, requiring the separation of milk and meat—the elaboration of this simple prohibition is very complex and is part of the Jewish literary tradition. Thus based on principles indicated by Gitlitz (1996:37–48), we should not be surprised that the crypto-Jewish practices are much less elaborate and extensive than the mainstream Jewish ones, both historically and currently. Gitlitz suggested that the practices would be both simpler and more biblically based than the rabbinically based forms of mainstream Judaism. Both of his suppositions seem to be borne out in crypto-Jewish practice.

The prohibition on the consumption of pork is one of the most common practices among crypto-Jews. While sometimes it is tied to crypto-Jewish identity, it also is attributed to dislike, allergy, or merely family tradition. Several individuals highlighted the way their mothers made frijoles as a way to indicate this practice, particularly stating that they never used pork or lard when preparing the beans. Others stated that they were not allowed to eat at other people's houses because they might serve pork. The prohibition on pork was clearly indicated in Inquisition lists of Jewish practice. Some families claimed that they raised pigs as a means of to hide the fact that they never ate them. This proscription also seems to be associated with family conflict, particularly when individuals who followed crypto-Jewish traditions married into families that did not. Thus several informants described conflict between parents and grandparents over this practice.

Within traditional Judaism, there are specific and detailed regulations concerning the ritual slaughter of animals for food. The process, *shechita*, involves slitting an animal's throat with a sharp knife and allowing the blood to drain away. The slaughter is done by specially trained butchers and has very precise specifications. Crypto-Jews from many parts of New Mexico describe ways of slaughtering animals that are similar.[9] While it is possible that a similar form of slaughtering—that is, slitting the throat and hanging the carcass to drain the blood—is practiced by the wider Hispano community, there are aspects particular to some crypto-Jewish families. The most common relates to the blood. The consumption of blood is prohibited in Jewish food rules. Blood was, however, an important source of protein in subsistence-farming communities, often eaten as blood sausage or pudding—called *morcilla* in New Mexico. Many crypto-Jews described the blood being drained away rather than eaten and claimed that their families never ate *morcilla* or made any other use of the blood. Others mentioned bringing their animals to a particular slaughterer who would kill them in a special part of his yard, where pigs were never killed, and pour away the blood rather than retain it. This excerpt from an interview with *Maria* reflects some common themes:

> We had our own kosher meats, and our person that did the slaughtering for us was Don Silverio Gómez. He did it for the community. We also ate fish. Mother would say that that was the cleanest food you could have. (*Maria*, August 2002)

Although this statement shows knowledge of mainstream Jewish practice, similar descriptions were provided by individuals who had little or no knowledge of it.

Atencio (1996) describes a very similar process, suggesting that particularly designated slaughterers used specially shaped knives and that there was a "rabbi to lead the ritual" (64). This aspect has not been mentioned by anyone interviewed for this study. He also mentions that sometimes the blood was drained away and covered and that some butchers removed the nerve from the thigh without knowing the biblical basis for doing so (Atencio 1996:64).

Traditional Jewish food rules also include the separation of milk and meat and the prohibition on the consumption of a much wider range of food, including shellfish. Although these practices are present in New Mexico, they are less widespread than the prohibitions on pork and blood. The relative absence of these strictures matches the historical evidence. Gitlitz (1996:540–541) suggests, for example, that the separation of milk and meat was not widespread among the crypto-Jews.

Alongside these food traditions, which are similar to those practiced by some mainstream Jews, crypto-Jews discussed some distinctive ones. Two foods were related to Passover. A few informants from the Taos region described a cake made from sprouted wheat. Although they did not remember its name, they said that it was eaten in the spring and thought that it was associated with Passover. One of them suggested that sprouted wheat was used because it cannot rise, which the interviewee knew was forbidden in Passover foods. Many informants specifically mentioned *capirotada*, a pudding made with flour or bread, sugar, nuts, and raisins. No yeast was used, which some informants suggested was to prevent the pudding from rising. Nonetheless, the use of flour or bread would have been against rabbinic law. Some informants thought that their mothers added cheese to the pudding, which they believed distinguished it from a similar food eaten by others in the Hispano community at the same time of year. It seems likely that *capirotada* is not a food specific to crypto-Jews; rather, it is a common Easter or spring food. But for many crypto-Jews, it has become associated with Passover and thus through a process of bricolage has become part of their practice of Passover and their identity as crypto-Jews.

Some of the practices associated with the cleaning of houses also fit into this category. Sweeping the floor from the walls to the center of a room has been explained by the belief in house demons and, by those who associated the practice with their crypto-Jewish heritage, by the knowledge that God's name should be on the doorpost in the form of a mezuzah. While I am not aware of any traditional basis for this practice, Schulamith Halevy (1999:80–82) suggests that there is one, and the practice also has been reported by Gitlitz (1996:321) and discussed by Yosef Hayim Yerushalmi (1971:37). Yerushalmi associates the practice with an essay by the seventeenth- to eighteenth-century rabbi and scholar Moses Hagiz, who specifically suggests that it was done this way because of reverence for the mezuzah.

Many crypto-Jews also report cleaning practices associated with Friday. Their mothers and grandmothers would specially clean the house and change the bed linens in some families, this was the only activity that distinguished Friday nights; in others, it was associated with lighting candles or drinking wine. Other individuals mention getting new clothing or having their clothes washed for Friday. Gitlitz (1996:321) reports similar practices by *conversos* in Spain.

Practices with Secrecy as the Key Element

Secrecy is the key component of many of the practices discussed thus far. The explanation given for the form of the practice or the location of its performance is often specifically to prevent others from identifying the individuals as practicing crypto-Jews. Thus the recitation of the Rosary while lighting candles on Friday night, the slit rather than the full circumcision, and the collection of spinach on Yom Kippur are examples of rituals that incorporate secrecy. Many crypto-Jews describe lighting eight candles in December, which they associate with Hanukkah, and doing so in a back room, again with the specific goal of keeping the practice secret.

To a large extent, secrecy is a constituent part of all crypto-Jewish practices—perhaps the most important identifying feature—and the way that most crypto-Jews express their identity. Many outsiders ask why secrecy is still important, given that the Inquisition no longer exists.

The answer to this question is complex. In part, many crypto-Jews fear rejection by or hostility from their families or communities should they publicly express their Jewish identity. This concern is evident in several of the extracts from interviews presented here. Others regard crypto-Judaism as incompatible with Hispanic political identity and wish to continue their activities in that sphere. While these are important motivating factors, based on the pervasiveness of the expression of secrecy, many of these explanations seem to rationalize a need for secrecy that is in fact inseparable from crypto-Jewish identity.

This is illustrated in the following statement from *Anna*, a resident of Albuquerque who was born in the 1950s:

> I cannot discuss this openly or tell people about my family. We are part of a land grant. If the church knew we were Jews, we would lose our rights to be part of it. (*Anna*, August 2001)

Anna's statement reflects a common view, also expressed in a very similar way by *Maria*, that justifies the need for both secrecy and anonymity. Her family claimed to be part of a Spanish land grant that, she believed, was open only to Old Christians (as opposed to New Christians, who were of Jewish descent). She thought that she would lose the opportunities connected to the increasing value of the land should her identity and crypto-Jewish practices be revealed. While it is unlikely that the clause about descent would have any legal standing, this justification was used by *Anna* and many others whom I interviewed to explain their continued secrecy.

Tomás Atencio's (1996) discussion of secrecy is also helpful in understanding this aspect of crypto-Jewish culture. He utilizes the work of Georg Simmel (1906) relating to the stranger and marginality. The stranger is marginal to the society in which she finds herself; she is on the periphery of her new culture, Catholicism, and in a way of her former culture, Judaism. Secrecy and inwardness become the means of protecting the now forbidden Jewish aspects of identity. The secrecy becomes an enduring way of life. The social by-products of secrecy shape both the individual's practices and his way of interacting in society. Atencio particularly focuses on one particular outcome: the nature of communication. He emphasizes that writing was not an appropriate means of communication among crypto-Jews; rather, both practice-based and verbal transmission of cryptic messages was the primary avenues. This cryptic aspect remains and in part leads to the distortion of meaning and form that is found in many crypto-Jewish practices (Atencio 1996:59).

David Gitlitz's (1996) discussion as a whole highlights the fact that transformations of Jewish practices related to secrecy were among the earliest and most pervasive. This is not surprising because fear of the Inquisition was an important motivating factor. In this initial stage, it would not be appropriate to speak of secrecy as part of bricolage; rather, it was a catalyst based on the need to hide the performance of practices from the public gaze. As the rituals and *converso* and crypto-Jewish culture developed over the following centuries, secrecy became one element among others that were unconsciously combined to create crypto-Jewish practice. Today, secrecy is both a key part of the rituals and of crypto-Jewish identity as a whole. Thus crypto-Judaism is still a secret tradition because it is inseparable from that secrecy, which is as much a part of the tradition as are Judaism and Catholicism.

This element in the processes of bricolage has had various effects on crypto-Jewish practice. On the one hand, it has led to Catholic elements being joined to Jewish elements as a means to hide the Jewish aspect of a practice. Interestingly, this amalgamation facilitated the breakdown of barriers created by early compartmentalization. Thus, almost ironically, the effects of secrecy were only in part to preserve Jewish identity; to an even greater extent, they led to the creation of a distinct crypto-Jewish identity, which includes elements from several cultural contexts. On the other hand, secrecy also resulted in the narrowing of crypto-Jewish practice to the private sphere, ceding the public sphere to the wider Spanish Catholic cultural forms.

Practices with Anglo-Jewish Elements

Crypto-Jewish practices that include elements that may have been taken from the current mainstream, or Anglo-Jewish, environment—rather than having roots, at least arguably, in early modern Spain—are both complex and prone to misunderstanding. This form of bricolage brings together the issues of interpretation and reinterpretation and of the use of modern Jewish symbols in the broader range of practice. This may lead some critics to argue that these practices are inauthentic and reflect a broader pattern of cultural invention, but I consider them to indicate cultural vibrancy.

Interpretation is fundamental to understanding this form of bricolage. We have touched on practices that may have originated in the wider Hispano or Hispanic communities—for example, eating *capirotada* around the time of Passover. While it is important to contextualize the genesis of a practice, it is even more important, for the understanding of crypto-Jewish culture, to discern the role of interpretation as part of bricolage in transforming the practice into one that is part of crypto-Jewish culture. Interpretation is thus one element in the complex set of elements brought together to create the cultural object. This process also occurs when an analogy is made between a Hispano or folk practice and a Jewish practice; through the reinterpretation, the resulting practice, although not originally Jewish, becomes in crypto-Jewish culture identical to the Jewish practice.

The interpretation of the four-sided top commonly used in New Mexico provides a very good example of this process, with several possible avenues of appropriation and reinterpretation. The *pon y saca*, or *trompito*, is a top

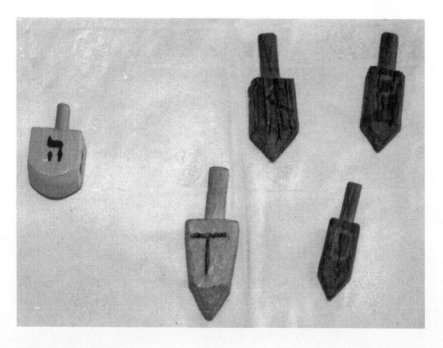

Dreidel and *pon y saca* from northern New Mexico. (Photograph by author)

with which children play around the month of December. Many crypto-Jews and some scholars have associated it with the dreidel used by Jews during the festival of Hanukkah. The following statement from *Marta*, although including a range of explanatory aspects not found in other interviews, is characteristic of many descriptions by crypto-Jews:

> Okay, you know what a dreidel is? Everybody knew how to make a dreidel. That was the way it was. Well, the top came, the new top, and everybody started using the top instead of the dreidel. So my sister used to say about my grandfather, "You know, you really shouldn't play with the top"—they called it the *trompa*—and *trompa* the translation almost means like a snout, to the *trompa* that is made [*inaudible*] had an [*inaudible*] now that's the nose of the devil. You can go ahead and play with it; you can even [*inaudible*] he did not forbid anybody from playing with it, but the dreidel was a different thing. That had the nose of God. Little things that you remember. (*Marta*, August 1999)

This explanation is interesting because it places, at least in *Marta*'s memory, the identification of the *pon y saca* with the dreidel back into her childhood. Other respondents of similar age also suggested that they viewed the top as being a particular Jewish symbol when they were children.

Due to its pervasiveness in the descriptions of practice by both observers and crypto-Jews, the dreidel is commonly assumed to have been part of Spanish Jewish practice and brought to New Mexico by the ancestors of modern crypto-Jews. Other scholars, however, have pointed out that the dreidel as a toy associated with Hanukkah originated in eastern Europe several centuries later than the expulsion of the Jews from Spain (which is suggested by the Yiddish name given to the top). These observers have also noted that a four-sided top is a common folk toy used extensively in the Hispanic community in the autumn and winter (Neulander 1996:22–23).

The coincidence of an existing folk toy and the historical discrepancy have led scholars like Judith Neulander to see the identification of the *pon y saca* with the dreidel as a false analogy, and thus they discount it as a significant feature of crypto-Jewish culture or as an expression of identity. While it is likely that the origin of the use of the *pon y saca* as a Jewish practice is indeed in the shared folk toy, and thus is not Jewish or crypto-Jewish, it is important to emphasize that today, and based on the statements of many crypto-Jews for much of the past century, the *pon y saca* has been an important part of crypto-Jewish cultural practice and regarded as an expression of identity.

There are a number of routes through which the "dreidel" (that is, the toy identified in this way) may have entered into crypto-Jewish practice. While it is clear that the modern false-analogy route suggested by Neulander is one of them, another is by way of Ashkenazic Jews. It is important to emphasize that both this possibly and Neulander's involve a form of reinterpretation characteristic of bricolage.

It is possible that the dreidel, both as an object and as an idea, was borrowed from Ashkenazic Jews, perhaps in the nineteenth or early twentieth centuries. Historical evidence indicates that Jews did come to New Mexico after the annexation of the region by the United States following the Mexican War, and some family traditions among crypto-Jews from Albuquerque suggest that there was some social intercourse and occasional marriages between them and the Ashkenazim. Synagogues were established in 1886 in Las Vegas and in 1896/1897 in Albuquerque. Thus certainly with the establishment of formal Jewish communities, ritual items like dreidels would have been available and may have been associated with Jewish identity. Through a process of bricolage, the dreidel could have been adopted or associated with the *pon y saca*. The suggestion is that crypto-Jews, through a process that may have included both unconscious and conscious elements, borrowed the dreidel because it was publicly identified with Jews and, over time, through the unconscious process of bricolage, integrated it into their practice. Lacking formal evidence, this can be seen as only one supposition among many.

Even if we assume, with Neulander and others, that this process of appropriation was much more recent, and even if its initial impetus was from a false analogy by either insiders or outsiders, the process of bricolage I have described could still have been operative. The interviews indicate clearly that for crypto-Jews today, the *pon y saca* is a dreidel and is expressive of Jewish identity. Thus as a Jewish ritual item, it has clear cultural authenticity even if its historical authenticity is in question. A dreidel or any other object or practice is a crypto-Jewish object or practice if it is so understood by the people who use or perform it—just as a dreidel can become merely a top if that is how it is used and understood.

Several other examples of this form of bricolage have been mentioned in interviews. Thus *Marta*'s grandfather, whom she described as being strongly conscious of his Jewish identity, had brought back from journeys in the western part of the United States objects that were from the mainstream Jewish community. She specifically mentioned his having owned a siddur (printed prayer book) and a tallit (prayer shawl). *Marta* stated that he chose these items and used them as expressions of his connections with Judaism. He wore the tallit, for example, only at weddings. The important point of this example is *Marta*'s explanation for the presence of these objects in her family. From her point of view, although they were not historically part of her family's crypto-Jewish practice, they became part of that practice due to their appropriation and introduction by her grandfather.

A few other objects lack this family context and are more difficult, or perhaps impossible, to properly interpret. A case in point is the mezuzah case described by Stanley Hordes (2005:267). Dating from the 1960s, it was found in the wall of a house that had apparently been lived in by a Hispanic family from 1949 until its sale. If, for the sake of argument, I assume that no Jewish family had lived in the house, I am left with the conundrum of the presence of this specifically Jewish ritual object. The mezuzah case, however, provides no direct or necessary evidence about the motives of those who put it up. Hordes attempted to follow up with the family to find a reason for the presence of the object, but was not able to get an explanation. Thus while the mezuzah case is a possible example of the form of bricolage discussed here, it is also possible that it was put in the wall for entirely different and undiscoverable reasons.

Utilizing the concept of bricolage, this chapter has attempted to outline the complexities of crypto-Jewish practice. Only a subset of the variety of practices found in that community were used to illustrate the various forms of bricolage. While they utilized different elements out of which to build structurally coherent practices, it is the shared structure(s) of the practices that makes them crypto-Jewish, rather than the particular elements. The resultant practices are somewhat more complex and fluid than might have been expected because of the significant variations in the expression of crypto-Jewish identity. The nature of the constituent elements out of which the process of bricolage occurs facilitates the possibilities of fluidity and differential emphasis. Thus certain practices may be used by different parts of the crypto-Jewish culture and carry these variations in structure.

One of the important aspects of the bricolage model is that it is ongoing. The process of cultural creation is not fixed at some point in the past. This is particularly illustrated in the inclusion of interpretation as an aspect of bricolage, thus providing an important theoretical insight—that is, how an object or a practice is interpreted is an object with which the *bricoleur* constructs meaningful rituals in the same way as is any other element of a ritual or a riteme. It is important to emphasize that since the process of cultural creation and appropriation (in all cultures) is continual in present-day practice, it does not provide strong evidence for past practice. This is true of both what people are doing and what they are remembering, as memory is shaped by similar process. It is only to the extent that we can show that present practices were performed in the same way in the past that we can gain insight into how modern crypto-Jews may link to their forebears in terms of practice and culture.

Appendix: Material and Symbolic Culture

Throughout the discussion in this chapter, I have touched on aspects of material culture.[10] Thus, for example, I examined some issues relating to the *pon y saca* and the mezuzah. This appendix explores some wider issues about material culture by focusing on the use of symbols on gravestones. This is done for two reasons. First, the discussion allows us to explore problems in the interpretation of symbols that are found in relation to all aspects of material culture. Second, and perhaps more important, gravestones were the most important objects of material culture used by crypto-Jews in their arguments about authenticity. The search for unambiguous material cultural evidence to provide validation in the face of challenges to authenticity continues to be a significant part of crypto-Jewish argumentation and leads to both a misunderstanding of the material culture identified as Jewish and, perhaps, a search in the wrong places for meaningful crypto-Jewish artifacts.

As noted in chapter 3, gravestones have been used to provide hard evidence for the presence of crypto-Jews in New Mexico. The arguments have utilized two main features of the stones—symbols and names—that have important differences. I will address each in turn.

Many visitors to New Mexican cemeteries have noted the presence on gravestones of a number of symbols commonly associated with Judaism.

Gravestone from eastern New Mexico. Two seven-branched candelabra flank the central cross. (© Cary Hertz Photography)

The most common is the six-pointed star, which is equated with the Star of David. Other symbols include the seven-branched candlestick and hands. Some individuals have gone much further, suggesting that a wide range of symbols used in Jewish cemeteries and occasionally found in New Mexico are also indicative of crypto-Jewish identity. While this contention is the most clearly problematic, as many of the symbols selected would not be identified by most observers as specifically Jewish, there are fundamental problems that challenge the useful interpretation of all this material.

The unstated premise behind these arguments is that symbols have stable meanings and that they express and are understood to express those specific meanings—in other words, that is there is a one-to-one fixed correspondence between the symbol and its meaning. Thus, by focusing on the six-pointed star, it is assumed that this symbol is always the Star of David, in any context, and that this interpretation by the observer is also the interpretation of the person who chose to have the star carved on the stone. Symbols, however, do not intrinsically hold any meaning; the relationship between the signifier (the symbol) and what it signifies (what it means or how it is interpreted) is arbitrary. Their meaning is relative to a specific community (and can vary within a community) and often to a specific time and place. The six-pointed star became a symbol used by Jews in the Middle Ages. It has been used as a marker of Jewish identity on tombstones in Europe for hundreds of years and is even found on a gravestone in Jamaica. However, the symbol is not uniquely Jewish. It frequently appears in Islamic geometric art and not infrequently as a decorative motif, as in the National Cathedral in Washington, D.C. This range suggests that while the six-pointed star (broadly within western European culture) often has a specific Jewish meaning attached to it, due in part to its presence on the Israeli flag, this has not always been the case, either historically or currently.

In New Mexico, we find three types of gravestones on which the six-pointed star is carved. The first, and the most common, are vernacular stones individually carved. Many of them appear to date to the early to mid-twentieth century. Occasionally, the star on these stones is associated with other symbols, including crucifixes and hands. These stones usually are relatively simply carved, with the symbols presented in relief using lines. What can be made of these symbols? As suggested, while the star may indicate Jewish identification, that is only one possible interpretation. The six-pointed star is relatively easy to carve using lines, as it is composed of two intersecting triangles. Thus for a relatively unskilled stone carver, it would

Gravestone from northern New Mexico. Two six-pointed stars are visible under the transverse bar of the cross. (Photograph by author)

be a very simple decorative motif to use. It could equally well have been a design chosen by the family for its own aesthetic reasons, having nothing to do with crypto-Jewish identity.

The second category of stones includes those made by professional stone carvers. Again, the six-pointed star frequently is associated with other symbols, usually of an overtly Christian nature. These stones have the same problem of interpretation as the first, as it is impossible to know from the stone itself how the symbol should be understood. Six-pointed stars were in design books and could have been chosen for a wide range of reasons.

It is clear that, at least in regard to these two categories of stones, the use of a particular symbol is, in and of itself, insufficient to demonstrate crypto-Jewish identity or tradition. The only way to understand the historical meaning of the symbol is either to find appropriate documentary evidence associating the family with crypto-Judaism or, even more important, to interview living family members to determine why they chose to use a particular symbol. Without such evidence, the symbol can be at the most only suggestive of a line of inquiry, but not on its own evidence for that inquiry.

The final category of stones is small but, to my mind, significant. It includes stones on which a six-pointed star either is carved in association with unambiguous Jewish markers or required a choice that was clearly marked as being Jewish. The first of these is exemplified by a stone in northern New Mexico from 1971 (for a photo of the gravestone, see Hordes 2005:257). It has a six-pointed star and the name of the deceased in Hebrew and English, as well as two acronyms, in Hebrew, specifically associated with Jewish burials. The stone has no other symbols. It is in a cemetery with stones bearing the full range of Christian symbols. Although it is impossible, from the stone itself, to know the views of the person buried, the stone must have been carved with the clear understanding of the symbol and the Hebrew words used. Stanley Hordes and I interviewed the brother of the woman buried there, who clearly stated that at the time of his sister's death, their mother had informed him of the family's "Sephardic" identity:

She said "That's who we are. We're Sephardic Jews." (*Juan*, August 2001)

It was this statement that had led the mother to select the stone (Hordes 2005:256). The brother knew that the symbols were Jewish, but did not know what the Hebrew on the stone meant.

The second type of stones in this category is military headstones. At least two examples are mentioned by Hordes (2005:256–259), dating to 1975 and 1983. The significant factor in regard to these gravestones is that the application form required for these stones to be erected offers a choice of religious identifiers, and it is necessary to select "Jewish" to get a stone with the six-pointed star. On both military headstones is a Star of David. Neither of the families that chose these stones was available for interview, and thus it is difficult to fully contextualize them. Both families chose to identify themselves in the official document as Jewish, but it is impossible to provide a context for that understanding and thus difficult to know whether the six-pointed star was understood by the family members as a statement of Jewish identity.

The problems inherent in interpreting the six-pointed star clearly hold true for other symbols. The historic meaning and interpretation of these symbols can be determined only through associated data. This argument, however, does not exhaust the value of these symbols in relation to crypto-Jewish identity. The historical meaning is one cultural horizon that, in many cases, is no longer recoverable. The interpretation given to the gravestones by modern crypto-Jews is a second and equally important cultural horizon. As I have indicated, modern crypto-Jews look on these stones as validating their crypto-Jewish identity. In this sense, the symbols on the stones become crypto-Jewish symbols; the six-pointed star becomes the Star of David. Thus the value of these symbols is not only in their original meaning, but, perhaps even more important, in their current meaning. Just as the meanings of symbols are not fixed, allowing us to interpret their original meaning based on our current understanding, so is the current meaning conceptually separable from the original meaning. Thus an object, such as a gravestone, can become an example of modern crypto-Jewish material culture even if it is no longer possible to determine if it was created as an expression of crypto-Jewish identity.

Names are the second important form of information found on gravestones. While most surnames are not indicative of crypto-Jewish identity (although a few may indicate Jewish origin), given names can be more suggestive. This is particularly true when a family exhibits a pattern of selecting names from the Hebrew Bible as opposed to the New Testament, which is the more common source for names in the Hispanic community. Hordes (2005:224–228) discusses the use of names and demonstrates that the significant increase in the use of names from the Hebrew Bible could not be associated with Protestant missionary work and thus may indicate an expression of crypto-Jewish identity. While that argument is suggestive, it cannot be directly supported by other evidence. Thus when names on gravestones indicate such a pattern, it cannot be viewed as evidence, but provides a direction for interviews and other forms of research.

It is worthwhile highlighting one example touched on in chapter 3. In several cemeteries gravestones can be found with the name Adonai as a given name. The word "Adonai" is the pronunciation of the Hebrew word for "God," often written in Christian texts as "Jehovah." The use of this name is surprising, as Jews traditionally do not pronounce the name of God (although the use of the word "God" as part of biblical names is common). Some have argued that this demonstrates that the deceased could not have been crypto-Jews, as Jews would never ignore this tradition. This, however, seems to be a particularly weak argument, since this type of custom could easily be forgotten, particularly as the surrounding Catholic community used Jesus as a given name. The name Adonai, though, could have been used in the same way that the name Jesus is—but expressing crypto-Jewish rather than Catholic identity. I was able to trace the family connected to one of these gravestones near Cuba, New Mexico. I interviewed Adonai's brother, who clearly indicated that the name had been given as an expression of the family's Jewish identity and that they understood the meaning of the word. Like the other cases examined here, the material cultural object could not speak for itself. Through the use of appropriate alternative forms of data, I was able to come to an understanding of the implications of the cultural object.

The six-pointed star and other symbols are found not only on gravestones, but also on buildings and jewelry. Two examples indicate an approach to these objects of material culture.

Many visitors to Albuquerque have noted that six-pointed stars are used as a decorative motif in the Church of San Felipe de Neri. This is discussed by Hordes (2005:261) and Judith Neulander (2001:124–128). Neulander suggested that the stars are merely decorative, particularly due to the presence of the Sacred Heart in the center of each, and Hordes countered with a photograph of the altar taken before 1903 in which the Sacred Hearts are absent. Neulander's contention can be turned around, so that the presence of the Jewish symbol, the Star of David, renders the Catholic symbol, the Sacred Heart, merely decorative (or perhaps a cover). It is also possible that both symbols were used with their meanings attached; just because someone wishes to express a crypto-Jewish identity does not imply that he or she is fully or even partly rejecting a Catholic identity. The symbols in themselves, however, do not provide a basis for accepting any of these interpretations. Similarly, the absence of the Sacred Hearts before 1903, noted by Hordes, does not demonstrate that the use of six-pointed stars in the church was motivated by the desire to express Jewish identity; they may have been merely decorative. Although the addition of the Sacred Hearts to the decoration of the church in the 1930s or 1940s might indicate a rejection of Jewish aspects of Hispano society or the possible general association with Judaism, this too is purely supposition.

As in the case of the gravestones, the symbols do not speak for themselves. Since San Felipe de Neri is older than any living individuals, it is impossible to recover the original meaning of the six-pointed stars, unless it is found in documentary evidence. There are, however, examples of a living tradition of interpretation by individuals who are closely associated with the church and are practicing Catholics. *Jose*, a resident of Albuquerque who was born in 1920, worked in the church as a voluntary caretaker for many years:

> Well, they always said they represented the Star of David, you know. I remember going to some cemeteries, and you see the cross; others you see the Star of David—I wish I knew where it was, you know; one time I saw one like a cross and then a Star of David on top of it, you know, the star on [the] side.
>
> I'm saying what I was told, that the people who came here were Jewish. My aunt used to tell me all these stories of how it was. She was a smart lady. (*Jose*, September 2003)

Jose clearly associated the six-pointed stars not only in the church but also on gravestones with the Star of David. He was young when he learned about the stars, which he related to symbols used by a synagogue in Albuquerque. While this material does not prove that the stars were originally included to symbolize Jewish identity, it does suggest, in relation to similar narratives, a very strong tradition that understands these stars as expressing Jewish identity within the Hispano community (even by individuals who are practicing Catholics).

The six-pointed star or other symbols of Judaism are also occasionally found on jewelry (as well as pillows and household objects). These items tend to be of more recent vintage, and it occasionally is possible to find out how they are understood by the individuals who choose to wear or use them, or at least by very close relatives. A good example is a silver six-pointed star that was owned by *Juan*'s mother. In the first part of the interview with Hordes (2005:286) and me about his sister's gravestone, *Juan* showed us the star and described it:

> He was wearing that and had a little Star of David. A silver one [*referring to a six-pointed star*], I don't know if it's still in here or not. She gave me a gold one, and I let my second wife borrow it and she kept it. I wonder what happened to it. Oh, here it is.
>
> I think she had the gold one in the cheap box; it was a pretty one . . . woven . . . like a traditional Mogen David, no. It was real beautiful. I should have never let my ex-wife wear it. (*Juan*, August 2001)

Juan specifically referred to the six-pointed star by using both the English and Hebrew terms. Later in the interview, I returned to this, picking up his identification of the star as a Jewish symbol.

> INTERVIEWER: Do you know whether she ever talked about this as being a symbol of Judaism?
> JUAN: She knew what it symbolized. There was no question in her mind about this. She knew her history and everything. She just never talked about it much.
> I: So this just wasn't something that was a nice shape.
> J: She knew what she was getting. Because she bought that other one in gold. (*Juan*, August 2001)

This interview provides a clear interpretation in direct association with the material cultural object. The star in question, however, probably was made in the mid-twentieth century and thus is only a reflection of how recent generations of Hispanos have interpreted their identity and used material culture as a means to express it.

In the discussion of Christian elements in crypto-Jewish practice, I briefly examined Saint Esther. Many crypto-Jews have reported venerating (this is probably too strong a term) this saint, particularly in the spring. Neulander (1996) argued that as there is an authentic Saint Esther in the Catholic calendar, the Saint Esther revered in New Mexico has nothing to do with the biblical Esther and any material evidence relating to her is not proof of ongoing crypto-Jewish identity or tradition. I argue that the coincidence of names of a minor saint and a biblical figure associated with persecution would create a structural link between the two. Thus even though the saint was originally a different person, she became the biblical Esther for crypto-Jews. In a situation where secrecy was necessary, how better to preserve identity than by using an image for crypto-Jewish purposes that would be considered an appropriate Catholic religious object if seen by neighbors or priests. Ross Frank (2000) describes a similar process in relation to *retablos* and *bultos* associated in the 1930s with Saint Job (also called Saint Jo'). His discussion indicates that these objects were originally associated with Jesus and only later became identified with Job. While Frank (2000:228–233) suggests that this reidentification may have been theologically motivated, due to the similarities between Jesus and Job, in a telephone phone conversation reported by Hordes (2005:263), Frank accepted the possibility that this change may also have been associated with crypto-Judaism. David Gitlitz (1996:117) also mentions the use of Job by crypto-Jews in Mexico.

I reiterate this issue to highlight a more general one. At a number of points in the ethnography, critics have challenged the authenticity of crypto-Jewish culture or material culture because of either the mixture of Jewish and Catholic elements or the alternative Catholic interpretation of an object. While it is important to note these facts, they do not necessarily undermine the authenticity of the object as a part of crypto-Jewish culture. The evidence of crypto-Jewish understanding must be part of the discussion, as must other contextual issues. The range of evidence makes Saint Esther a compelling part of crypto-Jewish material culture. Other saints' names that have biblical associations also fit this category, as do particular saints who represent actual biblical characters.

Sometimes, though, the evidence takes us in a different direction. Some portable crucifixes have a slot in the back that originally was used to store a stand to hold the cross. While the crypto-Jewish evidence suggests that individual families considered these crucifixes to be important, the interpretation of these slots as compartments in which to hide religious scrolls or other Jewish ritual objects was being done by modern crypto-Jews. Their process of reinterpretation fits in with the arguments about bricolage, and thus these crosses become part of present-day crypto-Jewish material culture, having cultural authenticity in that sense. The context of their interpretation, however, indicates that the crucifixes are unlikely to have historical authenticity as part of crypto-Jewish material culture. This, however, does not make a blanket argument about all crosses, each of which should be looked at on its own terms and in relation to the traditions (such as hiding mezuzah scrolls) associated with it.

This discussion revolves around a key question: What would characterize crypto-Jewish material culture? Many scholars, Michael Carroll (2002) for one, seem to look for a smoking gun—that is, a piece of material culture that is undeniably crypto-Jewish or, indeed, Jewish. This might include the use of symbols on an object or the discovery of a diary that explicitly states that something is done for a crypto-Jewish reason. I would argue that a smoking gun either is unlikely to be found or, more correctly, is right in front of the critics, but they fail to recognize it.

While symbols are suggestive of cultural status, I have followed a route similar to that of Neulander, although for very different reasons, arguing that symbolic evidence per se does not provide the absolute historical validation that these scholars seem to demand. It might be that they require material evidence that predates the expulsion of the Jews from Spain and thus links present-day crypto-Jews with their direct Jewish ancestors. There are, however, problems with this. First, as it is highly unlikely that these types of material cultural objects would have been passed down and survived to this day, due primarily to the fear of being accused of Judaizing; material objects would have been very strong evidence. Second, the ownership of an object with Jewish provenance does not necessarily imply that it retained or retains Jewish symbolic value. It is possible that an object of Jewish origin could have been owned by a family that had no Jewish connections and was unaware of the original intention of the makers of the object and/or had no understanding of the symbols on it. If one is looking for a material connection between present-day crypto-Jews and fifteenth-century Spanish Jews, genetic testing would be a more reliable route and, indeed, is one that many crypto-Jews have taken. The evidence suggests that at least some of them carry a genetic smoking gun. It is clear that neither genes nor material cultural objects carry cultural meaning. They establish a physical link, but it is through understanding, use, and interpretation that cultural meaning arises. This smoking gun continues to be found in the words and practices of living crypto-Jews.

The second form of material culture, written diaries or similar historical documents, are largely absent from recent historical records. This, however, is not surprising in the context of crypto-Jewish ethnography. Secrecy is a significant, perhaps the significant, component of the identity. Thus the dearth of written evidence or testimony in the post-Inquisition period fits this ethnographic context. It is also possible that many crypto-Jewish practices were part of these individuals' and families' everyday activities and thus not recorded in diaries. It is only in the recent past that the practices and the identity have been highlighted and thus become worthy of special comment. But there are convincing written statements regarding the ancestors of modern crypto-Jews—Inquisition documents. They must be part of the context in understanding present-day crypto-Jews.

Given the paucity and problematic nature of historical material culture, should we abandon the search for material culture that can provide insight into present-day crypto-Judaism? The smoking guns do exist in the form of objects made by living crypto-Jews and perhaps their parents and of folk art. These objects, made for current use, often are ignored by material culture specialists because they clearly are of recent vintage and occasionally are unspecific. A number of examples came to light in the course of research for this study: candlesticks made of cactus branches intended to be used on Friday night, and eight-branched menorahs made of wooden spools and four-sided tops made of wood and of Bakelite intended to be used for Hanukkah. These objects are crypto-Jewish material culture, and in the context of their use and interpretation throw additional light onto crypto-Jewish practice.

We can also include folk art as material culture. A number of *santeros* from different parts of New Mexico utilize consciously Jewish motifs in their art. Thus, for example, some depict Moses and others use symbols like the Star of David. This work can be seen as crypto-Jewish material culture in at least two respects. First, some of the artists consider themselves to be crypto-Jews and use the symbols to express that identity. One *santero* in this group mentioned a range of practices that may be linked to crypto-Judaism in his family's tradition, including circumcision in both his and previous generations. Second, some crypto-Jews buy these objects because they portray symbols that they consider to be meaningful. In a wider sense, even artists who do not identify themselves as crypto-Jews state that they express these ideas in their art as a result of the presence of the Jewish strand in *manito* history. In a way, they are expressing in their art the same sentiment explored by Tomás Atencio (1996).

The use of overtly Jewish symbols, however, does not seem to represent an ongoing tradition of crypto-Jewish material culture. Some *santeros* from Taos, for example, claim that the depiction of Moses as a *bulto* (devotional

Candlesticks made from cactus. (Photograph by author)

sculpture) is only two generations old. Hordes (2005:264) quotes from an interview with Leo Salazar (1933–1991), who described the origin of his use of Moses not as a traditional figure, but as one emerging from a reaction to a specific piece of wood (this narrative was confirmed in a subsequent interview with his son, Leonardo, in 2000). Salazar subsequently carved a wide range of Moses *bultos*. The tradition apparently started by him was continued by his son and now has been carried into a third generation. Although the Salazars came from a long line of *santeros*, there is no evidence or suggestion by them that the Moses figure was made by members of the family prior its origin with Leo Salazar. The limited historical depth is also true of the use of six-pointed stars and other symbols associated with Judaism. Some *santeros* state that they were aware of the star as a Jewish symbol, but do not suggest that it had been used by previous generations. They

Retablo of Adam and Eve by Charles Carrillo. (Photograph by author)

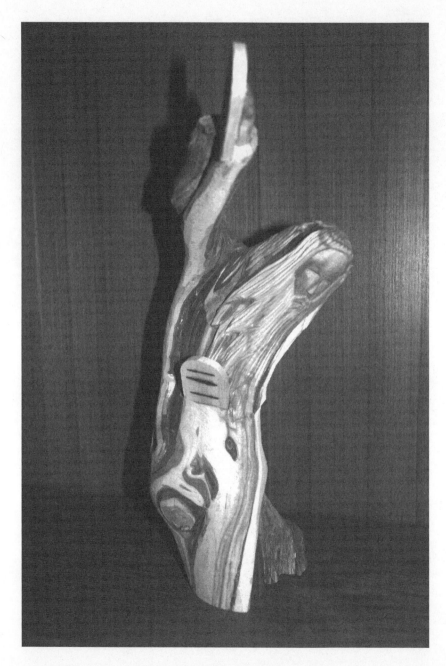

Bulto of Moses by Juan Salazar. (Photograph by author)

incorporated these symbols into their art because they want to either express their own crypto-Jewish identity or acknowledge the presence of crypto-Judaism in Hispano society. Some of the artists have indicated knowledge of Saint Esther or other similar saints and choose to utilize motifs from the Hebrew Bible as a connection with this tradition.

These objects are, however, only a small percentage of crypto-Jewish material culture. Most items do not display particular symbols associated with either Sephardic or Ashkenazic Judaism. Most of those used for crypto-Jewish practices are the vernacular objects of everyday Hispano life. A glass or cup becomes a kiddush cup not because it is adorned with symbols or was passed down from Jews in Spain, but because it is used and understood as a kiddush cup by a community. The smoking guns of material culture are in front of us; we just do not recognize them because we are looking for the wrong things—objects that will convince us of authenticity rather than those that actually express crypto-Jewish authenticity.

SIX

A POSTMODERN TAKE ON CRYPTO-JUDAISM

Thus far, the discussion in this book has worked largely within a modern framework of analysis, utilizing the paradigmatic theoretical approach of structuralism. It now moves in a postmodern direction, introducing concepts of fluidity and agency as well as subverting those of history and memory. The reality of crypto-Judaism is far too complex and individual to express in any static model.

Jonglerie

Through bricolage, cultural objects are unconsciously created and re-created. The fundamental aspect of bricolage is the underlying structure by which the different elements are organized. This structure is unconscious and relatively static, and thus not accessible or consciously transformed or manipulated by individuals or communities. Structure appears to be a given, with all cultural acts being predetermined. A problem with this classic formulation is that it leaves little room for agency (individual purposive action) and improvisation, and perhaps most tellingly it does not provide for a mechanism of transformation.

The discussion of ideal types of crypto-Jewish identity suggests that structures found among the crypto-Jews of New Mexico are more complex

and nuanced than might have been expected within the classical structuralist model. The variations on structure are clearly interrelated and, at least
in relation to the weak crypto-Jewish identity, contain aspects of fluidity
that suggest that individuals and communities can have some degree of
agency, at least in respect to emphasis. Thus some individuals with weak
crypto-Jewish identity may more or less strongly emphasize one side or the
other of the opposition between the Jewish and the Catholic elements of a
practice.

Pierre Bourdieu's (1977:72) concept of *habitus*, an unconscious "strategy
generating principle," provides a reinterpretation of underlying structure
that opens up possibilities for agency and transformation of the kind found
among the crypto-Jews. As a strategy-generating principle, *habitus* is less
monolithic than is underlying structure. It provides a basis for improvisation. Thus each instance of practice derives from structure, but does not
merely replicate it; each example allows for the pushing of boundaries and
thus agency and transformation. In a sense, the act of doing something is
both structured and creative at the same time. Following Bourdieu, I do not
regard improvisation as the outcome of "contradictory discourse" (Holland
et al. 1998:17), although this is the nature of the crypto-Jewish experience;
rather, I see it as the basic form of human practice, giving expression to
underlying structure.

The introduction of improvisation and therefore the potential for change
takes us some way down the path of explaining the ethnography of crypto-
Judaism; it does not, however, fully account for the fluidity that is found on
both the individual and communal levels. That is explained by the concept
of *jonglerie*, or identity juggling (Kunin 2001). Although *jonglerie* is closely
related to Bourdieu's notion of improvisation, it additionally reintroduces
bricolage and adds a much more dynamic role for individual conscious manipulation. *Jonglerie*, a French word that means "jugglery," emphasizes the
movement of elements in a possible circle, with one element (or perhaps
more) chosen to be emphasized at any one point. The circle emphasizes
that no element is intrinsically emphasized.

There are also associations between my understanding of the concept of
jonglerie and Bourdieu's understanding of the term "practice." For Bourdieu, practice mediates between the self and the environment (Holland et
al. 1998:39). In my approach, *jonglerie* and improvisation are aspects of
practice that mediate between structure and the environment (of the cultural field of action).

The ethnography presented here highlights the fact that the cultural repertoire available to crypto-Jews is very wide. Crypto-Jews participate in a range of overlapping cultures—minimally, Hispano, Jewish, and American—and have in their backgrounds other cultural influences as well. This context provides a very strong argument for moving away from a fixed and monolithic concept of culture. If we maintained such a model, it would suggest ongoing compartmentalization, which is not supported by the ethnography or by recent anthropological theorizing. The cultures with which the crypto-Jews interact are both overlapping and fuzzy; in reality, it is probably impossible to disentangle them. The ethnography does not suggest that individuals are consciously aware of meaningful cultural boundaries. These cultures, therefore, provide the substance out of which crypto-Jewish culture and identity are constructed, the elements that are the content of the process of bricolage. The complexity of the cultural objects themselves facilitates the possibility of alternative uses and emphases. It is likely that this form of bricolage is essential for the process of *jonglerie* and is characteristic of postmodern cultures, in which many cultures come together with similar overlapping and fuzzy boundaries.

This concept of culture is a key part of my analysis. If culture is relatively monolithic, we would expect an essentially consistent structuring process. If culture, at least in the case of this ethnography, is more complex, with significant overlaps and fuzzy edges, we might expect more complex variations of structure, which is in fact indicated by the ethnography. Thus individual crypto-Jews are not bound by a single structure, but in some way must work with fluid and ill-defined structures that may vary in different contexts. This is not to suggest that an individual has different compartmentalized structures, but that the individual can in different contexts move through a variety of structures that result from the complexity of cultures.

Jonglerie provides a mechanism that bridges bricolage with practice, or the unconscious with the conscious aspects of cultural action. It suggests that in a context in which identity and culture are contested, an individual may at different times select (both consciously and unconsciously) different aspects to emphasize or deemphasize and, based on that process of selection and emphasis, will instantiate a different aspect of the underlying structure. Within the complex mix that makes up crypto-Jewish identity, individuals at different times or in different contexts differentially understand or interpret their identity; this may have an effect on the aspect of a practice they emphasize or deemphasize. Thus if the practice includes

Jewish and Christian elements, there is a wide range of possible emphases that will lead to different interpretations. They will, however, also lead to different structural patterns. Each difference in emphasis changes the nature of the pattern of mediation between the Jewish and the Christian aspects of the practice.

The ritual of lighting candles and reciting the Rosary is a useful example of the possible variations. This practice includes two elements that have no intrinsic relation to each other. Depending on the process of *jonglerie*, they come into different relations with each other. Thus they can be regarded as opposed to each other, in either direction, which would emphasize either the Jewish or the Catholic element. Alternatively, they can be seen as having a more mediated relation, with one side or the other being emphasized but not exclusively. There clearly can be a very extensive range of variations on this form of emphasis, all of which are structurally related. This process, however, is not open-ended. The possibilities for variant structures are fixed in the system, perhaps to the range established in the discussion of the ideal types of crypto-Jewish identity, and this provides the boundaries within which there is the possibility of agency.

Jonglerie has clear implications for the four ideal types of crypto-Jewish identity. If *jonglerie* is an ongoing process, then we must reconsider the static nature of these categories. When a more fluid understanding of identity is introduced into the model, it provides a depiction of crypto-Jewish ethnography that fits better with the observations. This is not to suggest that the ideal types are not a necessary part of the model, but that while at particular times and in particular contexts an individual's expression of identity does approximate one of the ideal types, at other times and in other contexts, it they may relate to a different ideal type.

Our arguments suggest that identity is not essential or fixed. It is instead contextual and fluid. Transformations in self-identification engendered by the discovery of crypto-Jewish ancestors or the diagnosis of genetic illnesses prevalent among Jews may imply a single trajectory. With some individuals, although the trajectory was generally toward a form of crypto-Jewish identification, it could move between the weak type and the Christian type with *converso* elements. The structural relations between these two categories are very close, with only a shift in emphasis from the Jewish to the Catholic elements. We find similar shifts within the weak type itself, with individuals at different times placing more or less emphasis on either the Jewish or the Christian aspects of identification and practice.

The process of *jonglerie* also occurs in more dramatic ways. Thus individuals can move from the two Christian categories to the two crypto-Jewish categories (and back). For example, a woman from Albuquerque was interviewed on several occasions during the course of the study and expressed different forms of self-identification. When initially interviewed, she fit into the category of Christian type with *converso* elements. She had a very strong identification with the Catholic Church; members of her family were active in the church, and she considered herself to be part of a strong Catholic tradition. Alongside this identification, however, she was also aware of the Jewish roots of her family. This knowledge was based on genealogical research as well as family tradition. She also mentioned a range of Jewish practices that had been retained in her family, some of which were recognized as remnants of Jewish practice, while others were uninterpreted. In spite of these aspects of Jewish and perhaps crypto-Jewish heritage, she did not consider herself or her family to be crypto-Jews. The Jewish elements were interesting, but relevant to the past. In subsequent interviews, due in part to changed life experiences, she expressed a different emphasis in her self-understanding, with the crypto-Jewish aspect becoming increasingly important in her narrative; on some occasions, she clearly identified with the strong type, regarding crypto-Jewish identity as being her key and ongoing self-definition.

This case illustrates the possible fluidity within the system. The woman was not creating an identity from whole cloth; rather, the elements on which the fluidity was based are evident in the first interview. The change was not in the creation of elements, but in the interpretation of them and the importance given to one set of elements rather than the other. It is, however, equally possible that in individual cases reinterpretation also includes a degree of cultural re-creation. This is found when individuals seek to bolster a challenged identity with a selective reinterpretation of the past. Although many crypto-Jews clearly do interpret and reinterpret their past on the basis of present knowledge and self-understanding, most do not seem to consciously invent practices either for their own purposes or for those of the ethnographer. Thus it is unlikely that individuals would invent a conscious narrative of a strong identification with crypto-Judaism unless the rudiments of the identification and practices associated with it were actually present.

The processes around the negotiation of identity and its fluidity also attest to the potential vibrancy of crypto-Jewish culture. Although it is to some extent a culture of memory, the role of individuals in negotiating and renegotiating identity introduces a significant aspect of improvisation. While some of this improvisation is conceptual, it also shapes practice in the form of recounting narratives of self and past. Thus the processes outlined here are those of a culture that is continuing to develop, rather than a static creation or memory of the past that serves merely as the vestige of a culture. This view is seconded by Dorothy Holland and her colleagues (1998), who suggest that these processes are "potential beginnings of an altered subjectivity, an altered identity" (18). Improvisation and *jonglerie* are creative and potentially transformative acts, which potentially change not only the individual but the community and its use of structure.

A key part of this vibrancy and modern crypto-Jewish culture is found in the public and private changing narratives of self. It is these narratives that encompass memory, form oral histories, and present self-definitions through which the process of *jonglerie* occurs and the lenses through which we come to know and understand crypto-Judaism.[1] It is important to emphasize, following Holland and her coauthors (1998:4), that these narratives have two interrelated aspects: they are both expressive of self (that is, they say something about the understanding of self for others, including ethnographers), and expressive for self (that is, they say something to self and are guides for action).

Narratives of self are a key feature of both crypto-Jewish culture and the ethnographic study of that culture. Holland and her colleagues' (1998) development of the concept of figured worlds, which draws on the work of the developmental psychologist Lev Vygotsky, provides a useful way to view this process: "By 'figured world,' we mean a socially and culturally constructed realm of interpretation in which characters and actors are recognized, significance is assigned to certain acts, and particular outcomes are valued over others" (52).

They use this concept to bring together a range of cultural activities in which collective narratives are used and internalized. This process allows these worlds to "take shape within and grant shape to the coproduction of activities, discourses, performances, and artifacts" (Holland et al. 1998:51). The key point for our discussion is that this process both forms a set of meanings, or "takes shape," and gives form to meanings, or "gives shape." This is important, as it highlights the fact that while in some sense all cultural meaning is constructed and artificial—a fiction—it also makes use of what individuals experience and have experienced. This is particularly evident in Holland's discussion of the development of narratives in Alcoholics Anonymous (AA). Through telling stories about self in the context of the meeting, individuals learn to reconfigure their narratives to fit into the new world of AA in which they find themselves: "Newcomers to the AA must give up an old identity, that of a normal drinker, and develop a new one. They go through a process of identity devaluation followed by a process of identity formation. This process takes place through reinterpretation, as members come to understand that their pasts have been a progression of alcoholic drinking and alcoholic behavior" (Holland et al. 1998:96).

The narratives provide a new way of understanding self that reemphasizes elements of the past in light of the new understanding (Holland et al. 1998:66–97). Thus although as individuals move into the crypto-Jewish discourse their narratives of self may change in relation to this new figured world, this does not imply that their new narrative is necessarily made up of fictional elements. It may be composed of reordered or reunderstood factual elements—all cultures are in this sense "faction" (a mix of fact and fiction).

This concept is particularly germane to the understanding of crypto-Judaism and crypto-Jewish identity. While aspects of individual practice do persist, the most significant element of crypto-Jewish practice is the narrative presentation of self. Thus part of being a crypto-Jew is moving into the form and structure of this figured world—that is, telling the story in the correct way. This learning process is not one of inventing practices or even necessarily interpretations (although this may be part of it); rather, it is one of learning what is significant and what is not, what has to be emphasized and what does not. This process of enculturation occurs through participating in formal and informal meetings and conferences and, today, through using the Internet and its many forms of communication.

This process of enculturation and reinterpretation of the past within narratives of self has been one of the significant features of our research. It also has been observed, but misunderstood, by others looking at the field (for example, Ferry and Nathan 2000). While the particular details of these changes in narrative form can be highly individual, there is a range of common threads. The commonalities are somewhat more complex than the relatively simple narrative move made by members of AA. Within the crypto-Jewish context is a wider range of identities and thus a wider range of narratives. The structures of emphasis and deemphasis that are fundamental to the reinterpretation of the past are different for each person.

Barbara Ferry and Debbie Nathan (2000) discussed an individual whose narrative of self was presented in two very different ways. They attributed this change to invention, arguing that the initial presentation of self was factual and the subsequent presentation therefore was fictional. But the content of the two narratives indicates a move from the weak to the strong crypto-Jewish identity. This transformation, if we take Holland's arguments seriously, is not a move from fact to fiction (or, indeed, the opposite) but a process of reinterpretation of the past on the basis of a new understanding of the present. It represents a move from one figured world to another; each figured world represents an interpretation, and neither is more factual than the other.

Holland and her colleagues also introduce the process of identity devaluation to the discussion of identity formation (that is, devaluation of the former identity in favor of the new identity), overemphasizing it in light of their discussion of AA. Identity devaluation does occur to some extent in the context of crypto-Judaism. Thus at public meetings, hostility toward aspects of the former identity sometimes is expressed in a number of ways, particularly when priests or others speak of their Christian beliefs. For some individuals, the move to crypto-Jewish identity seems to involve a clear rejection of their former Catholic identity and sometimes to a denial that it was real. At a meeting of the Society for Crypto-Judaic Studies (SCJS), for example, three individuals who expressed both crypto-Jewish connections and Christian messianic beliefs presented their stories. The aspect of the talk that caused the most hostility was a description by one about her embrace of messianism: "[O]nce you have a relationship with Jesus, there is no going back." Many participants regarded this statement as a denial of their journeys to Judaism and as an attempt to proselytize. Similar statements about an individual's return to Judaism has been met with praise rather than anger.

The devaluation of the former identity, however, is not as unidirectional or absolute as suggested by Holland. The concept of *jonglerie* emphasizes that it is an ongoing process that moves in either direction and, indeed, may never fix on one identity or the other. Perhaps even the concept of figured worlds can be seen as too essentialist. For many crypto-Jews, the narratives are much more fluid and contextual, perhaps indicating that figured worlds should be regarded as overlapping and fuzzy.

The crypto-Jewish ethnography indicates a range of contexts in which the process of entering into new figured worlds is facilitated. Perhaps the most obvious is the annual meeting of the SCJS, whose sessions can be roughly divided into academic, nonacademic, and testimonial. The academic and nonacademic panels largely provide information that serves as a basis for a new self-narrative, particularly its interpretation. The narrative is offered in the testimony of crypto-Jews about their self-understanding and their journey to it. Although the conference as a whole is more nuanced (presenting a more nonjudgmental relativist position), these narratives often contain an aspect of opposition to the participants' Christian past and thus provide a way to construct self within the range of crypto-Jewish structures. This slant can lead to strong hostility toward the inclusion of testimony that emphasizes the Christian side of the equation. The informal aspects of the conference also provide a basis for further movement into the crypto-Jewish figured world.

Other formal conferences have recently been convened that are much more consciously aimed at bringing crypto-Jews back to Judaism. Their agenda is specifically targeted at providing both content and narratives. They often include some of the same speakers who appear at the SCJS conference, with the addition of a strong rabbinic element to both validate and support the Jewishness of the participants. While the narratives presented at the SCJS conference, particularly in the testimony, often have an oppositional aspect, the society's aim not to proselytize means that the underlying structures presented will have a higher degree of mediation (and validation of alternative choices). This specifically Jewish form of conference will clearly lead to a more strongly oppositional variation of the structure.

I have also observed informal meetings that serve a similar purpose. One woman in Albuquerque who had a very strong and public crypto-Jewish identity met with close relatives and some friends on an ongoing basis to explore their heritage and Judaism. They looked at traditions in their families and those discussed in publications, particularly *La Herencia del Norte*, a magazine that highlights the Hispano culture of New Mexico. They also explored mainstream Jewish traditions; some of them had joined local Jewish communities. Through the process of learning together, the members of this group were creating their own figured world, which valued Hispano tradition but was moving toward a very strong identification with Judaism through the utilization of shared family memories.

Finally, many crypto-Jews have chosen to join Jewish communities. Through rituals of return or conversion, which often involve education, they gradually move into the figured worlds that characterize mainstream

Judaism. While many of these individuals gain a degree of notoriety because of their backgrounds, and may be called on to speak about their personal histories, their narratives of self tend to be increasingly exclusive. Thus to the extent that Catholic content is mentioned, it is clearly minimized and presented as either negative or meaningless to self-identity.

Individual Memory, Social Memory, and Oral History

The concept of figured worlds and its role in reinterpretation raises important questions in relation to memory. We tend to think of memory as a relatively fixed set of images of the past that are evoked as necessary. The notion of figured worlds begins to problematize this popular understanding. It highlights two aspects of transformation that occur in relation to memory. As we move from one figured world to the next, we both reinterpret our memories and change our emphases to reflect our new self-understanding. While in one sense both of these changes are external to memory, it is questionable whether memory exists separately from them: Do we have memories to be interpreted and emphasized, or are the memories we evoke already interpreted and emphasized?

Before we address these questions directly, it is worthwhile to touch on some of the general issues relating to memory, interviews, and oral history.[2] Historians and other scholars have argued about the role of memory as a form of evidence, with an increasing number willing to consider it in conjunction with other types of evidence. They have been aware of the issues surrounding the reliability and veracity of memory, with the most substantial arguments relating to veracity rather than reliability. Memories seem to be consistent and reliable; they may, however, in certain circumstances not be factual. Daniel Schacter's (2001) analysis of some of the pitfalls relating to memory is particularly helpful in highlighting the potential problems in the use of memory as a source for history and other related disciplines. He suggests that memory has "seven sins": transience, absent-mindedness, blocking, misattribution, suggestibility, bias, and persistence. A subset of these sins has important implications to the study of crypto-Judaism.

The "sin" of transience specifically describes the process or curve by which remembering and forgetting are linked (Schacter 2001:12–17). It focuses on the differential speeds at which aspects of an event are gradually forgotten, suggesting that elements that are part of a consistent repeated pattern are more quickly forgotten, while those that stand out or have an emotional component tend to be remembered longer and in greater detail. Many of our informants spoke of events associated with a particularly important relative and experiences that were occasional rather than repeated. From Schacter's perspective, memories of these events probably would be more persistent than others, although they, too, would be subject to transience.

Schacter's discussion of his first and seventh sins, transience and persistence, suggests that the emotional content associated with a memory is fixed. If we move his discussion into the more fluid framework of identity presented here, however, we must question this static nature of emotional content. As individuals more into new figured worlds, they may transform the emotional content of different memories. If this is true, it is possible that as emotions change, the memories and the details evoked by them will change as well. Thus in one context, a memory may be more transient then it might be when triggered in a different context.

Schacter (2001) highlights one additional feature of the transience process: "But with the passing of time, the particulars fade and opportunities multiply for interference—generated by later similar experiences—to blur our recollections. We thus rely ever more on our memories of the gist of what happened, or what usually happens, and attempt to reconstruct the rest by inference and even sheer guesswork" (16). While many experiences described by crypto-Jews are one-shot, some events are ongoing and thus are subject to these processes. Perhaps ironically, those individuals with the strongest and most consistent set of crypto-Jewish identity and practice are most susceptible to transience. It is thus not insignificant that individuals in this category utilize inference and perhaps guesswork to provide details of some of their experiences. As they made up only a tiny subset of the interviewees, it seems unlikely that this process significantly shaped the result of the study. Our use of iterated interviews over several years also minimized this potential problem.

The "sin" of misattribution is the process by which a memory is falsely ascribed to one source when it should be attributed to another (Schacter 2001:88–111). A common example of this is linking a memory to an event rather than to a picture of the event (Charlton, Myers, and Sharpless 2006:286). It is possible that there is an aspect of misattribution in the material provided by some interviewees for this study. It might occasionally be the transference of a memory from something learned to an actual event. This process, however, seems from the interviews to relate to interpretation rather than practice. Thus over time, individuals may integrate into their memories interpretations of practices they performed and "falsely" consider the interpretation to be part of the memories. Most of the respondents did not seem to add to their narratives practices that they had learned about but did not perform. Most clearly stated what they did and did not do. Thus one interviewee who had a good knowledge base about Judaism clearly spoke of a range of practices with added interpretations, such as using modern Hebrew terms, but also stated that his family did not follow other traditions, such as abstaining from the consumption of pork.

The "sin" of suggestibility is closely related to that of misattribution (Schacter 2001:112–137). It refers to the potential of adding new interpretations or, indeed, false memories as a result of being asked leading questions. This problem is of great importance in assessing any form of ethnographic work. The ethnographer may be regarded as a figure of authority and thus shape the answers of his or her informants. This form of interference is very hard to avoid and in the context of a study on an issue like crypto-Judaism may be impossible to overcome. Many of the individuals interviewed knew that I were interested in crypto-Judaism—although many of them did not know what it is—which may have shaped the elements of their identities that they selected to talk about. By using open-ended interviews and following up leads given only by the individuals themselves, I hope to have minimized the impact of suggestibility.

The "sin" of bias has been touched on (although not by name) in many parts of this discussion. It refers to the process by which memories are "distorted" by present knowledge and understanding of self (Schacter 2001:138–160). It is, indeed, a statement in a negative way of the concept of figured worlds, but I consider it to be an ongoing means by which memory and self are reunderstood. If we focus on memory as merely a piece of evidence, taken from the subjective individual and used in an objective sense, we could understand Schacter's term "distortion," which no doubt Judith Neulander and others would subscribe to happily. If, however, we are interested in memory as part of ethnography, as a highly subjective expression of self-understanding, we would regard it as transformation rather than distortion. It is important to note that this process is one of interpretation; thus in the "use" of memories in relation to ethnographic or folkloric analysis, the content can be separated from the interpretation, and each examined and understood on its own terms.

Schacter's and similar approaches, due perhaps to their focus on oral history, tend to deemphasize the aspect of selectivity. Oral historians ask their informants to describe an event and thus expect a relatively complete depiction of it; the general content is preselected by the question. In the ethnographic interviews conducted for this study, we tended to be more general, although the focus was on family practices and self-perception. The interviews were unstructured, and thus the chain of memories evoked was less formal than might be the case in interviews conducted for oral histories. This informality placed a greater emphasis on the interviewees to select those elements that were meaningful and important to them. This approach perhaps placed a strong emphasis on the "sin" of bias. The individuals selected, consciously and unconsciously, the memories to evoke and share based on their level of knowledge and their understanding of self (as shaped by the context of the interview). This was clearly evidenced by those informants who were repeatedly interviewed over a number of years. The self-perception of some of these respondents markedly changed, which led them to describe a different set of memories in successive interviews.

While it is clear that some of these memories were consciously deployed, the interviews also suggested that there was a strong unconscious aspect to this process. The chain of memories and the level of detail and content were not entirely triggered by conscious choice, but were largely dependent on the context (of both the individual and the interview) and the process of unconscious, relatively free association. This unconscious aspect is possibly indicated in the description of a reinterview discussed by Barbara Ferry and Debbie Nathan (2000). At the original interview, conducted by Stanley Hordes, a set of memories had been elicited that were contextual to the time, place, and respondents. When the second interview was conducted, the context was very different. The description suggests that the interviewee did not actively evoke the same memories and thus had to be prodded, which was then taken as bad practice by Neulander (2001). If we regard the process of remembering and summoning memories as largely unconscious, then the issues encountered can be explained.

In certain respects, then, memory is fluid. While the specific content of a memory may be reliable, the aspects of interpretation and selectivity add to it a high degree of subjectivity and transformation. It is perhaps necessary in this context to distinguish between memory—the encoded contents of the brain—and memories—the particular thoughts and images that are evoked and are mediated by both the "seven sins" and, more important, selectivity. While memory exists as a category, we actually encounter only the mediated form of memories—and it transforms as we move within and between figured worlds.

Memories, both consciously and unconsciously triggered, are a key part of self-identification. They provide a model *of* self—that is, a basis on which we interpret and explain who we are—and a model *for* self—that is, a basis on which we act and interpret experience. The interrelated aspects of selectivity and interpretation are central to this process; both are shaped by current self-understanding, which provides a basis for both selection and interpretation, as well as a reciprocal validation and model of continuity and meaning. In this sense, memories are a myth of self, if myth is taken to mean a model by which we explain and give coherence to past, present, and future. As with any myth, a key part of its power is the perception of its essentialness—that is, both its validity and its permanence. To that end, we tend to think of memory and identity as fixed rather than fluid.

Alongside individual memory scholars have identified social memory. James Fentress and Chris Wickham (1992) define social memory: "In principle, we can usually regard social memory as an expression of collective experience: social memory identifies a group, giving it a sense of its past and defining its aspirations for the future. In doing so, social memory often makes factual claims about past events. . . . [T]he question of whether *we* regard their memories as historically true will often turn out to be less important than whether *they* regard their memories as true" (25–26). This definition of social memory is particularly relevant to crypto-Jewish ethnography. It emphasizes that social memory (which, by definition, must be learned) provides a shared basis on which a community builds its sense of self.[3] It shapes both interpretation of the past and patterns of behavior and interpretation in the present. For crypto-Jews, narratives of the expulsion from Spain and, particularly, the persecution by the Inquisition are particularly important in creating this type of identity. Fentress and Wickham also emphasize the internal point of view: the external validation of the collective memory is less important than its perception by those in the community. Thus that any approach that wants to understand crypto-Judaism cannot merely stand back and claim to judge its authenticity, but must look at the collective narratives of crypto-Jews and how they are understood without judging this historicity.

The work of Benedict Anderson (1983) deals with issues related to social memory and is occasionally introduced into the discussion of crypto-Judaism. He is concerned largely with the development of nationalism, which like any other aspect of culture is constructed and therefore is in some sense artificial. While some scholars have used Anderson's term "imagined communities" as an attack on crypto-Judaism, regarding it as referring to invented and perhaps fake communities, Anderson (1983) applies the phrase to all nations and nationalisms: "It is *imagined* because the members of even the smallest nation will never know most of their fellow members, meet them, or even hear of them, yet in the minds of each lives the image of their communion" (6). His discussion makes it clear that the word "imagined" has nothing to do with factuality or invention. Rather, it refers to the social connections among individuals, which are imagined and constructed on the basis of shared models of history and memory. As his arguments develop, Anderson introduces issues concerned with the rethinking of history in relation to different constructions of nationalism. If we regard crypto-Judaism in his sense as an *imagined* community, we can utilize Anderson's model to explain the selective processes of memory and forgetting. As a collective history and memory is constructed, it leads to the remembering of those elements that strengthen the boundaries and unity of a community—and, equally, the forgetting of those that do not. Anderson's approach does not suggest that the content of these shared histories is invented, but that the memories are culturally constructed (as are all histories and social memories) to serve the needs of a particular community (or nation) at a particular time and in a particular place.

Eric Hobsbawm and Terence Ranger (1992) present a variation on this theme that in some respects is closer to the misuse of Anderson's concept. Their idea of invented tradition might be regarded as encompassing the processes that crypto-Jews consciously (and perhaps unconsciously) have deployed to understand their identity in both the present and the past. The key aspect that differentiates Hobsbawm and Ranger's arguments from Anderson's is that invented traditions are specifically distinct from history. Whereas history is seen as expressing actual continuity, these traditions invent factitious continuity in relation to "a suitable historic past" (Hobsbawm and Ranger 1992:1).

In their summation of the types of invented traditions, Hobsbawm and Ranger (1992:9) suggest that there are three main types:

- Those that establish social cohesion
- Those that legitimize institutions or status
- Those that serve to inculcate systems of norms

Crypto-Judaism does not easily fit into any of these categories. While the history and traditions that form its basis do define a form of bounded community, it is not one with strong social cohesion; the "tradition" does not establish a strong link among behavior, group identity, and history. The other two types are not reflected in crypto-Judaism, unless the ethnography is forced to fit Neulander's (2001) argument that the identity is related to a claim of "whiteness." Even if it were true, there is no evidence that individuals who make the claim gain in status due to their self-understanding as crypto-Jews.

We have to ask Hobsbawm and Ranger if it is legitimate to distinguish so-called invented traditions from a more general concept of tradition or history. Their arguments imply that there are legitimate histories and traditions that can be conceptually set in opposition to invented histories and traditions. If we view all uses of history and concepts of tradition as contextual—that is, perceived and deployed by a particular culture at a particular time and in a particular place—it is not clear why this perspective should make any distinction between the legitimate and the invented. The difference between the two types of histories and traditions is merely one of awareness: we are aware of when the Boy Scouts were founded and when the celebration of Thanksgiving originated. We are not as easily aware of when other "traditions" emerged and thus give them a lesser status. Crypto-Jewish history is invented in the sense that it is consciously deployed by crypto-Jews in explaining their past; this invention, however, is no different from any other use of history or tradition.

The processes relevant to memory are also relevant to history and oral history, as I have begun to indicate with the introduction of Anderson's work. Like memory, history should be divided into two elements: history—the events that happened in the past—and histories—particular narratives of the past that mediate the events by means of documents and oral histories (and other artifacts that are accepted as meaningful). Histories, like memories, are mediated consciously or unconsciously. Conscious mediation occurs through the use of historical theories or models, such as a Marxist approach. Unconscious mediation occurs most significantly (although not uniquely) when there is no theorization. Mediation is impossible to avoid, as all histories are both selections and interpretations of the past; different forms of understanding lead to differences in selection and interpretation.

The processes that pertain to history are relevant to crypto-Judaism on several interrelated levels. Historians, ethnographers, and crypto-Jews rely on oral history to understand the recent past. Oral history is implicated in the issues that concern memory; it is also implicated in those, both conscious and unconscious, that concern history. Some crypto-Jews self-consciously bring together their memories and organize them into oral history, thus bringing in this second level of historical mediation. Other crypto-Jews and the academics also construct histories, although these are based on the canons of academic history. While our society views this process as objective (and that is an essential aspect of our society's understanding of self), histories are both consciously and unconsciously motivated.

This aspect of history is particularly interesting in relation to how some crypto-Jews who are not academic historians engage in writing histories. One example is the analysis by Mona Hernandez (2007) of La Conquistadora.[4] Hernandez's work focuses on the history of a statue, La Conquistadora, found in the Cathedral Basilica of Saint Francis of Assisi in Santa Fe. Her paper opens with a brief discussion of the kabbalah, suggesting that it was brought by Spaniards to New Mexico. It then moves to a description of the journey of the statue to New Mexico in 1625. La Conquistadora was brought to New Mexico by Fray Alonso de Benavides, in a wagon train led by Francisco Gómez, who later was accused of Judaizing—although, as Hernandez indicates, it was his son Francisco Gómez Robledo who was eventually tried by the Inquisition. Hernandez suggests that although there was strong evidence of his being a crypto-Jew, Gómez Robledo was released and eventually returned to New Mexico.

During the Pueblo Revolt (1680–1692), the statue was saved by a niece of Gómez Robledo, Josepha López Sambrano. Hernandez implicitly asks: Why would a woman of crypto-Jewish identity (as a niece of Gómez Robledo) save an idol? She responds with a quotation from Cecil Roth (1932), which indicates that crypto-Jews sometimes formed associations with Catholic objects as a cover for Judaizing. At this point, she reintroduces the mystical theme, suggesting that La Conquistadora represented the Shekhina, a mystical feminine aspect of God. Her narrative directly ties the mystical concept of the Shekhina in exile from God to the thirteen-year exile of the settlers from New Mexico in El Paso during the Pueblo Revolt. La Conquistadora returned to New Mexico in 1693. Hernandez's narrative significantly focuses on the genealogy of the returnees, tying the family of Gómez Robledo to the ancestors of her own family.

Hernandez then moves to the establishment of a confraternity connected initially with Our Lady of the Rosary and subsequently, in 1770, with La Conquistadora. It is again significant that she specifically associates leaders and members of this confraternity with her family. The change in patron was associated with a revival of the confraternity, with La Conquistadora being venerated as protector against the Comanches. Hernandez suggests that the revival of the confraternity and, by implication, the change of patron were again associated with the kabbalah. She describes the kabbalah as "originating from man's sense of inadequacy in dealing with life's problems." Thus in the face of Comanche and Apache raids, the residents of New Mexico had to look beyond human resources. She also details the messianic aspirations of the kabbalah and, by implication, of the confraternity. Hernandez concludes by identifying herself as a Jew, but expressing a wish to have some connection with the present-day La Conquistadora.

This material is fascinating from a number of perspectives. On the one hand, it makes use of a wide range of historical resources—for example, genealogical material and Inquisition documents. It also presents the material as a whole, utilizing a historical framework and attempting to contextualize the material and events. On the other hand, it introduces a wide range of speculative material, particularly the role of the kabbalah in crypto-Jewish ideology.

While it is not my goal to critique Hernandez's paper as a piece of history, in the context of this discussion it is important to see how self-identification and what might be called crypto-Jewish historiography shaped the selection and interpretation of the data. Hernandez importantly both identifies herself as a Jew and situates herself in relation to the events, at several points tying herself genealogically to the main figures in her narrative. Thus on the structural level, the narrative works in the same way as the narratives discussed in relation to the ideal types of crypto-Jewish identity. The structure sets up the opposition between Francisco Gómez (and his descendants), as Judaizers or crypto-Jews, and the Catholic Church, as embodied by the Inquisition. La Conquistadora seems to mediate between these categories; it was indirectly brought to New Mexico by Gómez and saved by his great-niece. Hernandez's analysis, though, removes this apparent mediation by rethinking La Conquistadora as the Shekhina and thus as a symbol of Judaism rather than Catholicism. La Conquistadora in effect becomes an object of crypto-Jewish rather than Catholic material culture. This observation does not intend to challenge either Hernandez's self-perception or historical analysis (which may have roots in a family tradition), but to demonstrate that historical argumentation is also structured in a way similar to that of other forms of narrative about past and self.

The example of Hernandez's paper also highlights issues relating to histories that are more consciously theorized. Even if we remove the speculative aspects of her analysis, her discussion is highly selective—as is any historical discussion. Thus the genealogical material focuses on the line that connects the historical actors to the present day; it ignores potential lines that are dead ends or irrelevant to the narrative. While other histories may not be so personalized, they also select events and movements that are regarded as relevant; the discarding of the irrelevant is clearly shaped by a theory or model of present and past that (pre)determines pertinence.

While Hernandez foregrounds the mystical interpretive aspect of her narrative, it is also present in stated or unstated ways in more academic histories. A good example of this is found in the work of certain Israeli historians whose arguments implicitly interpret all events that occurred before the founding of the state of Israel as either leading to its establishment or demonstrating that without the Jewish state, Jewish cultural and political life lacks real stability. These Zionist arguments and interpretations are often unstated, but nonetheless provide the basis of both selection and interpretation in these historians' analyses.

The fluidity of identity, the possibility of moving between figured worlds, and the implications of these on memory and history relate to the broader question of the ways individuals identity themselves and the basis on which they validate these choices. In the modern framework, there was a tendency to essentialize this process, with identities seen as being largely fixed. The postmodern framework has introduced a greater emphasis on selection and de-essentialization; the model utilized in some discussions of religion and culture have used terms like "spiritual shopping."

While I am not convinced that the spiritual-shopping model correctly describes the crypto-Jewish ethnography, it is clear that individuals, at different times and in different places, are choosing to utilize different aspects of their families' traditions in their own cultural repertoires and in the larger cultural contexts as a way to establish identity and, in the light of those choices, are interpreting past and present as means of validation. They make these choices in relation to other people and in a range of temporary social contexts. Thus the concept of networked relationships seems to be a better model than the ego-centric notion of spiritual shopping. The figured-world model indicates a more contextual and socially oriented construction of self-identification.

The concept of figured worlds and the importance of interpretation and selection emphasize an important role for learning, of both interpretation and content. Some might suggest that all the issues discussed might suggest that crypto-Judaism is therefore in some sense inauthentic. Individuals learn how to structure their world in a "crypto-Jewish" way and through a variety of means fill in the content of that structure. Viewing this as evidence of inauthenticity, however, would be a serious misunderstanding both of my arguments and of culture.

Enculturation and learning are features of all cultures at all times. If enculturation is strictly defined as the development of the patterns or structures inherent in a particular figured world, it is a process that all individuals go through at different points in their lives. We are not born with any aspect of culture, even if the community of which we are part has a genetic model of self. We are enculturated into the models and structures of the particular groups to which we belong. In this sense, all cultures—including crypto-Judaism—are enculturated. As we go through life and move into different communities and subcultures, we are enculturated into their variations on the wider shared structures.

On a different level, all content is gained through learning. In all communities, different individuals have access to different aspects of the shared culture. This includes the practices, the symbols, and (most important) the interpretations of both. As life progresses, individuals learn about new cultural content and add it to their store of cultural knowledge. One of the features of some parts of society today is a very conscious attempt to give added value to traditions. Thus in parts of the American Jewish community, there is a trend to widen both practice and understanding of practice—with traditional knowledge almost perceived as a department store waiting for shoppers (although this model again misses the fact that most shopping is done by groups rather than by individuals); this is exemplified by the various volumes of *The Jewish Catalog.*

Crypto-Jewish culture fits this pattern. Each family has an idiosyncratic set of traditions and of interpretations or lack of interpretations. Many crypto-Jews are seeking to fill in the gaps in their knowledge and understanding. This process is a problem for scholars only if they are looking for a static community that as a fossil provides evidence of its "prehistoric" origins. Crypto-Jews are not helpful to this neocolonialist desire for pure forms for scholars' academic interest. The individuals who participated in this study are not interested in being a missing link or a proof of authenticity, but in deepening their understanding of who they are and in making choices about how they can express their spiritual and cultural search.

CONCLUSION

The debate about authenticity, which has shaped much of the discussion of crypto-Judaism, has focused on the issue of historical authenticity rather than cultural authenticity. I have attempted to shift this emphasis, at least in part, from the historical to the cultural. Cultural authenticity, unlike historical authenticity, does not depend on an external observer passing judgment on whether historical or other documentation is sufficient to determine authenticity. It focuses on the internal view, asking whether a group of individuals have a shared self-definition, which becomes the basis of authenticity, and what are the parameters of that definition. On the basis of this form of argument, crypto-Judaism in New Mexico and in other parts of the Spanish and Portuguese diasporas has cultural authenticity and, as such, is appropriate for ethnographic study.

Focusing on cultural rather than historical authenticity has enabled us to examine a wide range of fascinating processes that are relevant not only to crypto-Judaism but to other ethnographic contexts as well. The primary emphasis has been on the issue of identity and self-identification. Two interrelated models allow for the conceptualization of these characteristics in the crypto-Jewish community. The first divides crypto-Jews into four ideal types. The key aspect of the model is its focus on self-identification, with genealogy, practice, and belief being secondary elements of identity. This allows us to take seriously the self-understanding of the individual and community, with the definition of a crypto-Jew someone who considers him- or herself to be a crypto-Jew. On this basis, the individuals who have a range of practices similar to those of crypto-Jews but no self-identification as crypto-Jews are not crypto-Jews because that is not how they understand their identity.

The identification of variations on underlying structure is an additional important aspect of this model. The analysis suggests that each of the ideal types represents a variant on underlying structure. Thus the strong crypto-Jewish identity is characterized by clear-cut opposition between Jewish and Catholic elements of identity, emphasizing the Jewish side. There was some mediation, indicated by the presence of aspects of Christian practice, but it was relatively negative (that is, the value of the Christian aspects was minimized). The weak crypto-Jewish identity is characterized by a more mediated structure. There is a weak opposition between the Jewish and Catholic elements of identity, with a relative emphasis on the Jewish side (based on self-identification as crypto-Jews, which could be cultural rather than religious). But the Christian elements are not rejected as insignificant. The Christian identity with *converso* elements is similar to the weak crypto-Jewish identity. It has a mediated structure, with the emphasis being on the Christian rather than the Jewish side. The Christian identity without *converso* elements is the mirror image of the strong crypto-Jewish identity. As ideal types, they represent a very wide range of variations; as points on continuum, one category imperceptibly flows into the next.

The second model, fluidity and *jonglerie*, attempts to de-essentialize identity. It suggests that identities are fluid and transformative based on a wide range of contexts, both personal and social. Individuals may move among the types of crypto-Jewish identity, depending on how particular contexts interact with their self-perception. As they make these moves, they might perform the same practices and have the same experiences, but reinterpret them and differentially emphasize them on the basis of their changed self-perception. The concept of *jonglerie* adds an aspect of agency to the structuralist understanding. It suggests that as individuals and groups move among different constructions of identity and within a specific identity, they differentially select, emphasize, and deemphasize elements of structure. This process has the possibility of transforming structure through evolution.

While the de-essentialization of identity and the related process of *jonglerie* are particularly evident in relation to the crypto-Jewish ethnography, they are characteristic of all individuals and communities. To an extent, I have defined these processes as postmodern. This suggests that they are characteristic of a particular time and place: the late twentieth century and early twenty-first century in the West. Although it may be that in the post-modern context these processes are relatively self-conscious, I would suggest that they are not limited to this context. It may be appropriate to utilize the concept of hot and cold societies in regard to these processes of trans-formation (in a related, although different way from that of Claude Lévi-Strauss [1966]). Arguably, postmodern Western society would fall into the hot category, with the term "hot" referring to the self-conscious aspect of the construction of identities. Premodern and modern societies would in some senses be relatively colder.

Although the construction and fluidity of identity are particularly appar-ent in examining crypto-Jewish ethnography, they do not lessen its cultural authenticity. All individuals and all societies undergo similar processes of construction, although they may be more or less hot and cold; thus in cul-tural terms, crypto-Jewish culture and identity are as culturally authentic as any other culture or construction of identity. Crypto-Judaism cannot be regarded as a social pathology because it includes elements or self-perceptions that a particular observer deems to be inappropriate or consid-ered less valuable as a subject of ethnographic consideration.

Emphasizing cultural authenticity does not lessen the significance of historical authenticity, especially because it is important to crypto-Jews. Of the arguments challenging the authenticity of crypto-Judaism, only those of Judith Neulander (2001) are directly germane to the issue. Michael Car-roll (2002) attacked primarily the scholarship and scholars rather than the issue of authenticity, and the journalists Barbara Ferry and Debbie Nathan (2000) only recapitulated Neulander's contentions.

Neulander's challenges can be divided into those relating to the inter-pretation of practice and those accounting for the claim of crypto-Jewish identity by individuals in New Mexico. Many aspects of her first set of argu-ments are important. She raises issues, particularly of false analogy and the possible bias introduced by an interviewer, that are clearly relevant to field research in New Mexico and must be taken seriously. The key problem with this point of her discussion is that it does not account for families that perform a very wide range of practices; accepting her contentions would require utilizing a range of sometimes incommensurate arguments to deal with the individual practices. Even if this were possible, many of Neulander's assertions rely on a presumption that the practices must be from an alternative historical source. While it is important to be critically objective, her argument takes this too far and moves away from objectivity to an automatically negative position. Her arguments are equally problematic in that they completely ignore the self-understanding of both past and present crypto-Jews, which she considers to be a form of false consciousness and not even worthy of discussion.

While Neulander's arguments relating to practice do make an important contribution to the study of crypto-Judaism, the same cannot be said for her general theory about the claims of crypto-Jewish identity. Her analysis has two key positions. First, she contends that the families that claim crypto-Jewish identity and/or practices were Pentecostal (or similar Protestant traditions), perhaps in the early to mid-twentieth century. They then returned to Catholicism, but retained aspects of practices similar to those of Judaism and an identity as the new Israel while forgetting (or lying) about their Pentecostal past. Second, she argues that these and other individuals wish to be considered white and Euro-American. Jewish identity is taken as a trope for whiteness, and therefore a claim of that identity allows them to socially transform themselves. They utilize the practices and identity that arose from their Pentecostal past to support their ethnic transformation.

The empirical base for Neulander's arguments is unsustainable. Most significantly, historical documents from the mid-twentieth century indicate that the penetration into New Mexico of the types of Protestant sects that follow Sabbatarian or Judaizing practices was minimal and cannot account for either the number or the geographic location in the state of individuals who claim crypto-Jewish identity. The spread of the Pentecostal groups mentioned by Neulander, none of which were significantly Sabbatarian, was equally small at that time. Thus the empirical data provides no support for Neulander's hypothesis, and, interestingly, she provides no direct data to support her supposition.

Neulander's contention that Hispanos wish to be considered white and use Judaism, a religion known to practice endogamy, as a trope for that racial purity attributes motives to individuals. It is good ethnographic practice to determine motives on the basis of ethnographic evidence collected from interviews and participant observation, and a serious analysis of the internal point of view, rather than hypothesizing and then attributing them without any substantial empirical information. Among individuals interviewed for this study and by Janet Jacobs (2002), those who claimed crypto-Jewish identity actually had a wide range of views on their families' traditions. While some stated that their families practiced forms of endogamy (and, where available, the genealogical evidence has supported some of these claims), others strongly emphasized their *manito* or mestizo heritage (even when the genealogies do not back up these self-perceptions). Thus this aspect of Neulander's theory remains just that, a hypothesis that finds little support in the data. On this basis, we can discount Neulander's analysis as an explanation of crypto-Jewish identification in New Mexico.

The primary alternative theory is that proposed by Stanley Hordes (2005), who believes that crypto-Jews were among the settlers of New Mexico in the sixteenth and seventeenth centuries and that many individuals who claim crypto-Jewish identity can include these colonists in their genealogies. Hordes's work provides substantial evidence that some settlers were descended from *conversos* and that some of them were themselves crypto-Jews, or at least accused by the Inquisition of Judaizing both before and after the settlement of New Mexico. He has provided documentary evidence that individuals who claim crypto-Jewish identity are descended from these colonists. In addition, he discusses the possible reasons for the movement of crypto-Jews initially to northern Mexico and ultimately to New Mexico. These suppositions, while suggestive, are unprovable given the data available. Although the second part of his argument remains speculative—there is no direct evidence for the persistence of crypto-Jewish identity or practice between the late seventeenth century, with the end of inquisitorial power, and the late twentieth century, with the emergence of modern crypto-Jews—Hordes convincingly demonstrates that the most likely reason that individuals are claiming crypto-Jewish identity is that the identity was passed down to them from ancestors who are documented as having had that identity.

There remain, however, significant questions about which elements of crypto-Judaism are part of an ongoing tradition and which may come from a variety of other sources. In exploring this, it is useful to look at the issues relating to two aspects of crypto-Judaism: identification and practice. Many factors provide strong evidence that identification is often part of an ongoing tradition. In the data collected for this and other studies are found several common patterns of transmission of crypto-Jewish or Jewish identification from one generation to the next. The most common occurs when an individual is an early adolescent. He or she is informed by an elderly relative (on either the male or female side) that "Somos judíos." While this identification sometimes is regarded as a statement about the past, it is also often seen as a statement about present identity. The repetition of this narrative in a wide range of data from all parts of New Mexico (and, indeed, in other areas of the Spanish diaspora) and the account of a similar practice in Inquisition documents suggest that this is most likely a long-standing family tradition. Other individuals have reported learning about their families' identification as Jews or descent from Jews from an elderly relative, sometimes on his or her deathbed. Adding this to the genealogical data that provides historical validation for such transmission of identity provides very strong evidence that these traditions, in many cases, are reliable and account for a segment of individuals who claim crypto-Jewish identity.

The issue of practices is less clear-cut. It is important that Neulander's specific arguments about practices be taken seriously. Thus it is possible that individuals both inside and outside the crypto-Jewish community have identified practices as being of Jewish origin that are merely similar to Jewish practices. It is also possible that practices were adopted from the mainstream Jewish community in New Mexico or through other sources of information and learning. Thus the presence of practices that appear to be Jewish does not provide strong evidence of an ongoing tradition of crypto-Judaism. They may be associated with individuals who have strong traditions of identity, but may not be directly related to that identity historically (although clearly, they are a very important part of that identity).

We do, however, find families that report a very significant range of practices for which genealogical data provides a link to *converso* ancestors. Even though there is no tradition of self-identification in many of these families, the level of practice reported and the genealogical data are suggestive evidence for the persistence of crypto-Jewish practices separately from identification. Some scholars, particularly Shulamith Halevy (1999), have suggested that some of these practices can be specifically identified with rabbinical practices and thus could not have been derived from biblical sources. While some of her examples are problematic because they are similar to common folk practices—for example, the burning of nail clippings or hair—others are more suggestive. It would be important to do a broad comparative study to determine if these practices are widespread or limited to crypto-Jews and their descendents. Although we have not sought to bring together this kind of data, as more genealogical and ethnographic evidence is compiled, it would be a very fruitful area for further study.

A very important issue relating to practice must be reiterated. Many who challenge the presence of crypto-Judaism in New Mexico use practice as a key piece of evidence for denying both the historical and the cultural identity of those who claim to be crypto-Jews. While practices may not be good evidence for historical authenticity, they are an important part of crypto-Jewish culture and self-identification and thus are important to understand from that perspective. This issue is particularly relevant to cases that are considered to be evidence of false identifications of practice. A particularly good example is the *pon y saca*, which may very well be a folk toy that was misidentified as a dreidel. The ethnography demonstrates that no matter what its origin, the top is regarded by many crypto-Jews as a dreidel—and for a proper understanding of crypto-Jewish culture, it must be understood in that way. The genesis of practices and objects of material culture is culturally less significant than their current performance and cultural use and understanding.

Perhaps a more pertinent question than authenticity is whether crypto-Judaism, as a largely oral culture of memory, will continue as an identifiable culture within the dominant society. There are clear cultural factors working against the persistence of crypto-Judaism. The Hispano community is increasingly becoming part of the wider, homogenized American culture. This is most clearly indicated by the changes in the Spanish spoken in New Mexico and ultimately in the loss of Spanish as the first or even the second language of some New Mexicans. Many individuals from older generations mention a form of Spanish that was typical of New Mexico. We have touched on this in relation to its interpretation as Judeo-Spanish, or Ladino. Whether it is Judeo-Spanish or another archaic form of Spanish is irrelevant to the trends that have occurred in relation to the loss of cultural distinctiveness. Many informants, older than fifty, specifically mentioned that their use of this form of Spanish was challenged as being poor usage. They were forced to change to a more acceptable version of Spanish. This reflects at least the perception of the beginning of a process of culture loss, which has continued into the present generation, whose use of Spanish as the first language, or even the second language, is increasingly rare. A similar process seemingly has occurred in relation to the transmission of crypto-Jewish identity. Even individuals who have a strong identity as crypto-Jews have not necessarily passed it to their children, some of whom consider crypto-Jewish identity to be irrelevant to their self-understanding as either Americans or, more frequently, Hispanic Americans. The modern

American society in which crypto-Jews find themselves and in which many of them play a very active part is not a strongly oral society, which makes the preservation and transmission of an orally based culture increasingly precarious, particularly when oral traditions are set against the wide variety of other increasingly strong outlets of cultural transmission.

A number of aspects of contested identity have led to the potential loss of crypto-Jewish identity. Mainstream American culture has a huge impact on minority identities. While in the past this influence was officially sanctioned and found in a variety of instruments of state power, particularly education, today it is unstated but still strong. The influence of mass media is only one example. Prejudice and racism, while potentially strengthening minority identities, can often have the opposite effect. The conflict between Hispanic and Anglo identities can also have an impact on crypto-Judaism. Some Hispanos regard arguments about crypto-Judaism as an example of divide and rule: distinguishing those who claim crypto-Jewish identity from those who do not may politically weaken the Hispanic community. Both individuals who are active in Hispanic politics and young people who are exploring crypto-Jewish identity have expressed their concerns about this particular conflict.

Perhaps, ironically, the movement of crypto-Jews into mainstream Jewish communities may also have a negative effect on the continued transmission of crypto-Jewish identity. A number of individuals with different levels of crypto-Jewish identity have chosen to join a variety of synagogues in New Mexico, other parts of the United States, and even in Israel. While some of them have maintained their identity within the broader Jewish communities and, at times, continued both privately and publicly to transmit crypto-Jewish identity and practices, others have embraced mainstream Judaism and thus marked the end of their secret identity as crypto-Jews. It is possible that in a generation, the crypto-Jewish past as a unique culture will largely be lost, except as a vague tradition or memory.

In spite of these trends, some developments suggest that a number of aspects of crypto-Jewish culture and identity may be preserved. The first is the increasing discussion of crypto-Judaism in the press and other media outlets. This public knowledge about what were hitherto secret traditions has led some individuals to speak about their own traditions and preserve them in written form. It has also inspired others to explore their own families' past to discover if there is a crypto-Jewish heritage. Thus the move from private to public has resulted in the preservation of culture, albeit in a transformed form that may be similar to other aspects of American ethnicity—that is, identities that are dipped into on occasion.

Organizations like the Society for Crypto-Judaic Studies, as well as a wide range of Web sites that pass on information, also play an important role in cultural preservation. They provide opportunities for individuals to explore their identities. Many of them are limited to the extent that they are not crypto-Jewish organizations or outlets; they are about crypto-Judaism, rather than places where crypto-Judaism can continue to grow and develop. This is not to criticize these organizations; study, research, and learning are important parts of culture, but cultural growth comes from inside a community rather than from outside it (although much cultural development and transformation comes in response to neighbors and context rather than being sui generis).

Most important, the crypto-Jewish community itself is working to preserve its culture and move it in new directions. One of the most effective means to do so is through informal networks that are in part supportive. Members help one another understand and, at times, deal with the conflicts that the crypto-Jewish identity can create in relation to other traditions, be they cultural (for example, Hispanic) or religious (particularly, although not exclusively, Catholic). These networks also actively transmit knowledge. Members share genealogical information and other tools for family research, because the networks often include individuals who are related; traditions and their interpretations of them; and forms of Jewish knowledge, particularly basic Hebrew and, at times, liturgy.

Crypto-Jews have also established a variety of formal structures. One group that is increasingly active is based in southern New Mexico and the region of Texas around El Paso. It has a learning center with books and other resources on crypto-Judaism and Judaism and has held conferences for the past several years. Although the main agenda of this group is to bring crypto-Jews back to mainstream Judaism, it is increasingly developing an independent identity because of its crypto-Jewish focus. Several synagogues specifically target crypto-Jews, and at least one of them has a rabbi who is of crypto-Jewish background. While these synagogues are largely within the framework of mainstream Judaism, it is possible that they will develop a specifically crypto-Jewish form of practice and identity because of their congregants.

It might also be argued that certain messianic traditions also help perpetuate a form of crypto-Jewish identity. Within our study, a range of individuals who are members of messianic Jewish communities associated their connection to these groups with their crypto-Jewish identity. Several suggested that joining the messianic communities allowed them to be Jewish but still believe in Jesus. Others came to their crypto-Jewish identity from the opposite direction. Three interviewees suggested that they originally considered themselves to be Christian and joined a messianic church out of Christian conviction. They then found that some of the Jewish aspects of practice were already part of their tradition. This led them to explore their genealogies and thereby discover Jewish roots. Some of these individuals now consider themselves to be crypto-Jews. It may be that because messianic communities tend to be more welcoming than many synagogues, crypto-Jews will find a meaningful way to maintain and construct their crypto-Jewish identity in this form of organization.

The evidence in favor of both the historical and the cultural authenticity of crypto-Judaism is very persuasive. Both the community and the processes of identity construction that are occurring within it are complex. The boundaries of the community are porous in terms of ideas and people. Crypto-Jews come out of an intricate matrix in which they are trying to come to an understanding of self that is meaningful in contemporary New Mexican society.

(NEO)-STRUCTURALISM

A BASIS FOR UNDERSTANDING THE TRANSFORMATIVE USE OF STRUCTURE IN CRYPTO-JEWISH CULTURE

This appendix considers the neo-structuralist approach developed and used in this book. While the discussion focuses on abstract theoretical questions, material from the crypto-Jewish ethnography is introduced to exemplify particular theoretical issues. These examples are indicative rather than fully developed and relate to more detailed discussions that are found throughout the book. While I am interested in general questions that relate to structuralist theory and methodology, this appendix is concerned with the relationship between underlying structure and identity and agency and with higher-level issues relating to structural development and transformation.

While the theoretical model and ethnographic analysis developed in this book is unashamedly structuralist (or, due to the changes suggested, neo-structuralist), drawing their inspiration from the work of Claude Lévi-Strauss (1963, 1966, 1969), several aspects of my approach either develop some of the implications inherent to that theoretical apparatus or take structuralist theory in new directions. One of the key areas of enhancement is in respect to levels of structure. As discussed later, I divide underlying structure into four interrelated levels: three unconscious structural levels and the narrative conscious level. This should not be seen as a deviation from the work of Lévi-Strauss. Although he does not distinguish among the levels of structure presented here, they are all implied by his analysis; that is, he uses structure in different ways through his discussions. Lévi-Strauss's different uses are analogous to my four levels.

The issue of diachrony (that is, specifically historical development of texts, rituals, or practices, rather than development within a myth, ritual, or practice), particularly in relation to structural transformation, is also a development of theoretical material implied by Lévi-Strauss's extended exploration of South American myth. Although his work rarely traced diachronic development of structure, it did substitute geographic movement for temporal movement; that is, he traced the development of mythological structures as they moved geographically from one society to the next in the Americas. It is likely that he used geographic in place of historical transformation due to the absence of accessible texts from different historical periods. While this analogy may be questionable, the theoretical issues that Lévi-Strauss raised in that respect can usefully be applied to diachronic transformation. This issue, however, does lead us to one of the significant differences between the analysis presented here and classical structuralism—that is, the distinction between hot and cold societies, or those that perceive themselves as experiencing rapid change and those that do not.

The argument presented here suggests that this is not a useful differentiation. The crypto-Jewish material is particularly significant in regard to both the issue of diachrony and the hot and cold distinction. Crypto-Jewish ethnography includes a diachronic aspect in respect to the transformation of practices both over the historical range and within individual life histories. In respect to the hot–cold distinction, it is argued that crypto-Judaism is perhaps the clearest example of the type of transformation indicative of a hot society, and one conscious of transformation, yet the underlying structural forms remain significant markers in understanding the processes of cultural creation and re-creation. It is further argued that due to individual manipulation, juggling, and transformation of cultural forms, crypto-Judaism and perhaps much of modern culture should be characterized as fluid rather than hot or cold.

There are two other key areas of difference. First, Lévi-Strauss often moves from offering culture-specific analysis to hypothesizing about universal underlying structure in an abstract sense or occasionally in a specific sense (that is, that a particular structural relation is universal). While I am not arguing against universal underlying structure in the former sense, I am arguing against the imposition of particular content or meaning on a biological or universal level. The discussion presented here also is more interested in the culture-specific rather than the biological aspects of structure. The crypto-Jewish material provides a fascinating insight into the interrelationship among multiple structural forms, and while they may have a simpler and more abstract common basis than is implied by the apparent multiplicity, it may (due to its simplicity) no longer have any real value or meaning even as a form of structure. Equally, the apparent binary basis of the various forms of crypto-Jewish structure may not indicate a broader, universal binary basis of structure, but may be an artifact of the fact that all the alternative forms arise within the same individuals and thus may have a common, culturally rather than biologically determined basis.

The second fundamental difference is in relation to agency. Many readings of structuralism viewed it as denying human agency both in the creation of cultural artifacts and in cultural practice. They saw it as suggesting a highly deterministic model for human behavior; that is, underlying structure was both fixed and unconscious, and thus individual actors could act on the basis of only these predetermined and consciously unavailable structures. While Lévi-Strauss's understanding that structure is unconscious and provides the foundation for culture in respect to both individuals and groups informs my theoretical perspective, I do see room for agency and structural difference. It is argued here that agency comes into play in emphasizing or deemphasizing aspects of structure, particularly in cases of cultural overlap. This process leads to possible transformation in structure and thus removes the static view of culture that is often associated with structuralism.

The concept of transformation underlies many of the analyses presented in this book. Due to my interest in underlying structure, I am concerned primarily in transformations at that level; these transformations must be examined in either a diachronic, as applied here, or a geographic context, as found in Lévi-Strauss's work. While many analyses, either anthropological or literary, focus on transformation at the narrative or surface level—for example, the movement of a hero from ignorance to knowledge—or changes in technology, these elements must be seen as separate from underlying structure; they are part of the conscious development in the text, practice, and ritual and should be understood as reflecting or being based on underlying structure rather than being underlying structure. Thus the inclusion in a crypto-Jewish ritual of Christian and Jewish elements, with a movement within the ritual that emphasizes the Jewish aspect, does not reflect a movement within structure; rather, the placement of the two elements together and the movement to or emphasis on the Jewish one reflect a structure that allows opposing elements to be placed together and possible movement from one to the other. A similar feature, discussed later, in a crypto-Jewish narrative brings together the contrary localities of the mountains and the city.

Although structure does not transform within a single myth or practice, it should not be understood as static. Its processes of change are usually slow and often associated with significant cultural changes that arise from or are associated with significant changes in the way the world is constructed—that is, changes in how we categorize the world and how those categories are related to one another. Cultural change, due to the complex nature of cultural interactions, is a given; thus structural transformation is found in all societies. Structure and its relationship with culture in this sense are relatively conservative but not petrified. Agency provides one of the motors for structural transformation. Agency, which is conscious, does not directly change underlying structure; rather, it privileges different aspects of the structural equation and, by so doing, leads to a slow process by which models of categorization and thinking can change.

Levels of Structure

Before developing arguments relating to the different levels of structure and the different possibilities of underlying structural relations, it is necessary to briefly discuss underlying structure in general. Structuralist theory suggests that all cultural objects will have as their foundation an unconscious underlying structure (conceived here as an abstract equation that defines the relationship between elements or more precisely categories). The unconscious in these terms should not be regarded as equivalent to the chaotic Freudian unconscious; the structuralist unconscious is largely structured and, while not itself rational, is the basis for rationality. Like the Freudian unconscious, it is unconscious in respect to access by the individual, who normally is not consciously aware of underlying structure. Thus underlying structure shapes the construction of cultural practices without implying or relying on conscious volition.

Underlying structure is largely culturally constructed and is thus shared by individuals from the same community. Cultural objects from the same context thus largely share an underlying structural equation. The analogy between underlying structure and structural linguistics, provided that the analogy is not taken too far, is helpful in understanding the nature of underlying structure. Structure is analogous to the logic that organizes the articulation of phonemes in the construction of words. Structural linguistics has tended to overemphasize the binary aspect of this process; while binary elements may be significant in underlying structure, more complex relations are also discernible. One aspect of the analogy that is particularly helpful is the independence of words from meaning; at its deepest level, structure organizes patterns of categories that are abstract and contentless—it is the pattern that is significant, rather than the meanings articulated by that pattern. The pattern, however, should also be seen as the basis for creating meaningful cultural objects. Structure provides the underlying logic that allows words to be said and to be understood. It creates the logical possibilities that determine how and what can be meaningfully communicated.

The holy grail of classical structuralism was the discovery of the underlying structures of the brain that are shared by all human beings. In a broader sense, structuralism can be defined as the attempt to establish the underlying patterns of the brain, which shape the way we categorize the world and thus ultimately the way we think and act. This second definition moves away from the necessarily unitary or monolithic implications of the first definition. The second definition does not deny the possibility that there is a common underlying structure, but it moves the argument to a position that does not depend on there being a universal underlying structure; it does, however, require that underlying structure(s) be found universally, on both the individual and communal levels.

The concept of underlying structure, although often seen as unitary, contains a number of levels of structure. Analytically and methodologically, it is useful to divide structure into three levels (plus the narrative [N] level). The levels come into play at different stages of analysis.

N	Culture and context specific
S^3	Culture specific
S^2	Culture group specific
S^1	Universal

Levels of structure.

In order to help explain how I am using these levels of underlying structure, it may be helpful to offer the analogy of a computer to clarify the differences among the four levels. It should be emphasized that the analogy is meant to be only illustrative rather than prescriptive. S^1, the lowest and most abstract level of structure, is analogous to the computer hardware before any software is loaded into it. The computer has hardwired, or built in, patterns or structures. These patterns, however, are meant to be flexible; they must be able to work in a number of ways. depending on the specific software used. The hardware may also establish a specific number of categories, partitions in the hard drive or other means of dividing information. S^2 is the most basic level of structure. It is analogous to machine language or other general software that tells the computer how to use information that is downloaded. It might, for example state that if x type of information is input, it will be placed in y category, and if y type of information is input, it will be placed in x category. This software has no specific informational content; rather, on an abstract level, it determines how content input or downloaded should be used. S^3 is analogous to the level in which specific data is input into the computer. This information is utilized or categorized based on the abstract programming already input. As new information is added, the programming determines how it should be appropriately categorized. It is important to note that no piece of information has a necessary category; as each new piece is added, its categorization is influenced by the information already input, and it will determine what happens to the next piece of information. The N level is the final product. It may be the image on the screen, a game, or a report. It takes the categories and information from the previous levels and puts them into a context that is meaningful for the user; that context, however, has no necessary relation to the type of information or categories found at the lower levels of programming. With this analogy in mind, we can now move to a more detailed discussion of the levels of structure.

The N Level

Although the N, or narrative, level is technically not a level of underlying structure (just as playing a computer game is not programming), and thus is conscious rather than unconscious, it is necessary to explore some of its aspects in order to understand the three levels of underlying structure. The N level is the specific cultural artifact being analyzed—for example, a myth, ritual, or custom. In relation to a myth, the narrative aspect is clear; myths are usually structured in a narrative way, with a clear aspect of diachronic progression. Rituals and customs also have a narrative level, which is that seen and acted within by the participants. Rituals, in particular, have an aspect of diachronic progression (most clearly seen in rites of passage). Other practices, such as food rules, are less clearly narrative or diachronic; nonetheless, there still is a level of practice that is consciously perceived by the actors, even though these practices may be ongoing and have no specific time or place set aside. The N level is that in which all elements have been shaped by underlying structure and have been placed into a culturally (rather than structurally) meaningful context in which they are presented as a coherent myths, rituals, or practices.

The order of elements found at this level is not of structural significance except inasmuch as it may indicate diachronic (textually or ritually) transformation of the symbolic elements being used. This transformation, however, is not structural; rather, it may be one of nuancing, emphasizing, or deemphasizing the structural element. The reason for the distinction between narrative and structural meaningfulness is that in order to tell a story or construct a ritual, the elements may have been reordered based on the needs of the narrative. Structuralist analysis suggests that at the underlying levels of structure, diachronic or narrative development is not significant; the elements and their interrelations can be reversed or reordered in different ways based on structural rather than narrative considerations. The analysis in this appendix illustrates a range of different processes of ordering at the narrative level, for example, inversion or doubling. While these processes seem significant on the narrative level, they have no significant impact on underlying structure. It is the repetition and use of the elements rather than their narrative order that is significant. Narrative needs may at times also seem to conflict with structural needs.

This aspect is seen to be a significant aspect of crypto-Jewish practice, particularly due to diverse levels of practice and identity in that community. One of the themes highlighted in this volume, and indeed characteristic of much of crypto-Judaism ethnography, is the disjunction between the understanding and the explanation of a practice, both aspects of the N level and the underlying structure or structures. On occasion, practices are understood or explained in ways that seem to be almost antithetical to the underlying structure. Nonetheless, the structural coherence of the practices is maintained and, in relation with other cultural practices that are similarly structured, can significantly shape the elements in the construction of diverse forms of crypto-Jewish identity.

The N level is highly culture and context specific. The contents of myths and other cultural artifacts are closely related to their cultural, geographic, and historical contexts. As myths and rituals move in time and space, elements move in and out of significance and new elements become significant or available. Thus the narrative level is particularly prone to transformation in content rather than in structure. As indicated, this cultural specificity also relates to the process of emphasis or deemphasis, which at different times may lead to different developments on the narrative level. These types of N-level transformations are best seen in relation to the replacement of ritual items or mythological elements with those more closely related to the cultural and contextual space in which crypto-Jewish practices developed and changed. An obvious example of this simple transformation is the substitution of ritual foods and objects not available in New Mexico with those that were available—for example, the use of quince instead of citron in the rituals of the festival of Sukkoth. Thus this level of transformation provides some of the clearest examples of bricolage.

The S^1 Level

The most basic level of structure, S^1, is the fundamental, biological aspect of underlying structure. It is understood to be part of the structure of the brain and thus is the common inheritance of all human beings. Although at times Claude Lévi-Strauss (1963, 1969) seems to suggest that this universal level may contain a specific structure or content, from the perspective of this discussion it is both contentless and nonspecific. In this sense, it is regarded as the most abstract level of structure, being the potential for structuring rather than a specific structure. The term "potential" should not be understood as suggesting that humans could do without structuring; from a structuralist perspective, structuring is fundamental to being human and is a necessary process underlying any form of communication (even self-communication) or understanding (even self-understanding).

Questions immediately arise about the nature of this structuring principle. Many discussions by both structuralists and nonstructuralists have seen it as being binary, or dyadic, in nature, often regarding it as a specific form of binarism (that is, strongly oppositional). It is possible, however, that the S^1

level is much more plastic. As the basis for structuring, it provides the foundation for the development of a range of structural possibilities; they could be binary, albeit with a wider range than merely oppositional, or more complex, such as triadic rather than dyadic. The possibility for triadic structures, although not specifically found in crypto-Jewish cultural practices, has been demonstrated in regard to Mormon cultural practices (Kunin 2004:143–146). The analysis suggests that these structures can be understood only as triadic, and thus the traditional binarism cannot be sustained.

An additional issue closely related to binarism is whether underlying structure is also monopolistic. On the community level, it is likely that this may not be the case in a strong sense: different interest groups may nuance structure in different ways. On the individual level, however, this question raises significant problems. Can an individual simultaneously maintain two possibly antithetical structures? This question is directly related to that of compartmentalization at a higher level of analysis. Both structuralist theory and the analysis presented here suggest that if structural compartmentalization occurs it can be only a fleeting phenomenon and that the default position is one in which a single structure, however complex, is maintained. Nonetheless, the crypto-Jewish material allows for a more nuanced understanding of how individuals and groups relate to underlying structure, leading to the significant differences and variations found in the process of individual and group diachronic development. The analysis suggests that since structure is very rarely black and white, the mediated aspect allows for different emphasis, particularly in relation to the level of mediation. Thus as individuals are placed in different contexts (or, more precisely, cotexts), their nuancing of the same structural equation will lead to different, albeit related, structural configurations.

This discussion raises a related question about the location of underlying structure: Is structure found in the cultural object or practice, or is it found in the individual? Although because of the nature and method of most structuralist analyses the emphasis often seems to be on the object rather than on the individual, it is clear that there must be a complex interplay between the two. While the role of practice is discussed later, it is useful here to highlight the observation from the crypto-Jewish ethnography that it is the presence of underlying structure in both the object and the individual that provides the locus for the considerable structural nuancing observed. The underlying structure found in the object provides a static base on which different individuals can selectively emphasize or deemphasize (unconsciously) aspects of structure based on the cotextually developed relation to structure in their own unconscious (in a structuralist rather than a Freudian sense).

Although, as suggested, this level of structure is the holy grail of structuralism, it cannot be the main goal of any specific structuralist analysis. If there is a shared underlying structure, whether of the abstract nature proposed here or of the more concrete forms suggested in other analyses, it can be determined only on the basis of comparative analysis. Thus to achieve this goal, there must be a wide range of highly detailed, specific structuralist analyses from a wide range of cultural contexts, which through comparative analysis (much the same as needed to determine the structure of a set of myths) will enable the discovery of the common underlying structural thread that links all human beings. Nonetheless, it is perhaps possible to see this level of structure as being the basis of a process that is clearly found in all human beings and all human societies—that is, the need to structure the world around us. While there is perhaps no single common structure or even structuring principle, structuring is universal. This basis for structuring that arises from the biological structure of the brain provides the foundation for the culture-specific structuring analyzed by structuralists.

The S^2 Level

The next level of structure, S^2, is understood to be unconsciously shaped by a culture (loosely understood) or, more likely, a culture group— that is, a group of closely related cultures rather than specific cultures. The terms "culture group" and "cultures" are ideological, political, or analytical constructs that do not reflect the complexity of human interactions. They suggest a boundedness that ignores the overlaps and gray areas. Nonetheless, if we accept the ambiguity and complexity that this suggests, it is still possible to speak of a shared, unconscious ("culture"-specific) structure if it is recognized that it is not monolithic or monopolistic. Indeed, it is the blurring or sharing of structures that may provide an explanation for structural transformation.

The crypto-Jewish material is particularly fruitful in the presentation of this more dynamic understanding of culture. Crypto-Jewish culture is highly nuanced and transformative. It is very clearly the product of individuals' interaction with their cotext and maintains very little coherence in terms of content or understanding within the diachronic movement of the individuals' self-understanding. The culture is also embedded in an equally transformative and dynamic context—Hispano identity in New Mexico and more broadly, various aspects of American culture and self-understanding. Nonetheless, the material presented here suggests that at the S^2 level, there are relatively coherent (although not monopolistic) structures that allow for communication and sharing of forms of practice and understanding.

Like S^1, the S^2 level of structure is abstract in that it does not include any specific content. The S^2 level of structure is that in which the potential for categorization is concretized into both the number of significant categories (for example, dyadic or triadic), and the nature of the relation between those categories (that is, the way the categories interact with each other). These two interrelated elements are the basis for the creation of culturally meaningful patterns.

The S^2 level builds on the S^1 in several respects. It is the context of the move from the biological potential for structure to the cultural actualization of specific structure(s). In this sense, it is a limitation on "natural" possibilities; the move to structuring is one of limitation of setting boundaries to allow for meaningful exchange and communication. This level also establishes the nuanced relationship between categories. The different categories—whether dyadic, triadic, or more complex forms—can be related to one another in a number of ways that have significant implications for both the nature and content of the categories; the relations determine whether the categories are able to overlap or whether information is able to move from one category to another. The analyses conducted thus far suggest three ideal types of relation. The term "ideal type" is used to indicate that the "pure" form exists only as an analytical construct; each specific culture or culture group develops relations that fall between the different ideal types. There also is variation within a culture, although the range of nuancing at that level is much more limited than at higher levels of cultural differentiation.

The three ideal types represent different relations of exchange between categories. Each has implications in terms of both the organization of data and the movement of data. The (–) ideal type represents a negative relation or model of exchange. The negative relation allows for no possible exchange between and no overlap of the categories. This can be characterized in relation to two categories: A and B. Anything in category A will never be in category B, and anything in B will never be in A. The model of exchange indicates that the categories are clearly articulated and unbridgeable. This

$$A-B$$
$$A \cap B$$
$$A+B$$

Ideal types of structural relations.

relation is best exemplified in the Jewish system of food rules, in which an animal is either kosher (edible) or *treif* (not edible). No animals fall outside this dichotomy. If an animal is *treif,* it can never move into the kosher category. A significant aspect of this process of categorization depends on the level of elements being used: thus a cow has a clear oppositional relation to a pig, while the hindquarters of a cow, which are forbidden, are in an oppositional relation to the permitted parts of the cow.

The (*n*) ideal type represents a neutral relation or model of exchange. The neutral relation allows for different degrees of exchange between and a range of variants of overlap of the categories. This relation suggests that elements of category *A* will also be in category *B* and vice versa. The overlap of elements in each may be unequal, depending on the nature of the neutral relation. The model of exchange suggests that elements can also move between *A* and *B*. An example of this type of relation in crypto-Jewish ethnography is found in the New Testament and much Christian mythological material. These structures allow movement between categories, while retaining the distance between the two. Thus a person can start out as a non-Christian in the rejected category and through a process of faith can move into the positive category.

The (+) ideal type represents a positive relation or model of exchange. The positive relation allows for a high degree of exchange between and overlap of the categories. In its ideal form, everything in category *A* will also be in category *B*. This congruity, however, does not imply that the categories are in fact one—that is, an *A/B* rather than *A* and *B*. Despite having the same content, the categories are often seen or used in different ways. While positive relations are not found in most of the crypto-Jewish ethnography, they are found in some cultural elements utilized by some crypto-Jews—for example, Buddhist and Mormon material.[1] While in Buddhism there is a clear distinction between the category of multiplicity and that of absolute unity, these categories can be regarded on a deeper plane as describing one and the same reality—thus providing a monistic rather than a truly oppositional use of the categories.

Two additional aspects of structural relation must be emphasized. First, the figure depicts and the discussion presents a dyadic model (which in part colludes with the stereotypical understanding of structuralism). In cases where more complex models are found, the categories might be differentially related to one another. Thus, for example, in the triadic structure of the Book of Mormon, there is a negative relation between A and C, a positive relation between B and C, and a neutral relation between A and B (Kunin 2004:145). The complex nature of some crypto-Jewish structures, discussed later, can be categorized as either multiple structures or triadic structure—this is seen in the apparent bringing together of a form of oppositional negative relations with a structure based on a mediated relation.

Second, in actual cultural formations, there is significant variation on these ideal types. Thus, for example, a variation on $A + B$ might be that anything in A is in B, while some things in B may not be in A. As suggested, the nature of variation is more complex than merely indicating nuances at the cultural level. In a cultural formation, there also is a range of variants on the ideal type of that formation. Thus each community is characterized by a shared pattern that is then nuanced in different ways by both subgroups and, to some extent, individuals.

It is in this area of variation that the flexibility arises that allows for the dynamic character of crypto-Jewish structure. As argued later, the S^2 level is essentially dyadic, with a negative to neutral relation. The different subgroups of the community are able to use this negative to neutral valence (unconsciously) to structure their use of cultural practices in different (albeit closely related) ways in relation to their construction of identity. The fact that structured practices and objects also include this nuanced and variable valence allows for their use by individuals whose identity falls on different ends of the range—that is, those who define themselves clearly as Jews with a Catholic background and those who identify themselves as Catholics (or, indeed, other forms of Christianity) with a Jewish background.

The S^3 Level

The final level of structure, S^3, is the least abstract. It is culture and context specific, using mythological elements that are appropriate and available in that context; the structural content of each myth and ritual thus is shaped to fit that context. The specific content that is added to structure, however, does not directly influence the structural configuration; whatever content is input into the structure it will be organized and made meaningful in a set way determined by the underlying structural equation at the S^2 level. The mythological and ritual content added at this level are referred to as mythemes and ritemes, respectively. On the level of myth, a mytheme can be defined as the relation between a particular structural element and another, as defined by the (narrative) actional element. It is thus a small element used in the construction of a myth. Similarly, a riteme is a small unit used in the construction of a ritual; it is a particular element set in active relation to another element (for example, candles and the Rosary are two ritemes set in relation by the action of being used together).

Mythemes and ritemes have no set meaning or value; they can be understood only in relation to other mythemes and ritemes. Their value is in part set by their co/contextualization; that is, the meaning of the first mytheme or riteme is open ended. Once it is categorized in a particular setting, it is fixed for that specific context. This occurs through the introduction of a second mytheme or riteme. Each is categorized in relation to the other. This aspect of mythological or structural co/contextualization is particularly illustrated in relation to Jewish food rules. A particular constituent of the system—for example, the pig—has no meaning on its own, but gains meaning through its relation to other ritemes and thus cannot be usefully examined on its own terms, either historical or cultural.

This aspect of co/contextualization is also significant in regard to the interpretation of specific elements. It is often assumed that a symbol has a consistent cultural value. If we take co/contextualization seriously, it is clear that the value is context specific and that if the symbol (in the same culture) is placed in a different structural role and set of relations, its value can be significantly transformed. A good example of this process is seen in crypto-Jewish practice. The cotextualization or contextualization aspect is found in respect to the same ritual practice in co/contextually different identity structuring. Thus a ritual that brings together lighting candles on Friday nights with reciting the Rosary can serve different structural purposes, depending on the co/context. For an individual who emphasizes the Jewish aspect of his or her identity, the Rosary may be relegated to purely the role of secrecy—that is, covering up the Jewish aspect of the ritual. For an individual (or in a different cotext, the same individual) who emphasizes the Catholic aspect of his or her identity, the Rosary may be the operative symbol, with the candle lighting serving as a remnant of Jewish family history.

This aspect of co/contextualization is built on the view that meaning is found in (or associated with) only the combination of mythemes. No individual mytheme has an essential or a necessary association with a particular meaning; meaning is attributed to the combination of mythemes, a process that works, as suggested here, on the basis of structural principles. The arbitrariness is closely related to that observed by Ferdinand de Saussure (1959:65–74; see also Sturrock 1979) in relation to words. The combination of mythemes is associated with signifiers, which stand in arbitrary relation with the signified. On the basis of this process, however, the combination of mythemes gains a culturally contextual relation with that meaning. As the sets of mythemes move into a new cultural context, this conventionality is removed and the mythemes may be renegotiated (restructured) and associated with a new arbitrary, culturally specific meaning.

237

This theme will be developed in some detail in relation to the use and the interpretation of symbols in crypto-Jewish culture. Much of the discussion of symbols like the six-pointed star and the four-sided top have assumed that these objects retain their meaning or have fixed meaning without specific regard to co/contextual issues. Thus there is a common assumption that a six-pointed star carved on a grave-stone is a Star of David and thus an indication of crypto-Jewish identity. But symbols can be understood only in a highly co/contextualized way and thus can move into and out of cultural salience and have meanings only within a narrow cultural framework. Thus, for example, the six-pointed star originally may have been used on grave-stones for decorative, nonsymbolic purposes, but in the modern context, with the star being given a very specific meaning, its use by individuals has a different and specific cultural value, identifying them and their families as crypto-Jews. This is relevant in regard to the broader analysis of material culture, particularly in relation to those approaches that seek to find identifiable "Jewish" objects as a means to prove or, indeed, disprove the authenticity of crypto-Judaism in New Mexico. If the approach suggested here is correct, there is no such thing as a "Jewish" object. An object becomes "Jewish" based on its use and the way a community or an individual chooses to understand it. Even a symbol as apparently specifically Jewish as the Hebrew name for God can be a Christian (or, indeed, nonreligious) symbol based on its use and understanding. A similar example is the use of Hebrew letters interpreted in the motto as "Light and Truth" on Yale University's coat of arms. Similarly, the Rosary functions not as a Catholic symbol but, for some crypto-Jews, as part of the Jewish ritual of lighting candles and as a statement of Jewish rather than Catholic identity.

Dan Sperber's (1975:119–123) approach to symbolism, although not specifically speaking of mythemes, provides a useful model for understanding some aspects relating to the possibilities of meaning inherent in mythemes (and ritemes) and the significance of co/contextualization. Sperber makes a clear distinction between symbols and both verbalization and conceptualization. Although mythemes are by their nature verbalized, because they are relations rather than narrative events, they can be regarded as distinct from the narrative products on the N level. They are used to construct the narrative level but, as suggested earlier, before being set into relation with other mythemes have no specific or fixed meaning. Ritemes are more clearly symbolic in this sense, as they are by their nature independent of verbalization and necessary conceptualization. This, however, does not mean that symbols, mythemes, or ritemes are not and cannot be verbalized or conceptualized. It suggests that they are independent of such processes, but can mobilize them in different ways.

Sperber also suggests that symbols gain their meaning through a process of evocation, which is open ended and results in a cone of meanings, feelings, memories, and the like rather than a specific meaning. The meanings constructed, however, include culturally defined and accepted meanings (public aspects of symbolism) and a wider range of individually defined and articulated meanings. Sperber's model allows for an understanding of the interrelated aspects of boundedness and unboundedness that is inherent to mythemes and ritemes. The role of context (other mythemes or symbols) provides the necessary structure that allows the combinations of mythemes to meaningfully communicate—that is, to construct meaning on both the S^3 level and the N level. On its own, a symbol has no meaning because there is no context of boundedness to "determine" its meaning. If, however, symbols or mythemes are placed in a structured relationship, the mythemes and the structure will, at least to some degree, allow for meaningful shared (public) communication. The fact that symbols or mythemes retain their unbounded aspect provides an additional basis for agency within a structured system.

We have already touched on the ethnographic example of the recitation of the Rosary during the ritual of lighting candles on Friday nights. These individual elements have no specific meanings on their own. The candle lighting gains some of its boundedness from the time it is performed—

that is, Friday evening rather than any other evening. It also is bounded by a relation of difference; that is, it is done in a way that is different from lighting candles on other nights of the week and from performing practices done by others in the Hispano community. The symbols are further bounded by bringing together the Rosary and the candle lighting, with the interrelation of the two having a different effect based on the bounding effect of interpretation, which is also part of the symbolic/ritual context. The meaning of the symbols is also further bounded in those cases in which a further blessing is used.

Mediation

Alongside the levels of structure and, specifically, the three forms of relation, mediation provides an element of nuancing that allows for differences both between and within cultural groups. Mediation is a subcategory of the structural relations; it comes into play on the abstract level of S^2, on the mytheme and riteme level of S^3, and in a slightly different way on the N level. It specifically defines the process of exchange whereby elements move between the categories. Mediation has two main ideal types: negative and positive.

In a system with negative mediation, there is a strong emphasis on the unbridgeability of the categories. Any object that appears to bring together the categories either by overlapping—that is, containing some elements of both categories—or by moving between them is considered to be culturally problematic and usually either defined out of the system or moved clearly into one of the defined categories. Although negative mediation may be interpreted as a self-contradictory concept, from a structuralist perspective the rejection of mediation inherent in the concept is a form of mediation. In systems that are characterized by this type of mediation, mediators are often present but are given a strongly negative quality (as in the pig in Judaism) as a means to deny mediation and thereby strengthen the opposing categories. As with the ideal types of structural relations, there are variations on the nature of negative mediation.

In a system with positive mediation, there are varying degrees of bridgeability between the categories. Those objects that bridge categories range in qualitative valence from neutral to positive, depending on the object and the particular cultural system. These systems often (or always) allow movement between the categories, and mediators are often the vehicles through which this movement takes place. Depending on the quality of the positive valence and the level of positive mediation, the objects that move need a greater or lesser amount of transformation. In a system with a strong negative aspect, transformation has to be relatively absolute. In a system with more positive valence, transformation is minimal—often of quantity or nuance rather than of quality.

Mediation plays an additional significant role and provides an important diagnostic tool in analysis. Many myths, rituals, or customs include or imply the existence of mediators—elements that seem to fit in both categories, often having some features from one category and some from the other. The mediator can, in Mary Douglas's (1978) terms, be seen as anomalous because it is not easily categorized. This, however, is only one structural possibility. In fact, the way a system treats its mediators—for example, considering them as anomalous and dangerous or seeing them as positive— is a clear indication of the nature of the underlying structural relation. The crypto-Jewish material discussed later is a good example of mediators and their diagnostic capabilities. Myth and folklore, oral histories, and ritual include mediators that are differentially interpreted by individuals and groups with different levels of crypto-Jewish identity. The way in which mediators are utilized or not is an indication of the nature of specific models of identity. What is significant is not the direction of transformation or emphasis, but the presence of mediation and the way in which it facilitates cotextual construction of identity. The use of mediators in crypto-Judaism is associated with both the strongly negative structural relation found in Jewish communities and the positive valuation of mediation found in many Christian communities and cultural practices. Nonetheless, as at other levels, there is a wide range of possible treatments and uses of mediators, each of which arises from and indicates a variant on structural relations.

In order to understand the structural role of mediation, it is necessary to distinguish between narrative and structural mediation. Thus far, I have discussed structural mediation or the implications of mediation for analysis. Mediation is also a common feature on the narrative level. Narrative mediation shares some features with the structural variety. The most significant factor is that the mediator contains aspects of both elements between which it mediates. It also provides a useful mechanism for moving elements from one state to the other or reducing the role of one element in the narrative.

One crypto-Jewish folktale provides a useful illustration of the different forms of mediation. The story describes the birth of a girl in the mountains of northern New Mexico. In order to hide the family's crypto-Judaism, the baby has to be baptized. This, however, cannot be done in the mountains, as there were no priests. The family journeys on a wagon down to Santa Fe to celebrate the baptism. During the journey, the wagon hits a bump and the baby flies out and onto the edge of the road. This, however, is not noticed and the journey continues. Upon arriving in Santa Fe, the family finds that the baby has vanished. Due to the difficulty of making the journey again, the baptism is performed in absentia and the family makes its way back the mountains. They find the baby happily sitting on the side of the road, waiting to be picked up. This narrative includes a significant aspect of mediation in the journey, which joins the two oppositional spaces: the mountains, identified as Jewish space, and the city, which is Catholic space. The journey allows or suggests the possibility of movement between the two domains, perhaps creating a liminal domain that joins the two oppositional domains. The journey itself and this liminal space, however, should be understood as narrative mediation, as they are included to allow the narrative to progress; the real elements being related are crypto-Jewish and Catholic identity, rather than the narrative spaces or movement. The journey does not create structural transformation, but allows the issue of structural transformation to be addressed. The potential structural mediator in the narrative is the baptism, which transforms one identity into another. This mediator is clearly rejected, and thus the narrative is characterized by negative structural mediation.

Interestingly, the progression of the narrative also denies the element of narrative mediation by removing the main object of transformation, the baby, halfway through the tale. Thus even the narrative presence of mediation is denied by the development in the story itself. On a different level, that of contextualization in the ethnographic interview, the story also provides a means of explaining why the name of the ancestor was in the baptismal registry while retaining her crypto-Jewish identity (which in this context is regarded as exclusive and oppositional).

One of the interesting aspects of the distinction between structural and narrative mediation in crypto-Jewish practice is the possibility of the same element playing either role, depending on the individuals utilizing a particular practice. In the practice discussed throughout this appendix, the Rosary can be seen as playing both roles. For those individuals who have a strong crypto-Jewish identity, the Rosary plays a narrative role, merely as a means to provide a cover for the underlying Jewish nature of the practice. For those individuals who have a weak crypto-Jewish identity, the Rosary plays a mediating role, linking their Jewish identity with the broader Catholic context. In other cases, the Rosary loses its intermediary status and, like the candle lighting, takes on the status of a riteme (and, sometimes, the privileged riteme) set in relation to the other ritemes in the practice. The significant elements of the distinction between narrative and structural mediators, for the purposes of this discussion, is that structural mediators are valenced while narrative mediators are not marked or not as clearly marked.

Mediation can also be used more broadly in relation to understanding the reception by different communities, Jewish and Christian, of both crypto-Jews and the general concept of crypto-Judaism. The crypto-Jew in relation to both communities is almost the perfect example of a mediator, containing elements of both and thus in some sense bridging them. It is suggested later that due to its general structural model of negative mediation, the Jewish community has greater problems assimilating crypto-Judaism than does the Christian community, which is characterized by positive mediation. It is also suggested that this process occurs during the construction of crypto-Jewish identity as individuals define themselves in relation to or in opposition to their Jewish and Christian heritage.

Structural Transformation

One of the important issues in structuralist analysis is structural transformation, either within or between cultures. It is particularly relevant to crypto-Judaism. Whatever its relation to historical Jewish structure, crypto-Judaism (in an ideal sense) represents a complex example of transformed structure: the structural models are an interesting mix of both Christian and Jewish structural elements. Transformation is also regarded as an ongoing process. It is found in individuals and groups as the cotext and relation to that cotext changes.

Transformation works on a number of levels; the two most relevant to this discussion are that which occurs as structured material moves from one community to another (or one part of a community to another) and that which occurs within a community as it changes diachronically (or geographically).

The transformations that arise from a move from one cultural context to another are not theoretically problematic. Structuralist theory suggests that as a myth, for example, moves from one culture to another, while its mythemes may be preserved (although they, too, often change), its underlying structure (S^2) is unconsciously adjusted to fit its new cultural context. The mythemes are reconstructed, reorganized, and particularly recategorized on the S^3 level in order to reconfigure the myth to the S^2 level of the new cultural context. This process may also include significant transformation on the N level.

This type of transformation is found in crypto-Judaism in regard to both Christian practices and, more particularly, those associated (either internally or externally) with Judaism. We have already touched on the use of the Rosary in a crypto-Jewish ritual context. This liturgical practice is restructured in two respects, both into a statement or practice associated with secrecy and into a powerful symbol devoid of specific Catholic content. The ceremony brings together two ritual practices, or ritemes, and through their co-relation provides a structural context in which their original valences are transformed. The transformation can work in either direction, depending on the individual or group that instantiates the practice. This aspect of transformation works on the S^3 level, in which specific information is input into the structure. The distinction is based either on an abstract equation, which divides everything into mutually exclusive categories, or on one in which mediation and thus validation of both elements is possible; both of these are developed on the S^2 level.

The transformation of underlying structure also occurs within a culture as it develops diachronically. This type of transformation works on three levels: N, S^3, and S^2. As stories are told and retold through time, the articulation or presentation of the structural relations can change at the N level. Often the structural relations tend to crystallize and become more clearly articulated, especially if the issues developed at the N level are not culturally problematic. Due to the absence of crypto-Jewish material of different diachronic depths, this aspect of structural transformation is difficult to illustrate. But it might be found in part in the utilization of ritemes associated with modern Judaism and thus the unambiguous association with Jewish as opposed to Christian identity. It is also possible that this process can be illustrated with material that describes crypto-Jewish practices in non-crypto-Jewish sources—for example, Inquisition records. A wide range of problems are associated with the use of non-crypto-Jewish sources in relation to both the nature of these documents and, theoretically, the con-

text in which they were produced (that is, the Catholicism of the secretaries and others who recorded confessions or listed Jewish practices) and thus might skew the underlying structures in line with their own cultural context. This structural process is much more apparent in textual traditions that have developed over an extensive period—for example, the rabbinic retellings of biblical narrative.

One potentially interesting variation on this type of transformation is found in individuals as they construct and reconstruct identity over a number of years. (The ethnographic research on which this analysis is based was conducted over twelve years, with many individuals being interviewed at different stages of the study.) The ethnographic material suggests a number of processes that are in some ways analogous to those found in cultural transformation.

One trajectory was taken by individuals who strongly emphasized either the Jewish or the Christian aspects of their identity. There often was very little noticeable change in structural markers; although based on more knowledge of crypto-Judaism, they sometimes marshaled additional material to illustrate their self-perception. Another trajectory was taken by those who moved to a stronger Jewish identity. There often was a hardening of structure, a process similar to that labeled as structural crystallization. The final trajectory was taken by those who moved from a clearly marked Christian identity to a strong Jewish identity. There was a transformation of structure in line with the strength of the transformed identity.

Although this transformation is analogous to cultural transformation, they appear to work in ways associated with transformations that arise through change in emphasis (and, indeed, this may be the primary driver of all structural transformation). As suggested, this type of development does not involve an actual transformation in structure, but, through the variations in possible emphasis within the mediatory aspect of structure, relates to a quantitative distinction rather than a qualitative change. As the culture develops, different ritemes or mythemes may be given greater or lesser prominence, often depending on the conscious manipulation of the text or ritual. Both these types of transformations, however, do not directly transform the underlying structural equations.

The transformation of underlying structure also works on the S^3 level. This is the process identified as bricolage (Lévi-Strauss 1966:16–36). It refers to the changes in the elements out of which myths or rituals are constructed, as the cultural or environmental context changes. It is through bricolage that new elements are unconsciously categorized and assembled to create new cultural constructs. The key point is that these elements, which constitute a finite set, are related to each other and are given cultural value through their being structured at the S^3 level. It is the structural pattern rather than the elements that is significant. Like the previously discussed types of transformation, to which this form is closely related, there is no necessary change in the underlying structural equations. While many cultural theories take into account this type of recycling process, the distinctive aspect of structuralism is that it emphasizes the structures that articulate the recycled elements rather than the recycled elements themselves.

Crypto-Jewish material provides a rich source for analyzing different forms of bricolage. There are four main types:

- The use of Christian material in relation to Jewish ritual practices (or the reverse)
- The use of alternative cotextual items to replace items not available in the new cotext (such as the move from Spain to the New World)
- The presence of secrecy as an important component of a practice
- The appropriation of modern Jewish elements into crypto-Jewish practice

The significance of these forms of bricolage is that each one, with the possible exception of the cotextual elements, is fundamental to the flexibility within the mediation aspect of structure, thus allowing for the practices to be nuanced and in effect restructured by individuals with different degrees of crypto-Jewish identity.

The most significant type of transformation occurs at the S^2 level. It is characterized by a change in the underlying equation—either a change in nuance or a change in valence. Two main processes cause this type of structural transformation: the occurrence of significant changes in the cultural context or culture contact and the bringing together of different structural patterns. Both of these causes can develop slowly over time or, depending on contingent factors, be more abrupt. This type of transformation can also include nontransformation, often characterized by the hardening of structural patterns and the reduction of structural flexibility.

Although there is a historical link between the Jews of Spain and the crypto-Jews of New Mexico, as is almost conclusively demonstrated by much of the genealogical and historical data, we do find a process of structural differentiation between them. The transformation from Jew to crypto-Jew suggests that the mixing of cultural forms and practices after 1492 was a significant enough driver to lead to the observed differences in underlying structure (from an essentially unmediated structure to a highly or variably mediated structure). This transformation suggests both a limitation on compartmentalization—with the two distinct sets of forms and practices ultimately being synthesized into a new, restructured set of forms and practices—and the developmental effects of nuancing and stretching of structural boundaries.

Claude Lévi-Strauss's (1966:233–234) distinction between hot and cold societies is closely related to this discussion of transformation. He suggests that hot societies perceive themselves as undergoing rapid change and thus have a concept of diachronic development and, therefore, of history. He assumes that structural transformation in hot societies is equally rapid, and thus they are less amenable to structuralist analysis than cold societies. Nonetheless, hot societies are still seen as structured, and in more recent work Lévi-Strauss (1981, for example) applies structuralist methodology to modern, Western literary works. Cold societies do not perceive themselves as changing. They usually do not have a concept of linear development, or history. Lévi-Strauss regards these societies as undergoing relatively slow change, and thus their structures tend to be more static and amenable to analysis.

This distinction, however, is problematic on several levels. Its concept of history privileges a particular Western view as a means to distinguish between cultures. If history is seen as a model of self and time, rather than as something qualitatively distinct, there seems little reason to see it as fundamentally different from other models of self and time. Thus history, or perception of diachrony, cannot be the basis for distinction. If change is the significant factor, the distinction becomes slightly more supportable. While all cultures are constantly undergoing process of transformation, it is likely that some are changing more quickly than others. Nonetheless, provided that the material under analysis is specifically contextualized, there seems little reason to make a strong distinction between cultures.

It seems likely that all societies include aspects that reflect these two models of self and time in regard to both different subgroups having different models and the community as a whole being relatively hot or cold. This critique is supported by Jonathan Hill (1988:5; see also Turner 1988:235–246), who suggests that all societies are conscious of both myth and history—that is, cold and hot perceptions of self. Although I do not agree with Hill's use of myth and history as distinct categories, his view of the relative and composite nature of societies fits closely with the approach taken here.

Crypto-Jewish ethnography is particularly relevant to the distinction between hot and cold. distinction. As suggested earlier, crypto-Jews can be taken as a paradigmatic hot society. Most individuals are highly conscious of their choices in relation to the construction of identity. They are also often more conscious of the transformations in identity than might be expected in even a hot society. In some respects, crypto-Judaism might call for the additional category of fluid societies, with cold representing premodern societies; hot, modern societies; and fluid, postmodern societies. In this categorization, fluid societies are those in which individuals consciously and purposefully shape or believe they shape their identities through their choice of elements that have different degrees of cultural authorization. Nonetheless, as with the original distinction between hot and cold, fluid is relative—with all societies being relatively hot, cold, and fluid. As with the other categories, there is no evidence that underlying structure is consciously articulated in fluid societies and thus no argumentative basis for excluding it from structuralist analysis.

Myth and History

One of the issues raised by the discussion of hot and cold societies is the conventional distinction between myth and history, particularly and more broadly between myth and other forms of construction of the past—for example, oral history and memory.[2] In order to deconstruct this distinction, it necessary to introduce the definition of myth used here. It works on two levels, both of which arise from structuralist theory. The underlying structure of the definition is "highly structured narrative (or related) material." This definition arises from the understanding of the structuring process discussed earlier, which sees myth as that body of material in which the structures are most strongly articulated. The definition at this level is open ended; it makes no determination of either content or function. The next level of the definition narrows this range to narrative or related material (for example, genealogies) that is used by a particular community to structure its understanding of self and the world. This level builds on the structuring principle inherent in the underlying structural level and focuses on a particular range of structuring.

On the basis of this definition, there seems little value in the dichotomy between myth and history. Both types of narrative are means to structure reality and define the place of self in that reality. There are two primary areas of apparent difference:

- The diachronic framework of history, as opposed to the nonlinear models of some mythological systems
- The aspects of factuality—that is, history as perceived or understood as being built on documentable objective facts

The first area of difference, the very notion of diachrony, is a model of past and present. Thus history should be examined in the context of other models. On this basis, there seems no logical reason to privilege it by defining it as categorically different from myth, particularly if the category that it defines is taken as being in some sense qualitatively distinct: the term "history" implies a certain legitimacy that is not given to the word "myth." This difference is also weakened by the observation that even in societies whose model of self is seen as myth, there is evidence of a linear understanding of time. This is specifically the case of biblical narratives, which are given a historical framework, but seem to work in the same way as myths.

The distinction between myth and history is particularly weak in respect to crypto-Jewish narratives of self, which also undermine the distinction among myth and folklore, history, and memory. In the story of the baby missing from her baptism, for example, the operative elements are the need to be baptized—that is, to publicly be Catholic—and the subversion of this public identity by some means—in this case, accidental. The narrative creates opposition between two spaces and two identities and, through the fortuitous loss of the baby in the middle, denies the possible movement or transformation from one space or identity to the other. This narrative is set in the remote past, a great-grandmother's generation, and was understood to be true by the informant. But it might be considered by many scholars to be a folktale. This identification is based on a false distinction between peasant and nonpeasant cultures, with folklore (that is, peasant lore) being a deprivileged form of narrative relative to normatively authorized (by the elite) narratives, such as history and myth.

Identical structures and even form are found in a range of other narratives that function on different cultural levels. Thus, for example, a set of stories—in which the protagonists for various reasons are required to attend church—was identified by informants as fiction rather than history. In each narrative, the protagonists are fortuitously prevented from arriving in time for the religious ritual or service. These stories include mythemes that are structurally identical to those in the story about the unbaptized baby, identified by the interviewee as history. Narratives identified as memories—that is, stories of self—are also similarly structured. One respondent told the story of events in her childhood:

> This is about a special herb my mother gave us. When I was little we lived in Albuquerque, and we had to go to church. We did not want anyone to know we were Jews. Before we went to church on Sunday, our mother gave us some of this herb from a bag; I don't know what it was. We went in the church, but just before the father gave the bread and wine we all became violently sick and had to go out. I guess my mother did not want us to eat that bread. (*Maria*, June 1997)

As in the other narratives mentioned here, we find the same mythemes and underlying structural form. I am not suggesting that the informant was consciously shaping the story to fit a conventional form, for the story was not told in that way. Rather, I am arguing that all the genres of narrative share an underlying structure and, due to their use of common mythemes, are fundamentally identical. This identity of narrative in differing genres suggests that the distinctions among genres are not useful or significant from a structuralist perspective.

The suggestion that memory is a structured entity in the same way as other forms of narrative is worthy of elaboration. As structuring entities, humans create structural models of self not only at the societal level, but also at the individual level. This model making is structured in the same way as the higher levels of model making, with the interplay of the different levels shaping the underlying structure; this interplay is on both the conscious and the unconscious level. (The conscious aspect is discussed in relation to agency.) It is due to the unconscious aspect of this process that when individuals create cultural objects—for example, tell their own stories—these constructs are structured in the same way as traditional stories.[3] The presence of structuring is also evident in constructions of self, with memory a form analogous to myth. Memory is a selection of events, factual or fictional, that are used to construct a model of self or an explanation of self. The events chosen are constructs and viewed through the mediation of current understandings of self. Memory, like other aspects of myth, is culture specific: in different contexts, different content may be privileged as significant or insignificant. Perhaps the only distinctive quality of memory is that it appears to be much more fluid than other forms of myth. This fluidity is particularly evident in a postmodern cultural situation in which individuals, on the conscious level, are reflexively attempting to redefine themselves; such redefinition leads to a restructuring of memories in line with the perception of self (Kunin 2001).

The second area of difference between myth and history is equally problematic. It privileges a concept of objective fact as a qualitative or categorical marker. It is possible to deconstruct the concept of historical fact. All events in histories (as opposed to the objective events) are models of the past, choosing or privileging events on the basis of an understanding of significance. Some models—for example, the Marxist—make explicit this process of selection, while it is implicit in others. Nonetheless, all descriptions of events are artificial constructs, isolating particular moments in the ongoing flow of time. This is to deny not that the past occurred, but the possibility of recovering the past in an unmediated or unstructured form.

On the basis of these brief observations, I suggest that both myth and history are highly structured narratives that model self and the world and thus are functionally identical. The difference is in content: myth uses events that may or may not be fictional (it can use historical events), while history uses events that are understood to be factual. This difference in content suggests that the two forms are based on cultural choices; our society chooses to privilege fact, and therefore we construct our significant narratives out of factual/objective (self-defined) data. Thus science as a model of causality uses "objective" data to create its understanding of reality, and history uses analogous information. In other societies that do not have the same emphasis on "objective" reality, other material may be privileged. On this basis, myth, history, and science can be distinguished only on the basis of an ethnocentric privileging of our model of understanding. From a structuralist perspective, they are identical; I choose to apply the term "myth" to all these cultural objects.

One of the interesting aspects of the emphasis on a scientific, factual model is its cultural pervasiveness. Most realms of modern Western society attempt to utilize this type of model to validate their views or principles. Perhaps surprisingly, this is found even in various forms of fundamentalist Christianity. One of the most obvious uses is in relation to the concept of creationism or its close relation, intelligent design. Both of these challenges to Darwinism utilize (pseudo)-scientific arguments to support their particular views. The significant feature is the prevalence of a model of knowledge that is shared by both scientific and religious argumentation. If we look at the legitimizing use of religious experience, it can also be seen as requiring "empirical" data as the basis for truth. Religion must be legitimized through experiences that are accepted as objective, not merely on the basis of faith.

This aspect of factuality is also, not surprisingly, due to its cultural context, a significant feature of crypto-Jewish ethnography. Increasingly since the beginning of the twenty-first century, crypto-Jews have been looking to different forms of genetic testing as a means to prove their identity (both to the wider world, especially the Jewish community) and to themselves (to establish a particular identity). The testing is replacing less tangible and more subjective ways to determine identity and a sense of history—that is, family practices, traditions, and genealogical research. To a large extent, this change is related to the challenging of crypto-Jewish authenticity in the popular and academic media. It is, however, also closely associated with a need for an objective and scientific basis for culture and identity.

Agency

One aspect of the process of transformation at all levels involves individual agency. Agency comes into play through an individual's conscious and unconscious emphasis on or privileging of aspects of the underlying structural equation. Thus, for example, in a system like that of the crypto-Jews—characterized by a negative relation between categories (that is, two categories set in opposition to each other) but with some degree of positive mediation (that is, some overlap and potential movement)—individuals or groups can differentially emphasize either the negative or the positive side of the equation. Thus, to return to the example mentioned throughout this appendix, some crypto-Jews strongly emphasize the ritual of lighting candles on Friday nights and consider the recitation of the Rosary to be only a form of camouflage. Others might privilege both elements, seeing the practice as bringing together the Jewish and Catholic aspects of their identity. The individuals' differing emphases shape their own conscious and unconscious use of the underlying structure and can, through pushing at the edges of the system, shift it as it transforms through time. This process is facilitated in cultural situations in which different cultural equations come into contact, particularly where there are dominant and subordinate cultural systems. In such cases, individuals can unconsciously work, to some degree, within both systems, leading to the structural transformation of both models and the creation of new structural forms. It is assumed, however, that long-term compartmentalization is not possible and that the differing structural equations will have to be synthesized or in part rejected.

The conscious articulation of this form of agency is found in *jonglerie*, or identity juggling. This concept encapsulates the process by which individuals privilege different elements of their cultural repertoire at different points in time, depending on context and individual choice. *Jonglerie* is not a random process, but allows individuals to emphasize or select different aspects of their identity and thereby to shape and reshape different levels of their use and experience of structure. The theoretical concept of *jonglerie* highlights the constant process of conscious and unconscious negotiation of identity and the fact that all identities are in some sense contested. It is through this process that underlying structural patterns, and to some degree culture on a broader level, are transformed through time. As individuals and groups push the envelope, different types of development can occur. These include the levels of change highlighted earlier and, possibly, a reaction against change, characterized as nontransformation.

Although the type of agency suggested here is not found in traditional structuralist theory, which sees underlying structure as deterministic and autonomous, the arguments presented here should not be understood as undermining the original model. Structure is unconscious and shapes cultural understanding, communication, and action. Nonetheless, neither culture nor structure is static; both transform in response to new contexts. The concept of *jonglerie* provides one of the mechanisms for cultural transformation. It suggests that individuals, by articulating and defining their identity, emphasize or deemphasize different aspects of the underlying structural equation. While one individual's choice does not change the equation, it can, if it is shared by a large segment of the group to which the person belongs, lead to a process by which the model of thinking is transformed. It seems likely that this process is facilitated in contexts in which cultural boundaries are weak or people have the ability to move between several cultural or subcultural identities.

Practice

Practice, or lived experience (in terms of both historical experience and practices), is the forum that brings together the conscious and the unconscious level of structural articulation: bricolage and *jonglerie* are linked through action. Practice, or acting on, enables individuals and groups to structure, organize, or relate underlying structure to the materials of the contextual, or lived, environment. It equally and simultaneously allows the actors to relate the elements from which practices are constructed to the underlying structure. Neither the structure nor the practices can be given priority; both are common features of the system. Although I have suggested that structure has its basis in the biological nature of humanity, specific structures have their locus in individuals and communities; they exist not solely in the cognitive models or the practices, but in the interrelationship of the two.[4]

The implications of the relationship between structure and practice, or bricolage and *jonglerie*, has important implications for crypto-Jewish ethnography. While the role or perhaps the location of practice can be clearly identified in many cases, in others they are more problematic—such as for those individuals for whom crypto-Jewish culture is essentially one of memory and recounting memories. Memory itself is not a cultural practice, but the process of remembering and the social context of recounting may be similar to cultural practices and thus the location of the interaction between the conscious and the unconscious.

Due to the theoretical move away from fixed biological structures, my position moves closer to that of Pierre Bourdieu, particularly in his definition of *habitus*. *Habitus* can be regarded as the unconscious "strategy-generating principle" (Bourdieu 1977:72) through which individuals and groups respond to different situations—leading to the creation of meaningful practices. The creation of these practices and their interrelated *habitus* arise from previous practices and thus serve as the basis for future practice. This suggests that subtle changes in practice can lead to the transformation of *habitus* and thus, in our terms, structural transformation. Although it is tempting to think of practice in relation to acts, or perhaps rituals, there is no reason why it cannot be extended to writing and thereby texts. Texts, particularly their potentially authoritative nature, are useful indicators of the underlying role of systems of legitimization and authority found in all forms of practice and reproduced by forms of practice.

Practice, however, not merely is reproductive or a source of conformity, but also allows or provides the basis for pushing and shaping the boundaries. Lived experience, or practice, both validates and is validated by structure; it also is shaped by and equally shapes underlying structural relations. Both action and narration (particularly, but not exclusively, spoken narrative or storytelling) are loci in which structure and content are articulated through interaction with the world, other individuals, groups, or texts. The significance of the role of practice is emphasized in a book review whose author describes the writer of the book under review: "[H]e constantly keeps in mind the ways in which the physical activity of painting can generate its own ideas and may be regarded as a form of thinking" (Flam 2001:10). This express the role of practice as a means by which structure is both expressed and transformed.

NOTES

INTRODUCTION

1. Stanley Hordes (2005:6–7) presents a useful discussion of the proposed etymology of the term *marrano*.

2. The Jewish community has been roughly divided into two: Ashkenazim and Sephardim. The Ashkenazim are the Jews who are descended from those who settled in Germany and northern, central, and eastern Europe. They make up the majority of Jews in the United States. The Sephardim are the Jews whose ancestors lived in Spain and Portugal. After the expulsions of 1492 and 1497, many of them settled in Amsterdam, North Africa, and the Ottoman Empire. This category also includes Jewish communities that are found in the Arab world—for example, Yemen—even though they are not descended from Jews who left Spain. Due to their claim of descent from Sephardic Jews, many crypto-Jews are making connections with the present-day Sephardic community and consider themselves Sephardim.

3. Franciscan friars were the official agents of the Holy Office in New Mexico.

4. See also Suzanne Stamatov (2003:10), who argues that although the society was stratified, even individuals who were identified as *español* were willing to give information about their ethnically mixed backgrounds.

5. See www.aaanet.org/stms/ird.hatm. It is important to note that the field data in a nonanonymized form is preserved in both field notes and tapes of interviews. Participants were aware of and consented to the taping of interviews. In some cases

individuals requested that the interviews not be taped, I have complied with their wishes.

6. The word "game" is used here in a metaphorical sense to describe a field of cultural activity with its own internal set of rules, distinct from other "games" with their own distinctive sets of rules.

1. DIVERSITY AND COMPLEXITY

1. Although some conferences have been held outside the Southwest, by and large the meetings have taken place there. The choice of location is often guided by a wish to be accessible to different Hispanic communities. Thus the conference has been held in Miami, San Diego, and Portland, Oregon. Although the society specifically does not engage in bringing individuals back to Judaism, the choice of location and the outreach to the local communities do indicate at the least its sense of mission to communicate knowledge of the subject to the crypto-Jewish "community" at large.

2. Although this chapter employs the conference as a device for introducing the issues covered in this book, the meetings are part of the ethnographic study and it is worthwhile to consider the role of the conferences in shaping and expressing crypto-Jewish identity, particularly in relation to the discussions of cultural construction and fluidity of identity.

3. The conference described here is an amalgam of recent conferences in order to cover all the significant elements, some of which might not arise at a specific conference. Although the names of speakers are in the public domain, both in the society's newsletter and on various Web sites, I am maintaining their anonymity. Although the structure of the society and the conference is used, it must be emphasised that they only played a small part in my ethnographic research. Most of the interviews, and the majority of the participant observation, were conducted outside of this context and with individuals who were not members of the society and, indeed, did not know even know about the society.

4. See, for example, the detailed discussion of La Conquistadora in chapter 6.

2. THE CASE AGAINST THE AUTHENTICITY OF CRYPTO-JUDAISM IN NEW MEXICO

1. While it is true that many of the early interviews were conducted by individuals without such training, this is not currently the case. Thus, for example, exten-

sive ethnographic work was carried out by Janet Jacobs (2002), a trained anthropological ethnographer. The individuals on whom her study was based had not been interviewed and thus, in Judith Neulander's terminology, cannot be considered contaminated. Our own work also was conducted by a trained ethnographer and included a majority of individuals who had not been interviewed by other academics or nonacademics. While Neulander is correct that it is essential that interviews be carried out by trained ethnographers, that is not the province of any one disciplinary field.

2. Neulander occasionally suggests that others use their disciplines as a way to make authoritative statements—that is, using the authority of their disciplinary expertise to support what she considers to be unsupportable statements. She apparently does not realize that this is an ongoing aspect of her own argumentative strategy, which is best exemplified in the opening section of her dissertation

3. This being said, it is difficult—given the nature of Neulander's arguments—to see whether any current community of crypto-Jews would meet her externally derived standards.

4. The source of Neulander's version of "The Padre and the Jew," *Cuentos Españoles de Colorado y Nuevo Méjico* (Rael 1957), includes both a Spanish and an English rendition of the story. Neulander uses the Spanish version, which includes the word "matrimony." The English summary of the tale, also written by the collector, Juan Bautista Rael, does not include this word and translates the concept as "Jewish religion" rather than "Jewish matrimony" (806). It is clear that Rael, at least, did not consider matrimony to be the operative concept in the tale.

5. Neulander's argument assumes that the individuals who claim to be crypto-Jews are aware that claims of descent from Spanish settlers have been disproved and thus descent from Jews is the remaining option. I have seen no ethnographic evidence to support this contention. Many individuals acknowledged a range of ancestors, who usually included Jews, non-*converso* colonists, and Native Americans.

6. Neulander's (2006) most recent article adds very little to the debate. Her argument continues to be based on her assumption that since she has proved crypto-Judaism to be false, any use of it must be equally false (Neulander 2006:385). Given that Neulander's only evidence that it is false is her own work, her blanket rejection of other scholars' research seems a bit overstated. Her contention as a whole suggests that both scholars and nonscholars have misused genetic information or genetic diseases as a means to lay claim to identity, especially "whiteness" among Hispanos. This final aspect of her argument is unsupported by the ethnography.

I am not a geneticist, so will not address Neulander's arguments in that arena. The key part of her discussion is the misuse of genetic data as being equivalent to the misuse of ethnic data. While her argument in relation to the construction of categories is sound, she has not taken it far enough. She accepts that there may be appropriate genetically based categories—that is, empirically based rather than folkloric categories. I would suggest that all categories are culturally constructed, using some form of data, "empirical" or otherwise. There seems to be no reason to privilege a category created by a scientist rather than one created by a community.

The question relating to the genetic data is ultimately one of health: Does the category created allow health professionals to give better advice to their patients or potential patients? At a conference in Albuquerque held in August 2007, several geneticists and medical researchers suggested that a range of genetic disorders in the Hispano population had to be examined. Whether these disorders can be traced to a mutation in Jews is a second-order issue. We should not allow prejudice against the idea of crypto-Judaism prevent the examination of categories of patients as a public health-measure. Neulander's contribution is precisely unhelpful in this respect.

7. It is important to place Michael Carroll's article on crypto-Judaism in the context of some of his other work. He uses a similar methodology, for example, in his exploration of alien abduction (Carroll 1987).

8. While Carroll does not do so, it would be interesting to consider the nature of the cultural context that led to this reconsideration. There is no reason to assume that the revised view of the Inquisition is any less affected by scholars' motives than the previous one.

9. Juan Sandoval (who is not related to Isabelle Sandoval) is also highlighted by Barbara Ferry and Debbie Nathan (2000), who imply that his claim of identity was spurious: "[F]or reasons that remain unclear, he became convinced that he was a Jew" (91). They suggest that his primary motives were publicity and the associated economic rewards. As a folk artist, he moved from making Christmas wreaths to making Jewish-themed items and increasingly participated in public crypto-Jewish events. Although he may have used his identity as a means of economic gain, this does not prove that his identity was false. More important, even if it does challenge his credibility, it in no way calls into question that of other individuals who claim to be crypto-Jews.

10. Ferry and Nathan mention Loggie Carrasco as one of the individuals who grew distrustful of outsiders. In fact, Loggie (as stated in an interview for this study) considered her distrust to be related to the misuse of her information by some scholars, who included it as part of their attacks on the authenticity of crypto-

Judaism. Before this (and, indeed, in synagogue contexts after this), she had been willing to share her understandings with both academics and nonacademics.

3. THE CASE FOR THE AUTHENTICITY OF CRYPTO-JUDAISM IN NEW MEXICO

1. This distinctiveness did not mean that the *conversos* were entirely cut off from their former co-religionists, however. Renée Melammed (1999:16–30) demonstrates the patterns of relations between these two groups, focusing primarily on the relations between women. The Edict of Expulsion of 1492 (quoted in Melammed 1999:16) clearly indicates that, at least in the view of the authors of the edict, such relations were ongoing and detrimental to the assimilation of the New Christians into the Catholic Church.

2. Although Janet Jacobs's book was published in 2002, one year after the submission date of Judith Neulander's doctoral dissertation, it is unlikely that the dissertation was available to her. Thus Jacobs cites only Neulander's 1996 publication, which includes only an abbreviated version of her arguments.

3. Neulander (2006) suggests that these genetic diseases are associated with Ashkenazic rather than Sephardic Jews and thus are not relevant to the issue of authenticity of the crypto-Jews of New Mexico. But the hereditary basis of some of these disorders is not as uncontentious as is suggested by Neulander. For example, scientists now consider the genetic mutation that leads to breast cancer to have a statistically higher prevalence in women of Jewish ethnicity. Once thought to be found primarily in women of Ashkenazic origin, it is now believed to predate the historical split between these two branches of the Jewish community.

4. The issues relating to the interpretation of both symbols and other material cultural objects are examined in chapter 5.

5. Some early scholars argued that specific names or types of surnames were markers of *converso* origin; current research suggests that this can be convincingly shown of a very small number of names.

4. IDEAL TYPES OF CRYPTO-JEWISH IDENTITY

1. Throughout this and the following chapters, the quotations taken from interviews are identified by informant and date. Each informant was given an identifying

random name, which is used consistently in the discussion. The names are italicized to indicate that they are merely identifiers and not the real names of the individuals.

2. *Duendes*, in Spanish folklore, are house spirits said to resemble old men.

3. Unfortunately, I was unable to tape that part of the interview and thus do not have a transcript of her narrative.

4. David Gitlitz (1996:273, 119) reports a similar ritual practiced by crypto-Jews in seventeenth-century Spain. Other purification practices were consistently found in the research. Many individuals mentioned general cleaning or purifying before Friday night, some specifically noting the washing of the genitalia.

5. CRYPTO-JEWISH PRACTICE

1. This issue is raised in the discussion of the views of Judith Neulander (2001) in chapter 2.

2. In my earlier discussion (Kunin 2001:53), I indicated that only one individual reported this practice. In the intervening years, other informants from the same general area of northern New Mexico have described very similar practices.

3. David Gitlitz (1996:201) reports a similar practice as having taken place in 1485 and states that crypto-Jews often gave babies secret Jewish names. *Marta* said that the additional names were sometimes biblical or Spanish and occasionally "Ladino."

4. Similar practices are reported by Fay Blake (1997:17–19).

5. This festival is reported by other crypto-Jews. The booths are called *cabanitas* as well as *jacales*. See also Blake (1997:20). Although one informant in this study used the term *jacal*, none used the word *cabanita*.

6. Gitlitz (1996:548) describes the practice of separating the challah as occurring in Spain as late as 1670.

7. Tomás Atencio (1996:63) indicates that certain *manito* Protestant families practiced circumcision before it was performed for public-health reasons. Stanley Hordes (2005:229–231) confirms the information found in my research, taking circumcision back at least into the late nineteenth century.

8. Gitlitz discusses the importance of circumcision as evidence of Judaizing and notes that alternative methods were used alongside full circumcision. Thus he states that in seventeenth-century Mexico, the foreskin was occasionally scarred rather than removed (Gitlitz 1996:206). See also Seymour Liebman (1970:76–77).

9. Neulander (2001) argues that this form of slaughtering was largely dropped by *conversos* and their descendents, thus making this a false analogy. But her contention is not supported by Gitlitz's (1996:542–548) analysis of the historical documents. His work suggests that practices of *shechita* were found in both Spain and Mexico well into the seventeenth century. His work also supports the presence of the prohibition on the consumption of blood.

10. Some of the issues explored here have also been examined by David Kunin (2007), who comes to similar conclusions.

6. A POSTMODERN TAKE ON CRYPTO-JUDAISM

1. This concept has been expressed in a different but related way by Dorothy Holland and her colleagues (1998): "People tell others who they are, but even more important, they tell themselves and then try to act as though they are who they say they are. These self-understandings, especially those with strong emotional resonance for the teller, are what we refer to as identities" (3).

2. A broad discussion of these issues is found in Thomas Charlton, Lois Myers, and Rebecca Sharpless (2006:275–296).

3. It is important to emphasize that social memories are constructed by society and transmitted through enculturation. Thus there are as many social memories as there are groups and subgroups.

4. Her real name appears here, as her analysis is in print. Rather than using the print version, though, this discussion is based on a presentation to the SCJS, since it includes some excursuses and additional material.

THEORETICAL APPENDIX. (NEO)-STRUCTURALISM

1. While Buddhism is not a significant cultural factor for most crypto-Jews, it is one in a complex mix of cultural forms available, particularly in New Mexico. Some crypto-Jews, particularly those who have gone on spiritual pilgrimages, have mentioned encounters with Buddhism and similar traditions. Nonetheless, Buddhism is used here as an example because it is somewhat more immediately understandable than the Mormon tradition and its triadic, rather than dyadic, structure. In fact, there is more significant influence of Mormon than Buddhist traditions and culture among crypto-Jews.

2. This discussion is necessarily brief, since it could encompass an entire book.

3. Dell Hymes (1977:224) analyzed material that was understood to be traditional and material of modern origin (in the same ethnographic context) and found that the underlying structure of both was identical.

4. Although the concepts developed here are different from those used by Pierre Bourdieu (1977:21), his discussion of the relationship between practice and the conceptual models used to explain or justify it is relevant.

Bibliography

Alberro, Solange. 1988. *Inquisición y sociedad en México, 1571–1700*. Mexico City: Fondo de Cultura Económica.

Alpert, Michael. 2001. *Crypto-Judaism and the Spanish Inquisition*. Basingstoke, Eng.: Palgrave.

American Anthropological Association. 2004. "American Anthropological Association Statement on Ethnography and Institutional Review Boards." Available at www.aaanet.org/stmts/irb.htm.

Anderson, Benedict. 1983. *Imagined Communities: Reflections on the Origin and Spread of Nationalism*. London: Verso.

Atencio, Tomás. 2003. "The *Converso* Legacy in New Mexico Hispano Protestantism." *El Caminante*, no. 2:10–15.

———. 1996. "Crypto-Jewish Remnants in *Manito* Society and Culture." *Jewish Folklore and Ethnology Review* 18, nos. 1–2:59–68.

Austin, Mary. 1919. "Social Survey of Taos County, New Mexico." Manuscript AU 543. Mary Austin Collection, Henry E. Huntington Library, San Marino, Calif.

Baer, Yitzhak. 1961, 1966. *A History of the Jews in Christian Spain*. Translated by Louis Schoffman. 2 vols. Philadelphia: Jewish Publication Society of America.

Bascom, William. 1969. *Ifa Divination: Communication Between Gods and Men in West Africa*. Bloomington: Indiana University Press.

Beinart, Haim. 1981. *Conversos on Trial: The Inquisition in Ciudad Real*. Jerusalem: Magnes.

Benedict, Ruth. 1935. *Zuni Mythology*. New York: Columbia University Press.

Blake, Fay Forman. 1997. "The Hidden Jews of New Mexico." *Journal of Progressive Judaism* 8:5–26.

——— Bourdieu, Pierre. 1977. *Outline of a Theory of Practice*. Translated by Richard Nice. Cambridge: Cambridge University Press.

Brayer, Herbert O. 1940. *Directory of Churches and Religious Organizations in New Mexico*. Albuquerque: New Mexico Historical Records Survey.

Carroll, Michael P. 2002. "The Debate over a Crypto-Jewish Presence in New Mexico: The Role of Ethnographic Allegory and Orientalism." *Sociology of Religion* 63, no. 1:1–19.

———. 1987. " 'The Castrated Boy': Another Contribution to the Psychoanalytic Study of Urban Legends." *Folklore* 98, no. 2:216–225.

Charlton, Thomas L., Lois E. Myers, and Rebecca Sharpless, eds. 2006. *Handbook of Oral History*. Lanham, Md.: Altamira Press.

Clifford, James. 1994. "On Ethnographic Allegory." In Steven Seidman, ed., *The Postmodern Turn: New Perspectives on Social Theory*, 205–228. Cambridge: Cambridge University Press.

Douglas, Mary. 1978. *Implicit Meanings: Essays in Anthropology*. London: Routledge.

Dozier, Edward. 1970. *The Pueblo Indians of North America*. New York: Holt, Rinehart and Winston.

———. 1961. "Rio Grande Pueblos." In Edward H. Spicer, ed., *Perspectives in American Indian Culture Change*, 94–186. Chicago: University of Chicago Press.

Fentress, James, and Chris Wickham. 1992. *Social Memory*. Oxford: Blackwell.

Ferry, Barbara, and Nathan, Debbie. 2000. "Mistaken Identity? The Case of New Mexico's 'Hidden Jews.' " *Atlantic Monthly*, December, 85–96.

Flam, Jack. 2001. "Space Men" [review of *Paths to the Absolute: Mondrian, Malevich, Kandinsky, Pollock, Newman, Rothko, and Still*, by Jack Golding]. *New York Review of Books*, April 26, 11–13.

Frank, Ross. 2000. *From Settler to Citizen: New Mexican Economic Development and the Creation of Vecino Society, 1750–1820*. Berkeley: University of California Press.

———. 1998. "Demographic, Social, and Economic Change in New Mexico." In Robert H. Jackson, ed., *New Views of Borderlands History*, 41–71. Albuquerque: University of New Mexico Press.

Gerber, Jane. 1992. *The Jews of Spain: A History of the Sephardic Experience*. New York: Free Press.

Gitlitz, David M. 1996. *Secrecy and Deceit: The Religion of the Crypto-Jews*. Philadelphia: Jewish Publication Society.

Greenleaf, Richard E. 1969. *The Mexican Inquisition of the Sixteenth Century*. Albuquerque: University of New Mexico Press.

Halevy, Schulamith C. 1999. "Jewish Practices Among Contemporary Anusim." *Shofar* 18:80–99.

———. 1996. "Manifestations of Crypto-Judaism in the American Southwest." *Jewish Folklore and Ethnology Review* 18, nos. 1–2:68–76.

Hernández, Frances. 1993. "The Secret Jews of the Southwest." In Martin A. Cohen and Abraham J. Peck, eds., *Sephardim in the Americas: Studies in Culture and History*, 411–454. Tuscaloosa: University of Alabama Press.

Hernandez, Mona. 2007. Afterword to *New Mexico's Crypto-Jews: Image and Memory*, by Cary Herz, 139–146. Albuquerque: University of New Mexico Press.

Hill, Jonathan D., ed. 1988. *Rethinking History and Myth: Indigenous South American Perspectives on the Past*. Urbana: University of Illinois Press.

Hobsbawm, Eric, and Terence Ranger, eds. 1992. *The Invention of Tradition*. Cambridge: Cambridge University Press.

Holland, Dorothy, Debra Skinner, William Lachicotte Jr., and Carole Cain. 1998. *Identity and Agency in Cultural Worlds*. Cambridge, Mass.: Harvard University Press.

Hordes, Stanley M. 2005. *To the End of the Earth: A History of the Crypto-Jews of New Mexico*. New York: Columbia University Press.

———. 1996. "Irrigation at the Confluence of the Río Grande and Río Chama: The Acequias de Chamita, Salazar and Hernández, 1600–1680." Report, State of New Mexico, on the relation of *S. E. Reynolds, State Engineer, Plaintiff,* v. *Roman Aragon, et al.*, Defendants, no. 7941—Civil, Río Chama Mainstream Section, Río Chama Ditches, June 24.

———. 1993. " 'The Sephardic Legacy in the Southwest: The Crypto-Jews of New Mexico,' Historical Research Project Sponsored by the Latin American Institute, University of New Mexico." *Jewish Folklore and Ethnology Review* 15:137–138.

———. 1982. "The Inquisition as Economic and Political Agent: The Campaign of the Mexican Holy Office Against the Crypto-Jews in the Mid-Seventeenth Century." *The Americas* 39:no.1:23–38.

Hoyo, Eugenio del. 1972. *Historia del Nuevo Reino de León (1577–1723)*. Monterrey: Instituto Tecnológico y de Estudios Superiores de Monterrey.

Hymes, Dell. 1977. "The 'Wife' Who 'Goes Out' Like a Man: Reinterpretation of a Clackamas Chinook Myth." In Janet L. Dolgin, David S. Kemnitzer, and David M. Schneider, eds., *Symbolic Anthropology: A Reader in the Study of Symbols and Meanings*, 221–242. New York: Columbia University Press.

Jacobs, Janet Liebman. 2002. *Hidden Heritage: The Legacy of the Crypto-Jews*. Berkeley: University of California Press.

———. 1996. "Women, Ritual, and Secrecy: The Creation of Crypto-Jewish Culture." *Journal for the Scientific Study of Religion* 35, no. 2:97–108.

Kunin, David. 2007. "When Is a Top Just a Top? How Did the Dreidel Become Part of Crypto-Jewish Culture of the Southwest?" *HaLapid* 14, no. 1:1, 12–14.

Kunin, Seth D. 2004. *We Think What We Eat: Neo-Structuralist Analysis of Israelite Food Rules and Other Cultural and Textual Practices*. London: Clark.

———. 2001. "Juggling Identities Among the Crypto-Jews of the American Southwest." *Religion* 31, no. 1:41–61.

———. 1998. "The Crypto-Jews of New Mexico: An Ethnographic Survey." *Journal of Progressive Judaism* 11:21–46.

Lévi-Strauss, Claude. 1981. *The Naked Man*. Translated by John and Doreen Weightman. New York: Harper & Row.

———. 1969. *The Raw and the Cooked*. Translated by John and Doreen Weightman. New York: Harper & Row.

———. 1966. *The Savage Mind*. Chicago: University of Chicago Press.

———. 1963. *Structural Anthropology*. Translated by Claire Jacobson and Brooke Grundfest Schoepf. New York: Basic Books.

Liebman, Seymour B. 1970. *The Jews in New Spain: Faith, Flame, and the Inquisition*. Coral Gables, Fla.: University of Miami Press.

Melammed, Renée Levine. 1999. *Heretics or Daughters of Israel? The Crypto-Jewish Women of Castile*. Oxford: Oxford University Press.

Netanyahu, Benzion. 1995. *The Origins of the Inquisition in Fifteenth Century Spain*. New York: Random House.

———. 1966. *The Marranos of Spain from the Late XIVth to the Early XVIth Century According to Contemporary Hebrew Sources*. New York: American Academy for Jewish Research.

Neulander, Judith S. 2006. "Folk Taxonomy, Prejudice, and the Human Genome: Using Disease as a Jewish Ethnic Marker." *Patterns of Prejudice* 40, nos. 4–5: 381–398.

———. 2001. "Cannibals, Castes, and Crypto-Jews: Premillennial Cosmology in Postcolonial New Mexico." Ph.D. diss., Indiana University.

———. 1996. "The New Mexican Crypto-Jewish Canon: Choosing to Be 'Chosen' in Millennial Tradition." *Jewish Folklore and Ethnology Review* 18, nos. 1–2: 19–58.

———. 1994. "Crypto-Jews of the Southwest: An Imagined Community." *Jewish Folklore and Ethnology Review* 16, no. 1:64–68.

266

Nostrand, Richard L. 1992. *The Hispano Homeland.* Norman: University of Oklahoma Press.

Okely, Judith. 1983. *The Traveller-Gypsies.* Cambridge: Cambridge University Press.

Patai, Raphael. 1983. *On Jewish Folklore.* Detroit: Wayne State University Press.

Rael, Juan Bautista. 1957. *Cuentos Españoles de Colorado y Nuevo Méjico: Spanish Tales from Colorado and New Mexico.* 2 vols. Stanford, Calif.: Stanford University Press.

Rodríguez, Jeanette, and Ted Fortier. 2007. *Cultural Memory: Resistance, Faith, and Identity.* Austin: University of Texas Press.

Roth, Cecil. 1932. *A History of the Marranos.* Philadelphia: Jewish Publication Society.

Said, Edward W. 2003. *Orientalism.* Twenty-fifth anniversary ed. New York: Penguin.

——. 1978. *Orientalism.* New York: Pantheon.

Sandoval, Isabelle Medina. 1996. "Abraham's Children of the Southwest." *Jewish Folklore and Ethnology Review* 18, nos. 1–2:77–82.

Saussure, Ferdinand de. 1959. *Course in General Linguistics.* Edited by Charles Bally and Albert Reidlinger. Translated by Wade Baskin. London: Peter Owen.

Schacter, Daniel. 2001. *The Seven Sins of Memory: How the Mind Forgets and Remembers.* Boston: Houghton Mifflin.

Schama, Simon. 1999. *Rembrandt's Eyes.* New York: Knopf.

Simmel, Georg. 1906. "The Sociology of Secrecy and of the Secret Societies." *American Journal of Sociology* 11:441–498.

Sperber, Dan. 1975. *Rethinking Symbolism.* Translated by Alice L. Morton. Cambridge: Cambridge University Press.

Stamatov, Suzanne. 2003. "Families and Community in Colonial New Mexico, 1694–1800." Ph.D. diss., University of New Mexico.

Sturrock, J., ed. 1979. *Structuralism and Since: From Lévi-Strauss to Derrida.* Oxford: Oxford University Press.

Sutton, Wesley K., Alec Knight, Peter A. Underhill, Judith S. Neulander, Todd R. Disotell, and Joanna L. Mountain. 2006. "Toward Resolution of the Debate Regarding Purported Crypto-Jews in a Spanish-American Population: Evidence from the Y Chromosome." *Annals of Human Biology* 33, no. 1:100–111.

Tobias, Henry J. 1990. *A History of the Jews in New Mexico.* Albuquerque: University of New Mexico Press.

Turner, Terrance. 1988. "Commentary: Ethno-Ethnohistory: Myth and History in Native South American Representations of Contact with Western Society." In

Jonathan D. Hill, ed., *Rethinking History and Myth: Indigenous South American Perspectives on the Past*, 235–281. Urbana: University of Illinois Press.

Yerushalmi, Yosef Hayim. 1971. *From Spanish Court to Italian Ghetto: Isaac Cardoso: A Study in Seventeenth-Century Marranism and Jewish Apologetics.* New York: Columbia University Press.

INDEX

academic history, panels on, at SCJS conferences, 27–28
academics, as SCJS members, 24, 25–26
Adam and Eve, *retablo* of (Carrillo), 189
Adonai, as name, use of, 55–56, 182
Adventism. *See* Seventh-Day Adventism
agency, 193, 214, 225, 226, 251–253
Alberro, Solange, 104, 105
Albert Congregation (Albuquerque), 13
Albuquerque (New Mexico): crypto-Jewish practices in, 105, 155, 158, 165, 166; establishment of, 10
Alonso, Hernando, 100
Alpert, Michael, 98, 99
Amsterdam (Netherlands), 157
Anderson, Benedict, 206
Anglos, 11
Anita (crypto-Jew), 57, 58, 59–60
Anna (crypto-Jew), 170
anusim, use of term, 3
art, at SCJS conferences, 43
Ashkenazim, 13, 118, 174, 255n.2
assimilationist identity. *See* Christian identity with *converso* elements
Atencio, Tomás, 76; on authenticity, 110; on circumcision, 260n.7; on conversions to Presbyterianism, 62; on dough, burning of, 163; on endogamy, 118; ethnographic practices of, 80; on ritual slaughter, 168; on secrecy, 170–171
Austin, Mary, 9

authenticity, of crypto-Judaism. *See also* memory; self-identification
ARGUMENTS AGAINST: overview of, 45–46; personal attacks in, 27; unpersuasiveness of, 81; use of practices to support, 219. *See also* Carroll, Michael; Ferry, Barbara, and Debbie Nathan; Neulander, Judith
ARGUMENTS FOR: by Atencio, 110; by crypto-Jews, 110–113; by Halevy, 108–109; importance of scientific evidence to, 111; by Jacobs, 90–96; by Melammed, 83–84; overview of, 82–83. *See also* Gitlitz, David M; Hordes, Stanley
CULTURAL VERSUS HISTORICAL, 213; external versus internal, 49; and genetics, 40; and ideal identity types, 144–145; of interpretation in personal histories, 29; Jacobs's indicators of, 90; question of, 20–21, 27–28; and self-identification, 116–117

Baer, Yitzhak, 4, 75, 89, 98
Bascom, William, 52
Beinart, Haim, 4
belief(s), 36, 87–88, 120–121, 131–132, 140
Benavides, Alonso de, 208
Benedict, Ruth, 52
Bernáldez, Andrés, 5
bias (memory "sin"), 203–204

Bible (Hebrew), 89, 106–107, 112, 181–182;
  narratives in, 36, 120, 131–132, 163, 248
binarism, 230–231
Blake, Fay, 153
blood, consumption of, 57–58, 167–168,
  261n.9
Book of Mormon, 61, 235
Bourdieu, Pierre, 193, 253, 262n.4
brain, 227, 230, 232
bricolage: classic form of, 161; and
  crypto-Jewish practice, 147–175; and
  dreidel's association with *pon y saca*, 174;
  evidence for, 153; interpretation as part of,
  172; and *jonglerie*, 194; nature of, 151, 176,
  192; and secrecy, 171; in Sukkoth
  practices, 161–163; and transformation on
  N structural level, 230; as transformation
  on S³ structural level, 245; types of, 245;
  and veneration of saints, 157
Buddhism, 234, 261n.1
Buechley, Robert W., 11
bultos (sculptural depictions of saints), 11,
  185, 187–188, 190

cactus, candlesticks made from, 187, 188
candle lighting: in observance of Hanukkah,
  34–35, 169; in observance of Sabbath,
  48–49, 100
  AND RECITATION OF ROSARY: and agency,
  252; and bricolage, 153–154; meaning of,
  237–238, 238–239; mediating versus
  narrative role of, 242; *Paulo's* mention
  of, 130–131; structural purposes of, 236;
  transformation in practice of, 243; and
  weak crypto-Jewish identity, 139–140
candlesticks, made from cactus, 187, 188
"Cannibals, Castes, and Crypto-Jews"
  (Neulander), 46–47
Canto, Alberto del, 102
Carrasco, Loggie, 258n.10
Carrillo, Charles, 189
Carroll, Michael, 66–76; on authenticity of
  crypto-Judaism, 45, 46, 66, 67, 68, 69;
  ethnographic analogy, use of concept,
  68–70; on Ferry and Nathan, 66; on
  Hordes, 97; on Jacobs, 94; on motives of
  academics supporting crypto-Judaism,
  75–76, 215; orientalist paradigm, use of,
  70–74; on supposed feminization of
  crypto-Jews, 73–74; on truth, 67–68
Carvajal, Lenore, 30
Carvajal y de la Cueva, Luis de, 7, 102–103
Carvajal y de la Cueva, Luis de (nephew),
  102–103
Castaño de Sosa, Gaspar, 7, 102, 103
Cathedral Basilica of Saint Francis of Assisi
  (Santa Fe), 29, 208–209
Catholicism, 41, 62, 87, 151

change. *See* societies, hot versus cold;
  transformation
Christian identity with *converso* elements
  (assimilationist identity; ideal identity
  type), 88, 141–143, 214
Christian identity without *converso*
  elements (ideal identity type), 88,
  143–144, 214
Christianity: Catholicism, 41, 62, 87, 151;
  fundamentalist, 251; and Judaism,
  mediation between, 48–49, 100,
  126–127, 141, 195, 242; Pentecostal, 56,
  57, 59–61, 80, 92; Protestantism, 61, 62,
  80, 92, 216. *See also* candle lighting: and
  recitation of Rosary; messianic
  congregations; Seventh-Day Adventism
Church of San Felipe de Neri
  (Albuquerque), 182–183
Church of the Nazarene (denomination), 61
Churches of Christ (denomination), 61
Churches of God (denomination), 61
circumcision, 100–101, 163–166, 187,
  260nn.7,8
Clifford, James, 68
co/contextualization, 236–237
cold societies, 215, 224, 246–247
collective memory (social memory),
  205–207
colonial paradigm, 47–48
Columbus, Christopher, 6
comparative analysis, 232
compartmentalization theory, 148–149, 231,
  246
conferences, 43–44. *See also* Society for
  Crypto-Judaic Studies: conferences of
La Conquistadora (statue), 208–210
conversion(s), 42, 61, 62, 114
conversos: Jewish identity of, 2; and Jews, 5,
  259n.1; literary culture, loss of, 89;
  migration of, to the Americas, 7; nature
  of community of, 83; numbers of, 4, 85;
  in Portugal, 6–7; and secrecy, 5–6, 83;
  self-identification of, 4; as settlers of
  New Mexico, 103–104, 217; in Spain,
  98–99; as subjects of Inquisition, 5;
  surnames used by, 91; use of term, 2, 3.
  See also crypto-Jews
creationism, 251
crosses and crucifixes, 154–156, 185–186
"Crypto-Jewish Remnants in *Manito* Society
  and Culture" (Atencio), 110
crypto-Jews: Adonai, use of as name by,
  55–56, 182; arguments of, for
  authenticity, 110–113; artworks by, 11, 43,
  185, 187–188, 189, 190; and baptism,
  158, 159; childhood experiences of,
  interpretations of by, 130; circumcision
  among, 100–101, 163–166, 187,

260nn.7,8; as community, 83; disclosure of ancestry among, 133–135, 218; endogamy, preference for among, 32, 100, 105, 117–118, 127–128, 137–138, 145; formal structures for, 221; games played by, 128–129, 172–174, 219, 256n.6; genetic diseases among, as evidence of Jewish ancestry, 41, 118, 136, 258n.6, 259n.3; as hot society, 247; housecleaning practices of, 49–50, 130, 169; Jewish ancestors of, 38, 64, 97, 119, 195, 218; and mainstream Jewish communities, 43–44, 88, 200–201, 242; as mediators, 242; mourning customs of, 135–136, 138; names and naming practices among, 55–56, 91, 106–107, 112, 158, 159, 181–182, 259n.5, 260n.3; purification rituals of, 154, 161, 260n.4; religious backgrounds of, 38–39, 60–62, 80–81; as SCJS members, diversity of, 24–25; transformation of, from Jews, 246; use of term, 2–3. *See also conversos*; culture, crypto-Jewish; dietary customs; identity, crypto-Jewish; New Mexico; New Spain; practice(s); *names of individual crypto-Jews*

crypto-Judaism: complexity of, 23; cultural mixing in, 54–55; as culture of secrecy, 2–3, 6, 34–35, 110, 169–171; future of, 219–220; mediators in, 240; as oral tradition, 89; public discussion of, 220–221; as religion versus cultural tradition, 131; study of, 71; terms used for, 1–3; as transformed structure, 242; as trope for whiteness, 50, 62–64, 81, 93–94, 216. *See also* authenticity, of crypto-Judaism; culture, crypto-Jewish

cultural change, 226
cultural construction, 14–15, 30–31, 40
cultural inheritance, 29–30
cultural memory, 54
cultural objects, 147–148, 226
culture: enculturation as feature of, 211; as "faction," 198; fluidity of, 54–56, 58; Hispano, 11; and identity, 30–31; nature of, 14–15, 36–37, 194

culture, crypto-Jewish: complexity of, 149–150, 232–233; construction of, 215; continuing development of, 196–197; diversity of, 25; Inquisition's influences on, 5–6; mainstreaming of, 44; men as transmitters of, 84, 95–96; nature of, 212; preservation of, 220–221; range of, 194; secrecy as element of, 2–3, 6, 34–35, 110, 169–171; transformations in, 88–90; women as transmitters of, 83–84, 90–91, 94–96, 150. *See also* practice(s)

culture groups, 232
customs. *See* dietary customs; mourning customs

David (crypto-Jew), 129
diachrony, 224, 248–250
dietary customs: blood, consumption of, 57–58, 167–168, 261n.9; bread and wine, rituals involving, 151–152, 260n.6; fasting, 100, 109, 166; meat, washing of, 130; milk and meat, separation of, 168; and N structural level, 229; and Passover-related foods, 163, 168–169; pork, consumption of, 129, 138, 167; transformations of, 166–167
Dio (God), use of, instead of Dios, 120, 152
diseases, as evidence of Jewish ancestry, 41, 118, 136, 258n.6, 259n.3
doorposts: crosses on, 154–156; mezuzahs on, 155–156
Douglas, Mary, 240
Down, Rena, 24
dreidels (tops), 172–174, 219

Edict of Expulsion (1492), 259n.1
Edicts of Grace, 86–87, 89, 121
El Paso (Texas), 41
Emma (crypto-Jew), 151–152
encomiendas (tributary awards), 10
enculturation, 198, 211
endogamy: of crypto-Jews, 100, 117–118; of families researched by Hordes, 105, 128, 137–138, 145; in SCJS conference attendees' families, 32; in strong crypto-Jewish identity type, 127–128; in weak crypto-Jewish identity type, 137–138
españoles (Spaniards), use of term in New Mexico, 12
essentialism, 40, 46, 113
estancias (land grants), 10
Esther, Saint, 156–157, 184–185, 191
ethnographers, 47, 203
ethnographic analogy, 66–67, 68, 69
ethnographic methodology. *See* research methods
ethnography: crypto-Jewish, 224, 251; interviews, potential problems with, 79–80
evocation, 238
Exodus story, as model for expulsion, 36, 120, 131–132, 163
exogamy, 32, 174. *See also* endogamy

factuality, 121, 248, 250–251
false analogy: as basis for existence of crypto-Judaism, 79, 119, 146; and bricolage, 148, 157, 161; *pon y saca* as dreidel as, 173

271

family narratives. *See* narratives
fasting, 100, 109, 166
Felipe II (king of Spain), 102
Fentress, James, 205
Ferdinand of Aragon (king of Spain), 6
Ferry, Barbara, and Debbie Nathan, 76–81;
    arguments of, flaws in, 76–77, 215;
    Carroll on, 66; on changed narrative of
    self, 199; crypto-Jews, attacks on
    credibility of, 77–78; on Hordes, 76; on
    Isabelle Sandoval, 77–79; on Juan
    Sandoval, 258n.9; on Loggie Carrasco,
    258n.10; on Neulander, 79–81; on
    reinterviews, 204; on secrecy, 78–79
Fidel (crypto-Jew), 163, 164
figured worlds: and changed narratives of
    self, 199; creation of, 200; description
    of, 197–198; and learning, 211; and
    memory, 201, 202
Flavio (crypto-Jew), 139
fluidity: of culture, 54–56, 58; of identity,
    39–40, 99, 115, 117, 214; of memory,
    250; of self-identification, 196; of
    societies, 247; of weak crypto-Jewish
    identity, 193
folk art, 11, 43, 156, 185, 187–188, 189, 190
folk narratives (folktales, folklore), 47,
    52–53, 126–127, 241, 248–249, 257n.4
food. *See* dietary customs
Fortier, Ted, 54
Franciscans, 255n.3
Frank (crypto-Jew), 139, 140, 154
Frank, Ross, 12, 185
Fridays, 151–154, 169. *See also* candle
    lighting: in observance of Sabbath

genealogy, 29–30, 117–119, 127, 137
genetic disorders, as evidence of Jewish
    ancestry, 41, 118, 136, 258n.6, 259n.3
genetics, 64–66, 112–113; panels on, at SCJS
    conferences, 40–41
genísaros (baptized Native American slaves),
    12
geography, 10, 105, 149
George (crypto-Jew), 163
Gerber, Jane, 98, 99
Gitlitz, David M., 82, 84–90; on
    circumcision, 260n.8; on *conversos*, 4, 7,
    85; on cultural transformations, 88–90;
    on dietary customs, 163, 168, 260n.6; on
    Edicts of Grace, 86–87, 89, 121;
    genetic evidence, use of, 118; on
    housecleaning practices, 169; on
    Inquisition records, 85–86; on Job, 185;
    on negative beliefs, 120; New Christians,
    taxonomy of, 87–88, 114, 115–116; on
    practices, transformation of, 167; on
    public sphere of Jewish practice, 150; on

purification rituals, 260n.4; on ritual
    slaughter, 58, 261n.9; on secrecy, 171; on
    syncretistic practices, 147
God: Dio, use of for, instead of Dios, 120,
    152; names of, as personal name, 55–56,
    182; names of, meaning of, 237;
    Shekhina, 209
Gómez, Francisco, 208, 209–210
Gómez Robledo, Francisco, 208, 209
gravestones, 20, 32, 33, 111–112, 177–182
Greenleaf, Richard E., 100

habitus (unconscious strategy-generating
    principle), 193, 253–254
Hagiz, Moses, 169
Halevy, Schulamith, 108–109, 169, 218
Hannah (crypto-Jew), 161–162, 163
Hanukkah, 34–35, 169, 173
headstones, 20, 32, 33, 111–112, 177–182
Hebrew (language), 152, 156, 162, 180, 184
Hebrew Bible, 89, 106–107, 112, 181–182;
    narratives in, 36, 120, 131–132, 163, 248
Herencia del Norte, La (magazine), 200
*Heretics or Daughters of Israel? The
    Crypto-Jewish Women of Castile*
    (Melammed), 83–84
Hernandez, Mona, 208–210
*Hidden Heritage: The Legacy of the
    Crypto-Jews* (Jacobs), 90–96
Hill, Jonathan, 246–247
Hispanos: artworks by, 11, 43; assimilation
    of, 219; and authenticity of
    crypto-Judaism, 45–46; culture of, 11–12;
    genetic disorders among, 40, 41, 118;
    Pentecostalism of, Neulander's
    interpretation of, 59–61; as SCJS
    conference attendees, 26
history: academic, panels on, at SCJS
    conferences, 27–28; as basis for
    validation of identity, 31–32; and
    historical truth, 66–67; histories versus,
    207–208; and hot versus cold societies,
    246–247; and invented tradition,
    206–207; myths versus, 247–251; nature
    of, 31; personal, panels on, at SCJS
    conferences, 28–31; validation of, 28
Hobsbawm, Eric, 206–207
Holland, Dorothy, 197, 198, 199, 261n.1
Holocaust, 68–69
Hordes, Stanley, 82, 96–108; Carroll on, 69;
    on Church of San Felipe de Neri, 182,
    183; on circumcision, 164, 260n.7; on
    crypto-Jews, numbers of, 4; crypto-Jews,
    theory on, 217; on crypto-Jews in New
    Mexico, 101–108; on crypto-Jews in New
    Spain, 99–101; on endogamy, 128,
    137–138, 145; ethnographic practices of,
    80; Ferry and Nathan on, 76–77; on

gravestones, 181; historical discussion by, 97–98; importance of, 107; Inquisition documents cited by, 6; interviews conducted by, 180, 184; on Jews in Spain, 98–99; mezuzah case described by, 175; on Moses, 188; on movement of *conversos*, 7; on naming practices, 106–107, 112, 181–182; overview of work of, 97; and SCJS, 24, 27; Sutton on, 65–66

hot societies, 215, 224, 246–247

Hoyo, Eugenio del, 102

Hymes, Dell, 262n.3

Iberian Peninsula, Jewish community in, 4–7, 158

identity: concretization of, 39–40; construction of, 215; as cultural phenomenon, 118; and culture, 30–31, 220; devaluation of, 199; ethnic, unified Spanish, 6; Ferry and Nathan on, 78; fluidity of, 39–40, 99, 115, 117; Hispano, 43; individual versus group, 25; Jewish, as trope for whiteness, 50, 62–64, 81, 93–94, 216; and mediators, 240; religion as defining element of, 115–116; and self-identification, 144; subjective nature of, 121. *See also* genealogy; *jonglerie*; memory; practice(s); self-identification

identity, crypto-Jewish: complexity of, 37–38, 114–115; factors used to construct, 31–32, 36–37; future of, 219–220; and Inquisition documents, 30; Neulander on, 50–51, 216; panels on, at SCJS conferences, 36–40; rejection of, 38; self-attachment to, 136–137; self-discovery of, 135–136; and syncretism, 89–90; transmission of, 217–218. *See also* authenticity, of crypto-Judaism; identity; crypto-Jewish, ideal types of

identity, crypto-Jewish, ideal types of: and belief, 120–121; Christian identity with *converso* elements, 37–38, 141–143; Christian identity without *converso* elements, 38–39, 143–144; and genealogy, 117–119; *jonglerie*'s implications for, 195–197; and New Christian taxonomy, 87–88, 115–116; and patterns of identification, 144; and practice, 119–120; and self-identification, 116–117, 213–214; strong crypto-Jewish identity, 37, 121–132; understanding of, 115; weak crypto-Jewish identity, 37, 132–141

imagined communities, 206

improvisation, 193. *See also* fluidity; transformation

Inquisition: Carroll on scholarship on, 68–69; and crypto-Jewish culture, 5–6; documents of, 30, 100, 104; Edicts of

Grace of, 86–87, 89, 121; establishment of, 4–5; in New Mexico, 9; in New Spain, 7; in Portugal, 7; reliability of records of, 85–86

intelligent design, 251

interpretation: authenticity of, 29; and bricolage, 172, 174, 176; and figured worlds, 199; and identity, 121, 137, 138, 139; internal, of groups, 21; and *jonglerie*, 196; of memories, 39–40; and memory, 203–205; of narratives, 52; and Neulander, 47, 48, 58–59, 97; retrospective, 130; of rituals, 49; of self, 96. *See also* meaning; memory; practice(s); symbols and symbolism

Isabel (crypto-Jew), 130

Isabella of Castile (queen of Spain), 6

Israel, 210

jacal (temporary booth-like structure), 132, 162

Jacobs, Janet, 5, 82, 90–96; on authenticity, 90–92; on ethnic identity, 93–94; experience of, 257n.1; genetic evidence, use of, 118; on Neulander's theories, 92–93; on status and crypto-Jewish identity, 63; on stereotypes, 121; support for hypothesis of, 94–96; supposed orientalism of, 73–75, 94

Jesus, 131, 140, 182

jewelry, 183–184

Jewish Catalog, The, 212

Jewish culture. *See* culture

Jewish objects. *See* symbols and symbolism

"Jewish Practices Among Contemporary Anusim" (Halevy), 108–109

Jews: and *conversos*, 5, 259n.1; and crypto-Jews, 88, 200–201, 242; expulsion of, from Spain, 5, 6, 36, 89, 150, 259n.1; mainstream, 26, 41, 42, 43–44, 220; New Christians as, 87; in Portugal, 6–7; in Spain, 4–7, 83–84, 98–99; transformation of, to crypto-Jews, 246. *See also* crypto-Jews; Judaism

Job, Saint, 157, 185

jonglerie (identity juggling), 193–201; and agency, 252; ideal identity types, implications for, 195–197; and identity devaluation, 199; mechanism of, 194–195; as model, 214

Joseph (crypto-Jew), 133–134, 183

Josephina (crypto-Jew), 160

Juan (crypto-Jew), 184

Judaism: and genealogy, 117; mainstream, 26, 41, 42, 43–44, 220; public versus private practice of, 84, 94; Reform, 42; as trope for whiteness, 50, 62–64, 81, 93–94, 216. *See also* crypto-Judaism

Judaizing, 30, 59–60, 80, 91, 216, 260n.8
Judeo-Spanish (Ladino), 122, 123, 142, 155, 219
judío (Jew), use of term, 59–60, 93. *See also* "Somos judíos"
Julio (crypto-Jew), 134, 135, 138

kabbalah (Jewish mystic tradition), 208, 209
kiddush (blessing over wine), 151
kiddush cup, 191

Ladino (Judeo-Spanish), 122, 123, 142, 155, 219
Lawrence (crypto-Jew), 135
Leah (crypto-Jew), 127
levels of structure, in neo-structuralism, 223, 226–239
Lévi-Strauss, Claude, 147, 223–225, 230, 246
Liebman, Seymour, 75
limpieza de sangre (purity of blood), 12, 81, 117
linguistics, structural, 227
literature and art, panels on, at SCJS conferences, 42–43
López de Mendizábal, Bernardo, 9
López Sambrano, Josepha, 208
lost tribes, 47–48
Luke (crypto-Jew), 136
lulov and *etrog* (Jewish ritual objects), 162

Manifest Destiny, 72
"Manifestations of Crypto-Judaism in the American Southwest" (Halevy), 108–109
manito (Indohispanos), 110
Manuel (crypto-Jew), 133, 138
Manuel I (king of Portugal), 6–7
Margaret (crypto-Jew), 141–142
Maria (crypto-Jew): on attending church, 249; on autumn harvest booths, 132; on games, 128–129; on Ladino, 142; on practices associated with bread and wine, 152; on practices associated with Yom Kippur, 166; on ritual slaughter, 168; on secrecy, 170; stories of, patterns of exclusivity in, 124–126; on yellow, 160
marrano, use of term, 1–2, 3
marriage patterns, 32, 117–118, 137–138, 158–159. *See also* endogamy
Marta (crypto-Jew): on baptism, 158; childhood experiences of, interpretation of, 129–130; on dreidels, 173; on Exodus story, 131–132; on grandfather's Jewish objects, 174–175; Judaism, awareness of, 122–123; on secret Jewish names, 260n.3

Martin (crypto-Jew), 127, 158–159, 165–166
material culture, 176–191; Carroll's misunderstanding of, 75–76, 186; current objects as, 187; as evidence of crypto-Jewish identity, 111–112; folk art as, 11, 43, 156, 185, 187–188, 189, 190; gravestone symbols as, 176–183; written documents as, 186–187
meaning: and false associations of symbols, 51; historical versus current, 181; locus of, 33; of mythemes, 236–237; narrative versus structural, 229; of objects, 157; possibility of multiplicity of, 53; of practices, 49, 147, 157; of ritemes, 236; of symbols, 178. *See also* interpretation
Mederos, Manuel de, 102
mediation: between Christianity and Judaism, 126–127, 141, 195; of history, 208; in ideal identity types, 214; in neo-structuralism, 239–242; structural versus narrative, 240–242
Melammed, Renée Levine, 82; on crypto-Jews, numbers of, 4; on public sphere of Jewish practice, 150; supposed orientalism of, 73–75; on women as transmitters of crypto-Judaism, 83–84, 94
memory: and crypto-Judaism, 15; cultural, 54; and cultural construction, 30–31; and cultural creation, 148; distortions versus transformations of, 203–204; emotional content of, 202; and ethnographic interviews, 79–80, 146–147; Ferry and Nathan on, 78; and figured worlds, 201, 202; and identity, 32, 39–40; individual, 201–205; memories versus, 205; myths versus, 250; and practice, 35–36; role of, in SCJS conference papers, 29; and selectivity, 204; and self-identification, 205; "sins" of, 201–204; social, 205–207, 261n.3; veracity of, 201
men, as transmitters of crypto-Judaism, 84, 95–96
messianic congregations, 38–39, 62, 140, 143, 221–222
mestizos, 12, 62–63, 93
Mexico (New Spain), 6, 7, 60, 99–101
mezuzahs (ritual scrolls), 155–156, 175, 186
mikveh (ritual bath), 139
misattribution (memory "sin"), 202–203
Montemayor, Diego de, 102
Mormonism, 231, 235, 261n.1
Moses, 187–188, 190
Moses, Saint, 157
motzi (blessing over bread), 151
mythemes, 236, 238

myths: definition of, 247–248; geographical movements of, 224; history versus, 247–251; and N structural level, 229; and S^3 structural level, 235–236; of self, 205; transformations of, 243

N (narrative) structural level, 227, 228–230
names and naming practices: and baptism, 158, 159; as evidence of crypto-Jewish identity, 55–56, 112, 182, 259n.5; on gravestones, 181–182; Hordes on, 106–107; as indicators of crypto-Jewish authenticity, 91; Neulander on, 55–56; secret Jewish, 260n.3
narratives: in Bible, 36, 120, 131–132, 163, 248; crypto-Jewish, of self, 248–249; folk, 47, 52–53, 126–127, 248–249; genres of, 249; as histories, 207–210; interpretation of, 52–53; of self, 197–200, 201; and social memory, 205–206; transformations of, 53; on transmission of identity, 218. *See also* history; myths
Nathan, Debbie. *See* Ferry, Barbara, and Debbie Nathan
nationalism, construction of, 206
negative beliefs, 120, 140
negative (–) ideal type of structural relation, 233–234
negative mediation, 239
neo-structuralism. *See* structuralism
Netanyahu, Benzion, 4, 98, 100
Neulander, Judith, 46–66; Anita (crypto-Jew), analysis of information from, 57, 58, 59–60; arguments by, flaws in, 50, 51, 58–59, 215–216, 257nn.2,5,6; on Church of San Felipe de Neri, 182; on colonial paradigm, 47–48; on crypto-Jewish identity, 39, 97; cultural model of, 54–55; on cultural practice, 114–115; ethnographic practices of, flaws in, 56–57, 216–217; on external authenticity, 49; Ferry and Nathan on, 79–81; on folktales, 52–53; on genetic disorders, 259n.3; genetics, claims based on, 64–66; on Hordes, 77; on interviewers, experience of, 257n.1; Jacobs on, 92; on Pentecostalism as basis for supposed crypto-Judaism, 59–62; on *pon y saca*'s identification with dreidel, 173, 174; popularization of, 110; on practices, 48–49, 53–54, 55–56; publications of, 46; on reinterviews, 204; rhetorical strategy of, 46–47, 50–51; on ritual slaughter, 261n.9; on Saint Esther, 156, 184–185; on status as basis for supposed crypto-Judaism, 62–64

neutral (*n*) ideal type of structural relation, 234
New Christians, 85, 87–88, 102, 157
new Israel identity, 59, 60, 61
New Mexico: crypto-Judaism in, Carroll on, 45, 46, 66–76; crypto-Judaism in, Hordes on, 97, 101–108; crypto-Judaism in, Neulander on, 46–66; economy of, 10–11; geographic distribution of SCJS member crypto-Jews from, 25; history of crypto-Jews in, 3–13, 104–105; Inquisition in, 9; Jewish institutions in, 13; Pentecostalism in, 59–60, 80; Protestant sects in, 61, 62, 80, 92, 216; settlement of, 9–11, 18, 102–104, 217; Seventh-Day Adventists in, 61; society, structure of, 12. *See also* Albuquerque
New Spain (Mexico), 6, 7, 60, 99–101
nidah (ritually unclean woman), 154
Noah, story of, 53
nomenclature, 1–3
Nostrand, Richard L., 10, 11–12
Nuevo León (Mexico), 7, 102–103

objects, meaning of. *See* symbols and symbolism
observer bias, 15–16
Okely, Judith, 19
Oñate, Juan de, 7, 9, 103
oral history, 29, 30, 207–210
oral transmission of traditions, 91, 220
orientalism, 66–67, 70–74
other, 71–72

Pablo (crypto-Jew), 123, 126, 129
"Padre and the Jew, The" (folktale), 52–53, 126–127, 257n.4
participant observation, 14, 15
Passover, 163, 168–169
Patai, Raphael, 60, 80
Paulo (crypto-Jew), 130–131
Penitentes, 11, 124
Pentecostal Christianity, 56, 57, 59–61, 80, 92
personal history, panels on, at SCJS conferences, 28–31
pigs, 167, 239
points of view, internal versus external, 13–14, 21
pon y saca (*trompito*; four-sided top), 172–174, 219
pork, consumption of, 129, 138, 167
Portugal, 6–7, 158
positive beliefs, 120
positive (+) ideal type of structural relation, 234
positive mediation, 239–240
postcolonialism, 48

practice(s), 146–191; authenticity of, 34,
48–49; and bricolage, 147–175; changing
nature of, 150; of Christian identity with
converso elements type, 142; complexity
of, 149–150; context for, 148; explanations
versus structures of, 229–230; as factor
in New Christian identity, 87–88; and
ideal identity types, 119–120, 145; as
indicators of crypto-Jewish authenticity,
90–91; influences on, 35; interpretation
of, 50, 114–115, 119–120, 161; with Jewish
and Catholic elements, 151–161; with
Jewish and local elements, 161–169; lack
of explanations for, 35; with mainstream
Jewish elements, 171–175; meaning of,
49; and memory, 35–36, 146–147, 203;
and narrative presentation of self, 198; in
neo-structuralism, 253–254; Neulander
on, 215–216; public sphere of, 89, 150;
public versus private, 84, 94–95, 124;
and secrecy, 2–3, 6, 34–35, 110, 169–171;
sources for, 87, 218; stability of, 53–54; of
strong crypto-Jewish identity type,
128–131; and structure, 193, 253–254;
transformations in, 86, 89;
understanding and interpretation of, 35;
of weak crypto-Jewish identity type,
138–140. See also *jonglerie*; rituals;
women
practice(s), specific: baptism, 158, 159;
circumcision, 100–101, 163–166, 187,
260nn.7,8; crosses on doorposts,
154–156; of housecleaning, 49–50, 130,
169; of marriage, 158–159; of
mourning, 135–136, 138; obscure
rabbinic, 108–109; of purification, 154,
161, 260n.4; ritual slaughter, 58,
167–168, 261n.9; and Yom Kippur, 166.
See also candle lighting; dietary
customs; endogamy; names and
naming practices; rituals
Presbyterianism, 62
Protestantism, 61, 80, 92, 216
Puerto Rico, 158
purity of blood (*limpieza de sangre*), 12, 81,
117

quince, 162

rabbis, 21, 41, 108–109
race, as factor in New Christian identity,
87–88
Rael, Juan Bautista, 257n.4
random sampling, 92–93
Ranger, Terence, 206–207
readers, and textual interpretation, 69–70
reconquista (Christian reconquest of Iberian
Peninsula), 6

religion: as component of New Christian
identity, 87; and identity, 31, 115–116; and
objective experiences, 251; panels on, at
SCJS conferences, 41–42. *See also*
Christianity; crypto-Judaism; Judaism
religious practices. *See* practice(s)
research methods, 13–17; authenticity,
question of, 20–21; differences of, from
Neulander's, 63–64; and interviewees,
17, 19–20; key markers in, 91; and
observer bias, 15–16; participant
observation as, 14, 15; Pentecostal
influences, exploration of possible, 62;
and points of view, 13–14, 21; and
random sampling, 92–93; and SCJS
conferences, 256nn.2,3; unstructured
interviews as, 15–17
retablos (depictions of saints), 11, 156, 185,
189
ritemes (elements of practice), 151, 236, 238
ritual slaughter (*shechita*), 58, 167–168,
261n.9
rituals: for Friday nights, 151–154; involving
bread and wine, 151–152, 260n.6; and N
structural level, 229; Neulander on, 47;
of purification, 154, 161, 260n.4; and S^3
structural level, 235–236. *See also*
practice(s); ritual slaughter
Rodríguez, Jeanette, 54
Roland (crypto-Jew), 160
Rosa (crypto-Jew), 134–135, 164
Rosary. *See* candle lighting: and recitation
of Rosary
Roth, Cecil, 1, 208
Ruth (crypto-Jew), 138

S^1 structural level, 227, 228, 230–232
S^2 structural level, 227, 228, 232–235
S^3 structural level, 227, 228, 235–239, 245
Sabbatarian churches, 60–61, 216
Sacred Heart, use of, in architecture,
182–183
Said, Edward, 67, 68, 70
saints, veneration of images of. *See retablos*;
santeros; *santos*
Salazar, Juan, 190
Salazar, Leo, 188
Salazar, Leonardo, 188
Sandoval, Isabelle, 77–78, 79
Sandoval, Juan, 258n.9
Santa Cruz (New Mexico), 10
Santa Fe (New Mexico), 10, 29, 105, 165,
208–209
santeros (depictors of saints), 11, 187–188,
191
santos (images of saints), 159–160
Santos, Richard, 77
Sarah (crypto-Jew), 131

Saussure, Ferdinand de, 237
Schacter, Daniel, 201–204
Schama, Simon, 157
science, factuality of, 250–251
SCJS. *See* Society for Crypto-Judaic Studies
secrecy: and *conversos*, 5–6, 83; in
    crypto-Jewish culture, 2–3, 6, 34–35, 110,
    169–171; Ferry and Nathan on, 78–79
*Secrecy and Deceit: The Religion of the
    Crypto-Jews* (Gitlitz), 84–90
secret Jews. *See* crypto-Jews
self, narratives of, 197–200, 201, 249–250
self-identification: and authenticity, 45; of
    Christian identity types, 141–144; and
    crypto-Jewish historiography, 209–211;
    as factor in ideal types of crypto-Jewish
    identity, 116–117, 213–214; as factor in
    New Christian identity, 87–88; fluidity
    of, 196; and genealogy, 127; and
    historical considerations, 115; and
    identity, 32, 144; importance of, 91; and
    memories, 205; public expressions of,
    77–78; of strong crypto-Jewish identity
    type, 121–132; transformations in, 195; of
    weak crypto-Jewish identity type,
    132–137
Sephardim, 255n.2
Seventh-Day Adventism: and Christian
    identity without *converso* elements
    identity type, 143; and crypto-Jewish
    identity, 38–39, 60–61, 80, 92; reasons
    for individuals choosing, 109
Seville (Spain), 4, 5
shechita (ritual slaughter), 58, 167–168,
    261n.9
Shekhina (feminine aspect of God), 209
Simmel, Georg, 110, 170
"sins" of memory, 201–204
six-pointed star, 33, 178–181, 182–183,
    183–184, 237
social memory, 205–207, 261n.3
social science, panels on, at SCJS
    conferences, 31–32
societies, hot versus cold, 215, 224,
    246–247
Society for Crypto-Judaic Studies (SCJS),
    24–44; founders of, 24; on
    mainstreaming of crypto-Jews, 44;
    members of, 24–26; and preservation of
    crypto-Judaism, 221
    CONFERENCES OF, 26–43; academic history
    panels at, 27–28; academic versus
    nonacademic presentations at, 33–34;
    attendees at, 25–26, 37–38; Christian
    clergy at, 41, 42; and figured worlds,
    199–200; genetics panels at, 40–41;
    identity panels at, 36–40; literature and
    art panels at, 42–43; personal history

panels at, 28–31; preconferences, 43–44;
    religion panels at, 41–42; social science
    panels at, 31–32; symbols and practices
    panels at, 32–36
"Somos judíos" (We are Jews), 29, 117, 133,
    137, 164, 218
South America, *conversos* in, 7
Spain: expulsion of Jews from, 5, 6, 36, 89,
    150, 259n.1; Jews in, 4–7, 83–84,
    98–99
Spaniards (*españoles*), use of term in New
    Mexico, 12
Sperber, Dan, 238
spiritual-shopping model, 210–211
Stamatov, Suzanne, 12, 255n.4
Stampfer, Joshua, 24
Star of David. *See* six-pointed star
status, 62–64, 81, 93–94, 216
stories. *See* narratives
strong crypto-Jewish identity (ideal identity
    type), 121–132; beliefs of, 131–132;
    endogamy, preference for, 127–128;
    exclusivity of, 123–126; and genealogy,
    127; geographic distribution of, in New
    Mexico, 127–128; Jewish or
    crypto-Jewish practices of, 128–131; and
    memory transience, 202; and New
    Christian taxonomy, 88; oppositional
    nature of, 132; patterns in elements of,
    132; religion of, 122–123; respondents in,
    overview of, 121–122; underlying
    structure of, 214
structural crystallization, 244
structural linguistics, 227
structural mediation, 240–242
structural relation, 233–235, 239
structural transformation, 225, 226,
    242–247
structuralism, 223–254; agency in, 225,
    251–253; classical, 224–225; definitions
    of, 227; levels of structure in, 223,
    226–239; mediation in, 239–242; myth
    and history in, 247–251; N structural
    level, 227, 228–230; practice in,
    253–254; S^1 structural level, 227, 228,
    230–232; S^2 structural level, 227, 228,
    232–235; S^3 structural level, 227, 228,
    235–239; structural transformation in,
    242–247. *See also* structure
structure: change in, 226; of cultural
    objects, 192–193; and culture, 194–195;
    locus for, 231–232, 253; monopolism of,
    231; narrative mediation in, 240–242;
    transformations of, 252; triadic, 231. *See
    also* structuralism
suggestibility (memory "sin"), 203
Sukkoth, 132, 161–163
Sutton, Wesley K., 65–66

symbols and symbolism: false associations and meanings of, 51; on gravestones, 20, 32, 33, 111–112, 177–182; Jewish, use of, in Spanish diaspora, 32–33; and meaning, 178, 237–239; panels on, at SCJS conferences, 32–36; six-pointed star as, 33, 178–181, 182–183, 183–184; Sperber's approach to, 238; variability of value of, 236
syncretism, 89–90, 139–140, 151

Taos (New Mexico), 105
Temple Montefiore (Las Vegas), 13
texts, 69–70, 254
To the End of the Earth: A History of the Crypto-Jews of New Mexico (Hordes), 97–108
Tobias, Henry, 13
tops, four-sided (*pon y saca, trompito*), 172–174, 219
tradents (conveyors of tradition): men as, 84, 95–96; women as, 83–84, 90–91, 94–96, 150
traditions: and invented tradition, 206–207; men's transmission of, 84, 95–96; oral transmission of, 91, 220; women's transmission of, 83–84, 90–91, 94–96, 150. *See also* practice(s)
transformation: and bricolage, 245; cultural, 252–253; and hot versus cold societies, 246–247; in individuals, 243–244; intercultural, 243; intracultural, 243–244; of Jews to crypto-Jews, 246; and mediation, 240; on N structural level, 229–230; structural, 242–247, 253–254; of structure, 225–226

transience (memory "sin"), 201–202
transmission: of crypto-Jewish identity, 217–218; men's role in, 84, 95–96; oral, 91, 220; women's role in, 83–84, 90–91, 94–96, 150
triadic structure, 231
trompito (*pon y saca*; four-sided top), 172–174

unconscious, 226

Venta Prieta (Mexico), 60, 80
Vera (crypto-Jew), 164–165
verbalization, 238
Vygotsky, Lev, 197

weak crypto-Jewish identity (ideal identity type), 132–141; complexity of, 137; fluidity of, 193; and genealogy, 137; marriage patterns of, 137–138; and New Christian taxonomy, 88; patterns in elements of, 140–141; practices of, 138–140; self-identification of, 132–137; syncretism in, 139–140; underlying structure of, 214
Weber, Max, 115
whiteness, Judaism as trope for, 50, 62–64, 81, 93–94, 216
Wickham, Chris, 205
wine, 151–152, 158–159
women: *nidah*, 154; as transmitters of crypto-Judaism, 83–84, 90–91, 94–96, 150

yellow, aversion to, 160–161
Yerushalmi, Yosef Hayim, 169
Yom Kippur, 166